The Sagas of Ragnar Lothbrok

Original Texts, Translations, and Word Lists

Translated by
Matthew Leigh Embleton

Copyright ©2025 Matthew Leigh Embleton. All rights reserved.

The Sagas of Ragnar Lothbrok

The Saga of Ragnar Lothbrok..4
The Tale of Ragnar's Sons 103
The Lay of Kraka 127
Word List *(Old Norse to English)*...137
Word List *(English to Old Norse)* 197

Cover: Old Norse text over an outline of a ravenr. Author's design.

The original Old Norse texts are in the public domain.
These translations ©2021 Matthew Leigh Embleton
©2025 Matthew Leigh Embleton (This Edition)

Acknowledgments

I have long been fascinated by languages and history, and I am very grateful to the special people in my life who have supported and encouraged me in my work. Thank you for believing in me. You know who you are.

Introduction

The legend of Ragnar Lothbrok, one of the best known heroes of the Viking Age, has been told and re-told in an increasing variety of media. The rich tradition of Icelandic literature survived by oral tradition over several centuries before being written down in the 13th Century.

Old Norse is a North Germanic language spoken by inhabitants of Scandinavia from about the 7th to the 15th centuries. Old Icelandic is a variety of Old West Norse that emerged during the Norse settlement of Iceland in the second half of the 9th century.

The meaning of the word 'saga' (plural: 'sǫgur' or 'sögur') translates as 'that which is said', or more widely: a 'saying', 'statement', 'story', 'tale', or 'narrative'.

This book contains:
- The Saga of Ragnar Lothbrok (Ragnars Saga Loðbrókar)
- The Tale of Ragnar's Sons' (Ragnarssona Þáttr)
- The Lay of Kraka (Krákumál)

The texts are presented in their original Old Norse, with a literal word-for-word line-by-line translation, and a Modern English translation, all side-by-side. In this way, it is possible to see and feel how the Old Norse language worked and how it has evolved. Also included is a word list with 3,583 Old Norse words translated in to English, and 2,860 English words translated into Old Norse.

This book is designed to be of use and interest to anyone with a passion for the Old Norse or Old Icelandic language, Old Norse history, or languages and history in general.

The Saga of Ragnar Lothbrok

Old Norse	Literal	English
1	1	1
Heimir í Hlymdölum spyrr nú þessi tíðendi, at dauðr er Sigurðr ok Brynhildr.	Heimir in Hlymdal learned now this news, of death had Sigurd and Brynhild.	When Heimir was in Hlymdal, he heard the news about the death of Sigurd and Brynhild.
En Áslaug, dóttir þeira, en fóstra Heimis, var þá þrévetr.	When Aslaug, daughter theirs, but foster Heimir's, was then three-winters.	Aslaug was their daughter, and Heimir's foster daughter, and she was three winters old.
Veit hann nú, at eptir mun leitat at týna meyjunni ok ætt hennar.	Knew he now, that afterwards would seek to destroy the-maiden and family-line hers.	He now knew that afterwards they would seek to destroy the girl and her family line.
Er honum svá mikill harmr eptir Brynhildi, fóstru sína, at hann gætti ekki ríkis síns né fjár, sér nú, at hann fær eigi meyjunni þar leynt; lætr nú gera eina hörpu svá mikla, at þar lét hann meyna Áslaugu í koma ok margar gersimar í gulli ok silfri ok gengr á brott síðan víða um lönd ok um síðir hingat á Norðrlönd.	Was his so much grief after Brynhild, foster his, that he guarded not kingdom his nor wealth, saw now, that he could not the-girl there secret keep; now made a harp so great, that there put he the-girl Aslaug in coming and many precious in gold and silver and went to away afterwards widely about the-lands and about eventually there in northern-lands.	His grief for Brynhild, his foster daughter, was so much, that he didn't care for his kingdom or his wealth, and realised that he could not keep the girl there in secret; he made a harp that was so large that he put the girl Aslaug inside, along with many precious things in gold and silver, and afterwards went away travelling widely across the lands, and eventually there in the northern lands.
Svá var harpa hans hagliga ger, at hana mátti taka í sundr ok saman at fellingum, ok var hann því vanr um daga, þá er hann fór í hjá vatnföllum ok hvergi í nánd bæjum, at hann tók hörpuna í sundr ok þó meyjunni, ok hann hafði vínlauk einn ok gaf henni at eta.	So was harp his skilfully made, that he may take it apart and together at joints, and was he therefore accustomed about days, then that he travelled to beside waterfalls and nowhere with close-to farms, that he took harp to apart and though the-maiden, and he had wine-leek one and gave her to eat.	His harp was so skilfully made, that he could take it apart at the joints, and it was his custom that when they reached waterfalls with no houses nearby, he would take the harp apart and bathe the girl, and he had a wine-leek that he would give her to eat.

Old Norse	Literal	English
En þat er náttúra þess lauks, at maðr má lengi lifa, þótt hann hafi enga aðra fæðu.	But so was the-nature of-this leek, that man may long live, though he had only else little.	And it was the nature of this leek that one could live long on it even though they had little else.
Ok þá er mærin grét, sló hann hörpuna, ok þagnaði hún þá, fyrir því at Heimir var vel at íþróttum búinn, þeim er þá váru tíðar.	And when was the-girl crying, struck he the-harp, and silenced she then, for because that Heimir was well about accomplished prepared, they as then was frequent.	And when the girl was crying, he stuck up his harp and she became quiet, because Heimir was accomplished at those skills which were common at that time.
Hann hafði ok mörg klæði dýrlig hjá henni í hörpunni ok mikit gull.	He had and many clothes dear beside her in harp and much gold.	He had many costly clothes in the harp beside her, and much gold.
Ok nú ferr hann þangat til, uns hann kemr í Noreg ok kemr til eins býjar lítils, þess er heitir á Spangareiði, ok bjó þar karl sá, er Áki hét.	And now travelled he from-there to, until he came to Norway and came to a farm little, this was named of Spangarheith, and dwelt there a-man he, was Aki named.	And now he travelled from there until he came to Norway, and came to a little farm that was named Spangarheid, and there lived a old man who was named Aki.
Hann átti konu, ok hét hún Gríma.	He had wife, and called her Grima.	He had a wife, and she was named Grima.
Þar var eigi fleira manna en þau.	There were no other people but them.	There were no other people but them.
Þann dag var karl farinn í skóg, en kerling var heima, ok heilsar hún Heimi ok spyrr, hvat manna hann væri.	Then-one day was the-man travelling in the-forest, but the-old-woman was at-home, and greeted she Heimir and asked, what man he was.	Then one day the man was travelling in the forest, and the old woman was at home, and she greeted Heimir and asked what kind of man he was.
Hann kveðst vera einn stafkarl ok bað kerlingu húsa.	He said was a beggar and asked the-old-woman for-lodgings.	He said he was a beggar and asked the old woman for lodgings.
Hún segir, at eigi kæmi þar fleira en svá, at hún kveðst mundu vel við honum taka, ef hann þættist þurfa þar at vera.	She said, that none came there many about so, that she said would well with him take, if he thought needed then to be.	She said that no one else came there any more, so she could welcome him, if he thought he needed to be there.

Old Norse	Literal	English
En er á leið, þá segir hann, at honum þætti þat mest beinabót, at eldr væri kveyktr fyrir honum ok síðan væri honum fylgt til svefnhúss, þar er hann skyldi sofa.	Then it-was about during, then said he, that he seemed that most benefit, that fire would-be lit before him and then was he followed to sleeping-house, then that he should sleep.	Then in the end, he said that he would benefit most from a fire being lit in front of him, and then he would follow to some lodgings where he could sleep.
Ok þá er kerling hafði kveykt eldinn, þá setr hann hörpuna upp í set hjá sér, en kerling var óðamálug.	And when that the-old-woman had lit a-fire, then sat he the-harp up to sit beside himself, but the-old-woman was un-talkative.	And when the old woman had lit a fire, he sat the harp beside him, but the old woman did not have much to say.
Opt varð henni litit til hörpunnar, fyrir því at trefr á einu dýrligu klæði kómu út á hörpunni.	Often was she looking at the-harp, for because that fringes of a dear clothing came out-from in the-harp.	She often looked at the harp, because there were fringes of costly clothing coming out of the harp.
Ok er hann bakaðist við eldinn, þá sér hún einn dýrligan gullhring koma fram undan tötrum hans, því at hann var illa klæddr.	And was he warmed with the-fire, then saw she one dear gold-ring coming from under rags his, because that he was badly clothed.	And as he warmed himself by the fire, then she saw a costly gold ring coming from under his rags, because he was poorly dressed.
Ok er hann hafði bakast sem hann kunni sér þörf til, þá hafði hann náttverð.	And when he had warmed himself he knew as-he needed to, then had he supper.	And when he had been warmed by the fire as much as he needed, then he had supper.
En eptir þat bað hann kerlingu fylgja sér þangat til, sem hann skyldi sofa um nóttina.	Then after that asked he old-woman to-follow him from-there to, where he should sleep about the-night.	Then after that the old woman asked him to follow her from there to where he should sleep for the night.
Þá segir kerling, at honum mundi betra vera úti en inni, "því at vit karl minn erum opt málug, er hann kemr heim".	Then said the-old-woman, that he should better be outside but inside, "because that with man mine are-we often talking, as he comes home".	Then the old woman said that it would be better for him to be outside than inside, "because my man and I are often talking when he comes home".
Hann biðr hana ráða, gengr nú út ok svá hún.	He invite hers agreed, to-go now back and so-did she.	He accepted her invitation to go outside, and so did she.

Old Norse	Literal	English
Hann tekr hörpuna ok hefir með sér.	He took the-harp and had-it with him.	He took the harp and kept it with him.
Kerling gengr út ok ferr þar til, er bygghlaða ein er, ok fylgir honum þar til ok mælti, at hann skyldi þar um búast, ok kveðst þess vænta, at hann mundi þar njóta svefns síns.	The-old-woman went out and travelled there to, where barley-barn one was, and followed he there to and said, that he should there about settle, and said that hoped, that he would there the-night sleep his.	The old woman went outside and travelled to where there was a barley barn, and he followed there and said that he would settle there and hoped to sleep well.
Ok nú gengr kerling í brott ok annast þat, er hún þurfti, en hann gerir sér svefn.	And now went the-old-woman to away and take-care-of that, which she needed, as he made himself sleep.	And now the woman went away to take care of things that she needed to do, while he went to sleep.
Karl kemr heim, er aptanninn líðr, en kerling hefir fátt unnit þat, er hún þurfti, en hann var móðr, er hann kom heim, ok illr viðskiptis, er allt var óbúit þat, er hún skyldi annast hafa.	The-man came home, when the-evening passed, but the-old-woman did little work that, which she needed, then he was tired, when he came home, and of-ill business, that all was not-done that, which she should taken-care-of have.	The old man came home as the evening was passing, but the old woman had done very little of the work that she had needed to do, and he was tired and unhappy when he came home and found that very little of what should have been done had been taken care of.
Sagði karl, at mikill væri munr sælu, er hann vann hvern dag meira en hann mátti, en hún vildi til einkis taka þess, er gagn var at.	Said the-man, that much was difference happiness, that he performed each day more than he might, but she willed to nothing take this, which of-use was to.	The man said that there was much difference between their happiness, because he did worked every day and did more than he was able to do, but she did not want to do anything that was useful.
"Ver eigi reiðr, karl minn", sagði hún, "fyrir því at þat kann at vera, at þú mættir nú skamma stund vinna til þess, at vit værim sæl alla ævi".	"Be not angry, man mine", said she, "for because that it can then be, that you might now short awhile deserve to this, that with being happy all our-lives".	"Don't be angry with me, my man", she said, "because it may be that you will only have to work a short while longer, and make the two of us happy all our lives".
"Hvat er þat?", segir karl.	"What is it?", said the-man.	"What is it?", said the man.

Old Norse	Literal	English
Kerling svarar: "Hér er kominn til herbergis okkars einn maðr, ok ætla ek, at hann hafi allmikit fé með at fara, ok er hniginn á efra aldr ok mun verit hafa inn mesti kappi ok er nú þó móðr mjök, ok eigi þykkjumst ek hans maka sét hafa, ok þó ætla ek hann mæddan ok syfjaðan".	The-old-woman answered: "Here has come to room ours a man, and suppose I, that he has all-much wealth with to travel, and is declined by over age and would been have the most champion and is now though tired much, and none think I his equal seen have, and though suppose I he-is tired and sleepy".	The old woman answered: "A man has come here to our room, and I suppose, that he has all the wealth to travel, and is declining with age, though he may have once been a champion, but now he is very tired, and I don't think I have seen anyone like him before, and I suppose that he is exhausted and asleep".
Þá segir karl: "Þat sýnist mér óráðligt at svíkja þá ina fá, sem hér koma".	Then said man: "That seems to-me un-right to betray then the few, who here come".	Then the man said: "It doesn't seem right to me to betray the few people who come here".
Hún svarar: "Því muntu lengi lítill fyrir þér, at þér vex allt í augu, ok ger nú annathvárt, at þú drep hann, eða ek tek hann mér til manns, ok munu vit reka þik í brott.	She answered: "Therefore should long little-be for you, that to-you grows all in eyes, and do now either, that you kill him, or I take him to-me to husband, and shall we drive you to away.	She answered: "That is why you will long be a little man, because everything looks too big for your eyes, now it will be either that you kill him, or I will take him as my husband, and we will drive you away".
Ok segja kann ek þér þá ræðu, er hann mælti við mik í gærkveld, en lítils mun þér þykkja um vert.	And say can I to-you then speech, that he said with me about last-night, though little shall you think about worthy.	I can say the words to you that he said to me last night, but they will seem unworthy to you".
Hann mælti kvensamliga við mik, ok þat mun mitt ráð vera at taka hann mér til manns, en reka þik í brott eða drepa, ef þú vill eigi eptir því gera, sem ek vil".	He spoke feminine-same-like with me, and that shall my plan be to take him for-me to husband, and drive you to away or kill-you, if you will not after then do, as I wish".	He spoke in a feminine way with me, and it shall be my plan to take him as my husband and drive you away or kill you, if you will not do as I wish".
Ok er þat sagt, at karl hafði kvánríki, ok telr hún um þangat til, er hann lætr at eggjan hennar, tekr öxi sína ok snarbrýnir mjök.	And was it said, that the-man had-been woman-ruled, and talked she about that until, that he allowed to encouragement hers, took axe his and sharpened much.	And so it was said, that the man was overruled by the woman, and she kept talking about it until he gave in to her encouragement, and took his axe and sharpened it very much".
Ok er hann er búinn, fylgir kerling honum þar til, er Heimir sefr, ok var þar hrytr mikill.	And when he was ready, followed the-old-woman he there to, where Heimir slept, and was there snoring much.	And when he was ready, he followed the old woman to where Heimir slept, and he was snoring a lot".

Old Norse	Literal	English
Þá mælti kerling til karls, at hann skyldi láta verða tilræði sem best, "ok skunda brott með hlaupi, því at ekki máttu standast lát hans ok óp, ef hann fær þik höndum tekit".	Then said the-old-woman to the-man, that he should do as advised as best, "and hurry away with running, because that not could stand-you have him and shouting, if he gets you hands taken".	Then the old woman said to the man that he should do as best he could, "and hurry away, because you won't be able to withstand his shouting, if he gets his hands on you".
Hún tekr hörpuna ok hleypr á brott með.	She took the-harp and ran to away with.	She took the harp and ran away with it.
Nú gengr karl þar til, er Heimir sefr.	Now went man there to, where Heimir slept.	Now the man went to where Heimir slept.
Hann höggr til hans, ok verðr þat mikit sár, ok verðr honum laus öxin.	He hewed to him, and became that much wounds, and became he loose axe.	He struck at him, and his wounds were great, and his axe came loose.
Hann hleypr þegar í brott sem hann mátti hraðast.	He ran straightaway to away as he could fastest.	He rain away as fast as he could.
Nú vaknar hann við áverkann, ok vannst honum at fullu.	Now awoke he with wound, and defeated him in full.	Now he awoke with the wound, and he was defeated.
Ok þat er sagt, at svá mikill gnýr varð í hans fjörbrotum, at undan gengu súlur í húsinu ok ofan fell húsit allt ok varð landskjálfti mikill, ok lýkr þar hans ævi.	And it was said, that so much din was of his death-throes, from under went the-pillars of the-house and down fell the-house all and there-was an-earthquake great, and ended there his life.	And it was said that there was so much din from his death throes that the pillars of the house fell down, and there was a great earthquake, and there his life ended.
Nú kom karl þar, sem kerling var, segir nú, at hann hefir drepit hann, "ok þó var þat of hríð, er ek vissa eigi, hvé fara mundi, ok þessi maðr var furðu mikill fyrir sér, en þó væntir mik, at hann sé nú í helju".	Now came the-man there, where the-old-woman was, said now, that he had killed him, "and though was that of awhile, that I knew not, how going would, and this man was surprisingly large before him, but though expect me, that he is-being now in Hel".	Now the old man came to the old woman and said that he had now killed him, "and for a while I didn't know how it would go, as this man was surprisingly large, but now I expect he is in Hel".

Old Norse	Literal	English
Kerling mælti, at hann skyldi hafa þökk fyrir verkit, ok væntir mik, at nú hafim vit ærit fé, ok skulum vit reyna, hvart ek hefi satt sagt".	The-old-woman said, that he should have thanks for work, "and expect I, that now have we plenty-of wealth, and shall we test, whether I have truth said".	The old woman said that he would have thanks for his work, "and I expect that now we will have plenty of wealth, and we will see if what I have said is true".
Nú kveykja þau eld, en kerling tekr hörpuna ok vildi upp koma ok mátti eigi annars kostar en hún varð at brjóta, því at hún hafði eigi hagleik til.	Now kindled they a-fire, as the-old-woman took the-harp and willed to-open come and could not any-other use except she was to break, because that she had not the-strength to.	Now they kindled a fire, and the woman took the harp and wanted to open it, but could find no other way to open it other than break it, because she did not have the strength.
Ok nú fær hún upp komit hörpunni, ok þar sér hún eitt meybarn, at hún þóttist ekki slíkt sét hafa, ok þó var mikit fé í hörpunni.	And now did she open came the-harp, and there saw she a baby-girl, that she thought nothing such seen had, and also was much wealth in the-harp.	And once she opened the harp, there she saw a baby girl, she thought she had not seen anyone like her, and there was much wealth in the harp.
Nú mælti karl: "Þat mun nú verða sem opt, at illa mun gefast at svíkja þann, er honum trúir.	Now said the-man: "It shall now be as often, that evil shall give that betray then, who in-him believes.	Now the man said: "This will go as it always does, that evil will come to those who betray someone who trusts them.
Sýnist mér sem komin muni ómegð á hendr okkr".	Seems to-me that come shall infancy upon hands ours".	It seems to me that a dependant has come into our hands".
Kerling svarar: "Eigi er þetta eptir því, sem ek ætla, en þó skal nú ekki um sakast".	The-old-woman answered: "Not is this after according, as I intended, but though shall now not about harm".	The old woman answered: "This is not going according as I had intended, but no harm shall come of it".
Ok nú spyrr hún, hverrar ættar hún væri.	And now asked she, whose family she was.	And now she asked whose family she was from.
En þessi in unga mær svarar engu, svá sem hún hefði eigi mál numit.	But this the young girl answered not, so as she had not speech learned.	But the young girl did not answer, as she had no yet learned to speak.
"Nú ferr sem mik varði, at okkart ráð mundi illa fara", segir karl.	"Now goes as my expectation, that our plan will badly go", said the-man.	"Now I expect that our plan will go badly", said the man.

Old Norse	Literal	English
"Vit höfum unnit glæp mikinn.	"We have committed a-crime great.	"We have committed a great crime.
Hvat skulum vit sjá fyrir barni þessu?"	How shall we see for child this?"	How shall we look after this child?"
"Auðvitat er þat", sagði Gríma.	"Obvious is that", said Grima.	"It is obvious" said Grima.
"Hún skal eptir móður minni heita Kráka".	"She shall after mother mine be-named Kraka".	"She shall be named Kraka after my mother".
Nú mælti karl: "Hvat skulum vit sjá fyrir barni þessu?"	Now said the-man: "How shall we see for child this?"	Now the man said: "How shall we take care of this child?".
Kerling svarar: "Ek sé gott ráð til: Vit skulum segja hana okkra dóttur ok upp fæða".	The-old-Woman answered: "I see a-good plan to: we shall say she-is our daughter and up foster".	The old woman answered: "I can see a good plan, we shall say that she is our daughter and foster her".
"Því mun engi trúa", sagði karl.	"That will no-one believe", said the-man.	"No one will believe that", said the man.
"Miklu er barn þetta geðsligra en vit.	"Greater is child this pleasing than we.	"This child is more attractive than we are.
Erum allóvæn bæði, ok munu engi líkendi á þykkja, at vit munum eiga því líkt barn, svá endemlig sem vit erum bæði".	We-are all-ugly both, and shall no-one likely to think, that we should have therefore like child, so strange as we are both".	We are both ugly, and no one shall think it likely, that we should have such a child, so strange as we both are".
Nú mælti kerling: "Eigi veistu, nema ek hafa í nokkur brögð, at þetta megi eigi óvænt þykkja.	Now spoke the-old-woman: "Not know-you, except I have a certain trick, that this may not unexpected seem.	Now the old woman spoke: "You don't know this, but I have a certain trick, and it may not seem so unexpected.
Ek mun láta gera henni koll ok ríða í tjöru ok öðru, er vænst er, at síst komi hár upp.	I would have made her shaved and smear about tar and other-things, it-is expected to-be, that at-least comes hair up.	I would have her head shaved and smear it with tar and other things when her hair is expected to grow back.
Hún skal eiga hött síðan.	She shall have a-hood afterwards.	Afterwards she will wear a hood.

Old Norse	Literal	English
Eigi skal hún ok vel klædd vera.	Not shall she also well clothed be.	She will not be well clothed.
Mun þá saman draga vár yfirlit.	Shall then together carry our appearance.	Then she shall take on our appearance.
Má vera, at menn trúi því, at ek hafa mjök væn verit, þá er ek var ung.	May be, that people believe therefore, that I have much fairness been, then when I was young.	Maybe people will believe therefore that I had been fair when I was young.
Hún skal ok vinna þat, er verst er".	She shall also do-work that, of the-worst is".	She shall also do all of the worst work".
En þat hugðu þau karl ok kerling, at hún mætti ekki mæla, er hún svarar þeim aldri.	Then that thought they the-man and the-old-woman, that she could not speak, as she answered them never.	Then the old man and the old woman thought that she could not speak, as she never answered them.
Nú er þat gert, sem kerling hefir fyrir hugat.	Now was it done, as the-old-woman had before thought.	Now it was done, as the old woman had planned.
Nú vex hún þar upp í miklu fátæki.	Now grew she there up in much wealth-taken.	Now she grew up there in much poverty.
2	2	2
Herruðr hét jarl ríkr ok ágætr á Gautlandi.	Herrud was-named an-earl rich and famous in Götaland.	There was an earl named Herrud who was a powerful and famous earl in Götaland.
Hann var kvángaðr.	He was married.	He was married.
Dóttir hans hét Þóra; hún var allra kvenna fríðust sýndum ok kurteisust at sér um alla hluti, þat er til handa má bera ok betra er at hafa en án vera.	Daughter his named Thora she was of-all women most-beautiful appearance and well-mannered as seen regarding all things, that is to hand may bear and better that to have than without be.	His daughter was named Thora, she was the most beautiful woman in appearance and well mannered in all things that it is better to have than be without.
Þat var hennar kenningarnafn, at hún var kölluð borgarhjörtr, fyrir því at svá bar hún af öllum konum at fegrð sem hjörtr af öðrum dýrum.	It was her nickname, that she was called Fortress-Hart, for because that so surpassed she over all women in fairness such-as the-hart over other wild-animals.	It was her nickname, that she was called Fortress-Hart, because she surpassed all women in fairness as the hart surpasses over other animals.

Old Norse	Literal	English
Jarlinn unni mikit dóttur sinni.	The-earl loved much daughter his.	The early loved his daughter very much.
Hann lét gera henni eina skemmu skammt frá höll konungs, ok um þá skemmu var skíðgarðr.	He had made her a cabin short-distance away-from hall king's, and around that cabin was plank-fence.	He had a cabin made for her a short distance away from the king's hall, and there was a fence around the cabin.
Þat lagði jarl í vanda sinn at senda dóttur sinni hvern dag nokkut til skemmtanar, en þat mælti hann, at því mundi hann fram halda.	This had the-earl to custom his to send daughter his each day something to entertain, and that said he, that since would he going-forward hold.	The earl had a custom to send his daughter something every day to entertain her, and said that he would continue to do so.
Frá því er sagt, at hann lét færa henni lítinn lyngorm einnhvern dag, ákafliga fagran, ok þessi ormr þótti henni góðr ok lét hann í sitt eski ok bar undir hann gull.	From-there accordingly was said, that he had brought to-her a-little heather-snake one day, extremely beautiful, and this serpent thought she good and put him in his box and placed under him gold.	From this it was said that one day he had a little heather-snake brought to her, extremely beautiful, and she thought it was good, and put him in his box and placed gold under him.
Skamma stund var hann þar, áðr hann óx mikit ok svá gullit undir honum.	Short while was he there, before he grew greatly and so the-gold under him.	After a short while the serpent grew greatly, and so had the gold underneath him.
Þar kemr, at eigi hefir hann rúm í eskinu, ok liggr nú í hring um eskit utan.	It became, that not had he room about the-box, and laid now in a-ring around the-box outside.	So it became that he did not have room inside the box, and now laid in a ring around the box.
Ok þar kemr of síðir, at eigi hefir hann rúm í skemmunni, ok gullit vex undir honum jafnt sem ormrinn sjálfr.	And then came of since, that none had he room about the-cabin, and gold grew under him equally as the-serpent himself.	And after that, it did not have room in the cabin, and the gold underneath him grew equally as the serpent.
Nú liggr hann utan um skemmuna, svá at saman tók höfuð ok sporðr, ok illr gerist hann viðreignar, ok þorir engi maðr at koma til skemmunnar fyrir þessum ormi nema sá einn, er honum færir fæðslu, ok oxa þarf hann í mál.	Now laid he outside about the-cabin, so that together took head and tail, and difficult was he dealt-with, and dared no man to come to the-cabin before this serpent except except one, who he brought food, and an-ox needed he as a-meal.	Now he laid outside around the cabin, so that his head and tail were together, and he was difficult to deal with, and no man dared come to the cabin before this serpent, except one that brought food, and he needed an ox each meal.

Old Norse	Literal	English
Jarli þykkir mikit mein á þessu ok strengir þess heit, at hann mun þeim manni gefa dóttur sína, hvat manna sem hann er, ef at bana yrði orminum, ok gull þat, er undir honum er, skal vera hennar heimanfylgja.	The-earl thought much harm of this and bound this pledge, that he would the man give daughter his, that man which he who, if to kill would the-serpent, and gold that, which under him was, should be her home-following.	The earl thought this was a great harm, and bound a pledge, that he would give his daughter to the man who killed the serpent, and the gold that lay under him, would be her dowry.
Þessi tíðendi spyrjast víða of land, en þó treystist engi til at ráða fyrir þessum mikla ormi.	This news spread widely about the-land, and though trusted no-one to that prevail before this great serpent.	The news spread widely about the land, but no one trusted himself to prevail over this great serpent.
3	3	3
Í þann tíma réð fyrir Danmörku Sigurðr hringr.	In that time ruled for Denmark Sigurd Hring.	In that time Sigurd Hring ruled Denmark.
Hann var ríkr konungr ok er frægr orðinn af þeiri orrostu, er hann barðist við Harald hilditönn á Brávelli ok fyrir honum fell Haraldr, sem kunnigt er orðit of alla norðrálfu heimsins.	He was powerful king and was famous become for their battles, which he fought with Harald Wartooth at Bravellir and before him fell Harald, as known of words about all northern-lands of-the-world.	He was a powerful king and had become famous from the battle which he had fought with Harald Wartooth at Bravellir. Harald fell before him, as became known in all the northern lands of the world.
Sigurðr átti einn son, er Ragnarr hét.	Sigurd had one son, which Ragnar named.	Sigurd had a son who was named Ragnar.
Hann var mikill vexti, vænn yfirlits ok vel viti borinn, stórlyndr við sína menn, en grimmr sínum óvinum.	He was great grown, handsome to-look-at and well knowing carried, generous with his men, but grim with-his un-friends.	He was large grown, handsome to look at, well knowing and keen, generous with his men and fierce with his enemies.
Þegar hann hafði aldr til, fær hann sér lið ok herskipa, ok gerist hann inn mesti hermaðr, svá at varla fæst hans maki.	When he had age come-to, got he himself men and a-warship, and became he the most warrior-man, so that hardly few him matched.	When he had come of age, he got himself some men and a warship, and became the greatest warrior, so that hardly anybody matched him.

Old Norse	Literal	English
Hann spyrr þetta, er Herruðr jarl hafði um mælt; gefr hann at engan gaum ok lætr sem hann viti eigi.	He heard-of this, what Herrud earl had about said; gave he this no heed and acted as-though he knew not.	He heard of what Herrud had said, and gave no heed and acted as though he didn't know.
Hann lætr gera sér föt með undarligum hætti, þat eru loðbrækr ok loðkápa, ok nú er ger eru, þá lætr hann þau vella í biki.	He had made himself clothing with strange ways, that they-were shaggy-breeches and shaggy-cape, and now were made they, then had he them boiled in tar.	He had made himself clothing in a strange way, they were shaggy breeches and a shaggy cape, and when they were made, he had them boiled in tar.
Síðan hirðir hann þau.	Then hid he them.	Then he hid them.
Þat er eitthvert sumar, er hann heldr her sínum til Gautlands ok leggr í leynivág einn skip sitt ok var skammt þaðan, þat er jarl réð fyrir.	Then was one summer, that he took warband his to Götaland and laid in hidden-creek one ship his and was a-short-distance from-there, that where the-earl ruled from.	Then one summer, he took his warband to Götaland, and laid his ship in a hidden creek, which was a short distance from where the earl ruled from.
Ok er Ragnarr hafði þar eina nótt verit, vaknar hann snemma um morgininn, ríss upp ok tekr þessi in sömu vápnföt, er áðr var frá sagt, ok ferr í ok tekr spjót mikit í hönd sér ok gengr af skipunum einn saman ok þar, er sandr er, ok nú veltist hann í sandinum.	And when Ragnar had there one night been, awoke he early about morning, rose up and took these the same weapon-clothes, that before were from said, and went to also take a-spear great in hand his and went off the-ship alone together and where, that sand was, and now rolled he in the-sand.	And when Ragnar had been there one night, he awoke early in the morning, got up and took these weapon clothes, that were mentioned before, and he took a large spear in his hand, and went off the ship alone to where there was sand, and he rolled in the sand.
Ok áðr hann gengr í brott, tekr hann geirnagla ór spjóti sínu ok ferr nú einn frá skipunum til borgarhliðs jarls ok kemr þar snemma dags, svá at allir menn váru í svefni.	And before he went to away, took he spear-nail from spear his and went now alone from ship to city-gates earl's and came there early in-the-day, so-much that all men were a sleep.	And before he went away, he took the rivet from his spear and went alone from the ship to the earl's city gates, and arrived so early in the day that all the men were asleep.
Nú stýrir hann til skemmunnar.	Now turned he to the-cabin.	Now he turned to the cabin.

Old Norse	Literal	English
Ok er hann kemr í skíðgarðinn, þar sem ormrinn var, leggr hann til hans með spjóti sínu, ok þá kippir hann at sér spjótinu.	And then he came to the-fence, there as the-serpent was, laid he towards him with spear his, and then drew he then his spear.	And he came to the fence, where the serpent was, and laid towards him with his spear, and then drew his spear.
Ok annat sinn leggr hann.	And another his laid he.	He stabbed with his spear again.
Þat lag kemr í hrygg orminum, ok nú vinst hann við hratt, svá at spjótit gekk af skaptinu, ok verðr svá mikill gnýr í hans fjörbrotum, at skemman skelfr öll.	The spear-shaft came to spine serpent's, and now won he with quickly, so that the-spear-head went off the-spear-shaft, and was such great din about his death-throes, that cabin shook all.	The spear shaft hit the serpent's spine, and he defeated it quickly, and the spear head came off from the shaft, and there was such a noise as the serpent died that the whole cabin shook.
Ok nú snýr Ragnarr á brott.	And now turned Ragnar to away.	Now Ragnar turned away.
Þá kemr blóðbogi milli herða honum, ok þat sakar hann eigi, svá hlífa honum klæði þau, sem hann lét gera.	Then came blood-gush between shoulders his, and that harmed him not, so protected his clothing then, which he had made.	Then a gush of blood struck him between his shoulders, but it did not harm him, because the clothing that he had made protected him.
En þeir, er í skemmunni váru, vakna við gnýinn ok ganga út ór skemmunni.	Then they, who about the-cabin were, woken with the-din and went out of the-cabin.	They those who were around the cabin awoke with the noise and came out of the cabin.
Nú sér Þóra ganga einn mann mikinn frá skemmunni ok spyrr hann at nafni eða hvern hann vili nú finna.	Now saw Thora walking a man great away-from the-cabin and asked him of name and who he willed now to-find.	Thora now saw a large man walking away from the cabin and asked him his name and what he had come for.
Hann nemr staðar ok kvað vísu þessa:	He took stand and spoke verse this:	He stopped and spoke this verse:
"Hætt hefik leyfðu lífi, litfögr kona, vetra vák at foldar fiski fimmtán gamall, mínu; hafa skalk, böl nema bíti, bráðrakinn mér dauða,	"Risked have-I laid life, Fair-Coloured woman, of-winters Fought the on-land fish Fifteen old, mine Sea rogue's, lair taken bite, Hastening to-me death,	"I have laid my life, Fair coloured woman, of winters Fought the on-land fish Fifteen age, mine Sea rogue's, lair took bite Hastening me to death

Old Norse	Literal	English
heiðar lax til hjarta hringleginn, vel, smýgra".	Heath's salmon to heart ring-like, well, piercing".	Heath's salmon to heart ring-like, well, piercing".
Ok nú gengr hann á brott ok mælti ekki fleira við hana.	And now went he to away and said nothing more to her.	And now he went away and said nothing more to her.
En spjótit stóð í sárinu eptir, en hann hefir skaptit með sér.	But the-spear-point stayed in the-wound afterwards, that he had the-shaft with him.	But the spear point remained in the wound from the shaft that he had with him.
Nú er hún hefir þessa vísu heyrða, skildi hún, hvat hann sagði til um sitt erendi ok svá hvé gamall hann var.	Now that she had this verse heard, understood she, what he said to about his errand and so how old he was.	Now that she had heard this verse, she understood, what he said about his business and how old he was.
Ok nú hyggr hún at fyrir sér, hverr hann mundi vera, ok þykkist hún eigi vita, hvárt hann er mennskr maðr eða eigi, fyrir því at henni þykkir vöxtr hans vera svá mikill sem sagt er frá óvættum á þeim aldri, sem hann hafði, ok snýr hún inn í skemmuna ok sofnar.	And now wondered she that to herself, who he could be, and seemed to-her not knowing, if he was human man or not, for because that to-her seemed grown he had-been so much as said was from monsters about their age, as he had, and turned she then to cabin and slept.	And now she wondered to herself, who he could be, and she seemed not to know, if he was human or not, because it seemed to her that he was as well grown as was said about monsters, and she returned to the cabin and slept.
Ok er menn koma út um morgininn, verða menn þess varir, at ormrinn var dauðr ok hann var lagðr með einu miklu spjóti ok þat stóð fast í sárinu.	And as men came out around morning, were many of-this aware, that the-serpent was dead and he was laid with one great spear-tip and that stood fast in the-wound.	And as people came out in the morning, many were aware of this, that the serpent was dead and lay with a large spear tip that stood fast in the wound.
Nú lætr jarl þat í brott taka þaðan, ok var þat svá mikit, at fám var vápnhæft.	Now had the-earl that to away taken from-there, and was it so large, that few were weapon-capable.	Now the earl had it taken from there, and it was so large that few could weald the weapon.

Old Norse	Literal	English
Nú íhugar jarl, hvat hann hafði um mælt við þann mann, er orminum yrði at bana, ok þykkist eigi vita, hvárt mennskr maðr veldr þessu eða eigi, ok réðst nú um við vini sína ok dóttur, hvé hann skal eptir leita, ok þykkir á því líkendi, at sá mun eptir leita at hafa verðkaupit, er til hefir unnit.	Now thought the-earl, what he had about said with the man, that the-serpent would to death, and seemed not knowing, whether a-human man wielded this or not, and discussed now about with friends his and daughter, how he should afterwards seek, and seemed it therefore likely, that he would afterwards seek to have worth-price, which to have earned.	Now the earl thought about what he had said about the man who would put the serpent to death, and he seemed not to know whether it was a human who wielded it or not, and now he discussed this with his friends and his daughter, how he would then seek the man, and how the man would now seek the reward that he had won.
Þat réð hún at láta kveðja þings fjölmenns, "ok bið þá svá, at þangat komi allir þeir menn, er eigi vilja hafa reiði jarls ok nokkurs kostar mega sækja þingstefnu, ok ef sá er nokkurr, er við gengr banasári ormsins, skal hafa þat spjótskapt þangat, er fylgt hefir spjótinu".	So advised she to have a-greeting the-assembly crowd, "and ask then so, to from-there come all they men, that not wished to-have anger the-earl's and someone benefit may seek the-assembly, and if so that someone, who with going death-wound serpent's, shall have that spear-shaft get, that followed had spear-tip".	She advised him to have all the people summoned to an assembly, "and then ask, that all men attend who do not wish to provoke the earl's anger, and who was able to answer the summons in any way, if there is anyone who will avow the serpent's death wound, he will have the spear shaft which fits the spear point".
Þetta líst jarli vænligt ok lætr nú þings kveðja.	This beheld the-earl promising and had now the-assembly called.	The earl thought this was a promising idea and now had the assembly called.
Ok er at þeim degi kemr, er vera skal þingit, kemr jarl ok margir höfðingjar aðrir.	And when that the day came-to, which to-be should the-assembly, came the-earl and many chieftains other.	And when the day of the assembly arrived, the earl arrived along with many other chieftans.
Þar verðr mikit fjölmenni.	There were many followers.	There were many followers.
4	4	4
Þetta spyrst til skipa Ragnars, at þaðan skammt var þing stefnt.	This heard about ship Ragnar's, that from-there short-distance was the-assembly located.	This was heard about on Ragnar's ship, that was a short distance from the assembly.

Old Norse	Literal	English
Ok nú ferr Ragnarr frá skipum náliga með allan her sinn til þingsins.	And now went Ragnar away-from ships near-lying with all warband his to-the-assembly.	And now Ragnar and all his warband went away from the ship to the assembly.
Ok er þeir koma þar, nema þeir staðar nakkvat frá öðrum mönnum, því at Ragnarr sér nú, at komit var fjölmenni mikit frá því, sem vani var til.	And when they came there, took they places somewhat apart-from other people, because that Ragnar saw now, that come were followers much from before, than usually were to.	And when they arrived, they took places somewhat apart from other people, because Ragnar now saw that there were many more followers before than was usual.
Þá stendr jarl upp ok kveðr sér hljóðs ok talar, biðr menn hafa þökk fyrir, er vel hafa skipast við hans orðsending, ok segir síðan atburð þann, sem orðinn er, fyrst frá því, hversu hann hafði um mælt við þann mann, er orminum yrði at bana, síðan, at "ormrinn er nú dauðr, ok sá hefir látit eptir standa spjótit í sárinu, er unnit hefir þetta frægðarverk.	Then stood earl up and called-for himself-to be-heard and talk, bid men to-have thanks for, that well have been-done with his word-sending, and said afterwards events then, that became were, first from according-to, how he had about spoken with then men, that serpent should-be to death, since, that "serpent is now dead, and so has laid after standing spear-tip in wound, which won has this famous-work.	Then the earl stood up and called for himself to be heard, he thanked the people for responding so well to his message, and then said what events had happened, from when he had promised to the man who would slay the serpent, then he said: "The serpent is now dead, and and a spear tip was found afterwards laying in the wound, from this famous deed.
Ok ef nokkurr er sá hér kominn til þingsins, er þat skapt hafi, er þessu spjóti hæfi, beri hann þat fram ok sanni svá sögn sína, þá skal ek þat allt enda, er ek hefi um mælt, hvárt sem hann er af meirum stigum eða minnum".	And if someone has so here come to assembly, who that shaft has, that this spear-tip has, bear he that forward and prove so say himself, then shall I that all conclude, as I have about said, whether as he is of greater level or lesser".	And if anyone has come here to the his assembly, who has the spear shaft, that fits this spear tip, let him come forward and prove it himself, then I shall fulfill what I have said, whether he is of a higher or lower degree".
Ok lýkr hann svá sínu máli, at hann lætr bera spjótit fyrir hvern mann, er á er þinginu, ok biðr sér segja, hverr sá er, er við þessu gengr eða þat skapt hefir, er hér hæfir til.	And ended he so his speech, that he had borne the-spear-tip before each man, that about was assembly, and bid he say, who so had, that with this going or that shaft had, that here fits to.	And when his speech had ended, he had the spear tip borne before each man, who was at the assembly, and he bid that whoever had the shaft that fit should say so.
Nú er svá gert.	Now was so done.	Now this was done.

Old Norse	Literal	English
Eigi finnst sá né einn, er þat skapt hafi.	Not found was the one, who that shaft had.	No one was found who had the spear shaft.
Nú er komit þar, sem Ragnarr er, ok sýnt honum spjótit, ok gengr hann við, at hann mun eiga, ok þar hæfir hvárt eptir öðru, skaptit ok spjótit.	Now were come there, where Ragnar was, and showed him the-spear-tip, and went it with, that he must own, and there had each after other, shaft and spear-tip.	Now they came to where Ragnar was, and showed him the spear tip, and so it went that he must own it, because the shaft and the spear tip fit together.
Nú þykkjast menn vita, at hann mun hafa orðit orminum at bana, ok verðr hann af þessu verki harðla mjök frægr of öll Norðrlönd, ok biðr hann nú Þóru, dóttur jarls, ok hann tekr því vel, ok nú er hún honum gift, ok er fengit at mikilli veislu með inum bestum föngum í því ríki.	Now realised men knowing, that he must have been serpent that killer, and became he of this work very much famous of all the-northern-lands, and asked-for he now Thora, daughter the-earl's, and he took with well, and now was she with-him married, and was had the biggest feast with the best provisions of in the-Kingdom.	Now the men realised that he must have been the serpent's killer, and from this deed he became very famous in all of the northern lands, and he now asked for Thora, the earl's daughter, and he welcomed her, and she married him, and there was the biggest feast with the best provisions in the kingdom.
At þessi veislu kvángast Ragnarr.	At this feast was-married Ragnar.	At this feast Ragnar was married.
Ok er lokit er veislunni, ferr Ragnarr til ríkis síns ok réð fyrir ok ann mikit Þóru.	And when ended the feast, travelled Ragnar to kingdom his and ruled for and loved much Thora.	And when the feast ended, Ragnar travelled to his kingdom and ruled, and loved Thora very much.
Þau eiga tvá sonu; hét Eirekr inn ellri, en Agnarr inn yngri.	They had two sons called Eirek the elder, and Agnar the younger.	They had two sons, the elder was named Erik, and the younger was named Agnarr.
Þeir váru miklir vexti ok fríðir sýnum.	They were great grown and handsome appeared.	They grew large and were handsome in appearance.
Sterkari váru þeir miklu en aðrir menn flestir, er þá váru uppi.	Stronger were they much than other men most, that then were about.	They were stronger than most other men who were about at the time.
Þeir námu alls konar íþróttir.	They took all kinds sports.	They learned all kinds of sports.

Old Norse	Literal	English
Þat var eitthvert sinn, at Þóra kenndi sér sóttar, ok andast hún ór þessi sótt.	Then was some one-day, that Thora felt herself to-be-sick, and died she from this sickness.	Then one day, Thora fell sick, and she died from her sickness.
En Ragnari þótti þetta svá mikit, at hann vill eigi ráða ríkinu ok tekr aðra menn til at ráða ríkinu með sonum sínum.	Then Ragnar thought this so much, that he willed not to-rule the-Kingdom and took other men to that rule kingdom with sons his.	Ragnar was so affected by this, that he would not rule the kingdom, and appointed other men to rule the kingdom with his sons.
En hann tekr nú til iðnar sinnar innar sömu, sem hann hafði fyrr haft, ok ræðst nú í hernað, ok hvar sem hann ferr, færr hann sigr.	Then he took now to trade his the same, as he had before had, and decided now to raiding, and everywhere which he travelled, accomplished he success.	Then he took up the same occupation as he had before, and decided to go raiding, and everywhere he travelled, he accomplished success.
5	5	5
Nú er þat eitt sumar, at hann heldr skipum sínum til Noregs, því at hann átti þar marga frændr ok vini ok vill þá hitta.	Now was it one summer, that he held ship his to Norway, because that he had there many kinsmen and friends and willed then to-meet.	Now it was one summer that he set his ship's course to Norway, because he had many kinsmen and frends there that he wanted to meet.
Hann kemr skipum sínum um kveldit í höfn eina litla, en þar var bær skammt þaðan, er hét á Spangarheiði, ok lágu þeir þar í höfn þá nótt.	He came ship his about evening to harbour one little, and there was farm short-way from-there, that named was Spangarheid, and lay they there in harbour that night.	He came in his ship to a little harbour about evening, and there was a farm a short way from there that was named Spangarheid, and lay there in the harbour that night.
Ok er morginn kom, skyldu matsveinar fara á land at baka brauð.	And as morning came, would the-cooks go on land to bake bread.	And as morning came, the cooks would go on land to bake bread.
Þeir sjá, at bær er skammt frá þeim, ok þótti þeim sér þat betr gegna at fara til húss ok vera þar at.	They saw, that the-farm was short-distance from them, and thought they that it better going to travel to the-house and be there to.	They saw that the farm was a short distance away from them, and they thought that it would be better to travel to the house and work there.

Old Norse	Literal	English
Ok er þeir kómu til þess ins litla bæjar, þá hitta þeir einn mann at máli, ok er þat kerling, ok spurðu, hvárt hún væri húsfreyja eða hvat hún héti.	And when they came to this the little farm, then met they a person that having-a-meal, and was it an-old-woman, and asked, whether here was the-lady-of-the-house or what she-was named.	And when they came to this little farm, they met a person having a meal, and it was an old woman, and they asked her whether she was the lady of the house and what was her name.
Hún segir, at hún sé húsfreyja, "ok nafn mitt óvant, ek heiti Gríma, eða hverir eru þér?"	She said, that she was the-lady-of-the-house, "and name mine not-lacking, I-am named Grima, but who are you?".	She said that she was the lady of the house, "and my name is not lacking, I am named Grima, but who are you?".
Þeir sögðu, at þeir væri þjónustumenn Ragnars loðbrókar, ok vilja þeir færa fram sýslu sína, "ok viljum vér, at þú vinnir með oss".	They said, that they were servants-of Ragnar Lothbrok, and willed they to-do from business theirs, "and will we, that you work with us".	They said that they were servants of Ragnar Lothbrok, and they wanted to be about their business, "and we want you to work with us".
Kerling svarar, at hendr hennar váru stirðar mjök.	The-old-woman answered, that hands hers were stiff much.	The old woman answered that here hands were very stiff.
"En verit hafði þat fyrrum, at ek kunna bjargvel sýslu mína, ok á ek mér dóttur þá, er at mun vera með yðr ok mun heim koma brátt ok heitir Kráka.	"But was had-been that before, that I could well-enough do-business mine, and that I my daughter then, who that could be with you and should home come soon and named Kraka.	"But before I could do my work well enough, and I have a daughter, who could work with you when she comes home, and she is named Kraka.
Er nú svá komit, at ek kem trautt ráði við hana".	But now so comes, that I come scarcely talk with her".	But now it has become such that I scarcely talk with her".
Ok nú er Kráka at fé farin um myrgininn ok sér, at skip váru komin við land mörg ok stór, ok nú tekr hún ok þvær sér.	And now was Kraka for cattle gone about morning and saw, that ships were coming to the-land many and great, and now took she and washed herself.	And now Kraka was gone for the morning with the cattle and saw that there were many large ships coming to the land, and she took to washing herself.

Old Norse	Literal	English
En kerling hafði henni þat bannat, því at hún vildi eigi, at menn sæi fegrð hennar, því at hún var allra kvenna vænst, en hár hennar var svá mikit, at tók jörð um hana, ok svá fagrt sem silki þat, er fegrst verðr.	But the-old-woman had her that banned, because that she willed none, that men saw beauty hers, because that she was of-all women fairest, and hair hers was so great, that touched earth about her, and so fair as silk that, the fairest was.	But the old woman had forbid her from doing that, because she did not want any men to see her beauty, because she was the fairest of all women, and her hair was so great, that it touched the ground around her, and it was as fair as the fairest silk.
Ok nú kemr Kráka heim.	And now came Kraka home.	And now Kraka came home.
En þeir matsveinar höfðu gert eld, ok nú sér Kráka, at þar eru menn komnir, þeir er hún hefir eigi fyrr sét.	Then the cooks had made a-fire, and now saw Kraka, that there were men come, they that she had not before seen.	Then the cooks had made a fire, and now Kraka saw that there were many men that had come, that she had not seen before.
Hún hyggr at þeim ok svá þeir at henni.	She looked at them and so they at her.	She looked at them and they looked at her.
Ok nú spyrja þeir Grímu: "Hvárt er sjá þín dóttir, in fagra mær?"	And now asked they Grima: "Is that seen your daughter, the fair maiden?"	And now they asked Grima: "Is that your daughter, the fair maiden?"
"Eigi er til þess logit", segir Gríma, "at sjá er mín dóttir".	"Not is to this a-lie", said Grima, "that seen is my daughter".	"It's no lie", said Grima, "she is my daughter".
"Furðu ólíkar máttu þit verða", segja þeir, "svá illilig sem þú ert.	"Surprisingly unlike might you be", said they, "so ill-like as you are.	"She is surprisingly unlike you", they said, "bad as you are.
En vér höfum eigi jafnvæna mey sét, ok enga sjám vér hana hafa þína mynd, því at þú ert it mesta ferlíki".	But we have not equal a-maiden seen, and none see we she has your image, because that you are the most monstrous".	As we have not seen a maiden equal to her, and none of us see your image in her, because you are the most monstrous".
Gríma svarar: "Eigi má nú á mér sjá.	Grima answered: "Not may now of me see.	Grima answered: "You may not see it of me now.
Brugðit er nú mínum yfirlitum ór því, sem var".	Brought-out are now my looks from what, they were".	My looks are not what they were".
Nú ræða þeir þetta, at hún vinni með þeim.	Now decided they this, that she work with them.	Now they decided that she would work with them.

Old Norse	Literal	English
Hún spyrr: "Hvat skal ek vinna?"	She asked: "What shall I work-on?"	She asked: "What shall I do?"
Þeir kváðust vilja, at hún teygði brauð, en þeir mundi baka eptir.	They said willed, that she stretch bread, and they would bake after.	They said that they wanted her to knead the bread, and they would bake it afterwards.
Ok tekr hún síðan til sinnar iðju, ok vinnst henni vel.	And took she since to this occupation, and worked she well.	And she took to work, and worked well.
En þeir horfðu á hana ávallt, svá at þeir gáðu eigi sýslu sinnar ok brenndu brauðit.	But they looked at her always, so that they looked not looking-after theirs and burned the-bread.	But they were always looking at her, so they were not looking at their work, and the bread burned.
Ok er þeir höfðu lokit verki sínu, fóru þeir til skipa.	And when they had ended work theirs, travelled they to the-ship.	And when they had ended their work, they travelled to the ship.
Ok þá er þeir skyldu brjóta upp vistir sínar, mæltu allir, at þeir hefði aldri jafnilla unnit ok væri hegningar fyrir vert.	And then when they should brought up food theirs, speaking all, that they had never equally deserved and would-be punished for be.	And when they brought up their food, everyone said that they had never done such a bad job, and the deserved to be punished.
Ok nú spyrr Ragnarr, hví þeir hefði þanninn matbúit.	And now asked Ragnar, why they had that-way food-prepared.	And now Ragnar asked them why they had prepared the food that way.
Þeir kváðust sét hafa konu svá væna, at þeir gáðu eigi sinnar sýslu, ok ætluðu þeir, at engi mundi henni vænni vera í veröldu.	They said saw they a-woman so fair, that they heeded not their looking-after, and supposed they, that no-one could her fairer be in the-world.	They said that they saw a woman so fair, that they did not look after the bread, and they supposed that there could be no one fairer in the world.
Ok er þeir tóku svá mikit af of hennar fegrð, þá segir Ragnarr ok kveðst þat vita, at sjá mundi eigi jafnvæn sem Þóra hafði verit.	And when they took so much from of her beauty, then spoke Ragnar and said that he-knew, that to-see could not equally as Thora had been.	And when they had finished talking so much about her beauty, then Ragnar spoke and said that he knew that she could not be as beautiful as Thora had been.
Þeir kváðu hana eigi óvænni.	They said she-was not less-fair.	They said that she was no less fair.

Old Norse	Literal	English
Þá mælti Ragnarr: "Nú mun ek senda þá menn, er gerla kunni at sjá.	Then said Ragnar: "Now shall I send then men, who completely know when seen.	Then Ragnar said: "Now I will send men who know what they see.
Ef svá er sem þér segið, þá er þetta athugaleysi yðr upp gefit, en ef konan er at nokkurum hlut óvænni en þér segið frá, munu þér taka hegning mikla á yðr".	If so is as you say, then is the carelessness yours up given, but if the-woman is for any less fair than you say from, shall you take punishment great upon you".	If it is as you say, then your carelessness is forgiven, but if the woman is any less fair than you say, you shall have great punishment upon you.
Ok nú sendir hann menn sína til fundar við þessa ina fögru mey, en andviðri var svá mikit, at þeir máttu eigi fara þann dag, ok mælti Ragnarr við sína sendimenn: "Ef yðr líst þessi in unga mær svá væn sem oss er sagt, biðið hana fara á minn fund, ok vil ek hitta hana; vil ek, at hún sé mín.	And now sent he men her to meet with this the fair maiden, but the-storm was so great, that they may not travel that day, and said Ragnar to his sending-men: "If you behold this the young maiden so fair as we are told, ask her travel to me meet, and will I to-meet her; wish I, that she be mine.	And now he sent men to meet with the fair maiden, but the storm was so great, that they could not travel that day, and Ragnar said to his messengers: "If this maiden is as fair as we have been told, ask her to travel to meet me, and I want to meet her, and I wish that she be mine.
Hvárki vil ek, at hún sé klædd né óklædd, hvárki mett né ómett, ok fari hún þó eigi ein saman, ok skal henni þó engi maðr fylgja".	Neither wish I, that she see-me clothed nor unclothed, neither sated nor hungry, and travelling she though not alone together, and shall she though no man follow".	I wish to see her neither clothed nor unclothed, neither sated nor hungry, and travelling not alone, but with no one with her.
Nú fóru þeir, þar til er þeir koma til húss, ok hyggja at Kráku vandliga, ok líst þeim sjá kona svá væn, at þeir hugðu enga aðra jafnvæna.	Now travelled they, then until that they came to the-house, and observed at Kraka closely, and beheld they so the-woman so fair, that they thought none other equal.	Now they travelled until they came to the house, and observed Kraka closely, and beheld that the woman was so fair that they thought that none were her equal.
Ok nú segja þeir orð herra síns, Ragnars, ok svá, hversu hún skyldi búin vera.	And now said they words lord theirs, Ragnar, and so, how she should prepared be.	And now they gave her Ragnar's message, and how she should be prepared.

Old Norse	Literal	English
Kráka hugði at, hversu konungr hafði mælt ok hvé hún skyldi búast, en Grímu þótti engan veg svá mega vera ok kveðst vita, at sjá konungr mundi eigi vera vitr.	Kraka thought of, what the-King had said and how she should prepare, but Grima thought no way so may it-be and said to-know, that seeing the-King could not be wise.	Kraka thought of what the king had said, and how she should prepare, but Grima thought that there was no way that this could be done, and said that this king could not be wise.
Kráka segir: "Því mun hann svá mælt hafa, at svá mun vera mega, ef vér skiljum eptir því, sem hann ætlar til.	Kraka said: "Therefore must he as said has, that so shall be-it may, if we understand after therefore, as his intentions towards.	Kraka said: "He must have said this because it can be done, if we can understand what his intentions are.
En víst eigi má ek í yðarri ferð vera þenna dag, en ek mun koma snemma á morgin til yðarra skipa".	But know not that-may I to yours travelling be this day, but I shall come early in the-morning to your ships".	But know that I cannot travel with you today, but I shall come to your ships early in the morning".
Nú fóru þeir í brott ok segja Ragnari svá búit, at hún mundi koma til fundar þeira.	Now travelled they to away and told Ragnar so prepared, that she would come to meet them.	Now they travelled away and told Ragnar how it was prepared, that she would come to meet them.
Ok nú er hún heima þá nótt.	And now was she home that night.	And how she was home that night.
En um myrgininn snemma segir Kráka karli, at þá mundi hún fara á fund Ragnars.	Then about morning early told Kraka the-old-man, that then would she travel to meet Ragnar.	Then early in the morning, Kraka told the old man that she was going to travel to meet Ragnar.
"En þó mun ek verða at breyta búnaði mínum nokkut; þú átt aurriðanet, ok mun ek þat vefja at mér, en þar yfir utan læt ek falla hár mitt, ok mun ek þá hvergi ber.	"But though should I be to change clothing mine somewhat; you have a-trout-net, and shall I that wrap about myself, and then over out let I fall hair mine, and should I then nowhere be-bare.	"But I must change my clothing somewhat, you have a trout fishing net, and I will wrap that around myself, and let my hair fall, so that I will not be bare anywhere.
En ek mun bergja á einum lauk, ok er þat lítill matr, en þó má þat kenna, at ek hefi bergt.	Then I will taste of a leek, and which that-is little food, but then may it be-known, that I have eaten.	Then I will have a taste of a leek, which is little food, then it may be known that I have eaten.

Old Norse	Literal	English
Ok ek mun láta fylgja mér hund þinn, ok fer ek þá eigi ein saman, en þó fylgir mér engi maðr".	And I shall have follow me dog yours, and travel I then not alone together, but though follows me no man".	And I shall have your dog following me, and then I will not be travelling alone, but there will be no one following me".
Ok er kerling heyrir hennar fyrirætlan, þykkir henni hún mikit vit hafa.	And when the-old-woman heard her intentions, thought her that-she great wit had.	And when the old woman heard her intentions, she thought that she had great wit.
Ok er Kráka er búin, ferr hún leiðar sinnar, þar til er hún kemr til skipa, ok var fögr tilsýndar, er hár hennar var bjart ok sem á gull eitt sæi.	And when Kraka was prepared, travelled she the-way hers, there until that she came to the-ship, and was of-fair appearance, that hair hers was bright and as of gold one seen.	And when Kraka was prepared, she travelled on her way, until she came to the ship, and was fair in her appearance, and her hair was as bright as gold.
Ok nú kallar Ragnarr á hana ok spyrr, hver hún væri eða hvern hún vildi finna.	And now called Ragnar to her and asked, who she was or who she willed to-meet.	And now Ragnar called to her and asked her who she was and who she wished to meet.
Hún svarar ok kvað vísu:	She answered and said a-verse:	She answered and spoke this verse:
"Þorik eigi boð brjóta, er báðuð mik ganga, né ræsis kvöð rjúfa,	"Deny not invitation break, That invite me to-come, Nor prove obligations broken,	"I do not break the invitation, That invites me to come, Nor prove my obligations broken,
Ragnarr, við þik stefnu; manngi er mér í sinni, mitt er bert hörund eigi, fylgi hefi ek fullgott, fer ek ein saman, mínu".	Ragnar, with your summons No-man is to-me of with, Mine is bare skin not, Followed have I full-good, Travelled I alone together, mine".	Ragnar, with your summons, No man is with me, My skin is not bare, I have been followed full well, My travel has been alone".
Nú sendir hann menn at móti henni ok lætr fylgja henni á skip sín.	Now sent he men to meet her and had follow her to ship theirs.	Now he sent his messengers to meet her and follow her to their ship.
En hún kveðst eigi fara vilja, nema henni sé grið gefin ok förunaut hennar.	But she said not travel willed, except she be mercy given and companionship hers.	But she said she did not want to travel, unless her companion and her were given safe conduct.

Old Norse	Literal	English
Nú er henni fylgt á konungs skip, ok er hún kemr í fyrirrúm, seilist hann í mót henni, en hundrinn beit í hönd honum.	Now was she followed to the-King's ship, and as she came to first, reached he to meet her, but the-dog bit to hand his.	Now she was followed to the king's ship, and as she came on to the deck first, he reached out to meet her, but the dog bit his hand.
Þeir menn hans hlaupa til ok drepa hundinn ok reka bogastreng at hálsi honum, ok fær hann af því bana, ok er eigi betr griðum haldit við hana en svá.	Then men his ran to and killed the-dog and drove bow-string about neck his, and got he of then death, and was none better safe-conduct held with her than that.	His men ran to the dog and killed it with a bow string around its neck, and he died from this, she got no better safe conduct than that.
Nú leggr Ragnarr hana í lypting hjá sér ok hjalar við hana, ok varð honum vel í skap við hana ok var blíðr við hana.	Now seated Ragnar her about the-deck beside himself and talked with her, and was he well of mood with her and was pleased with her.	Now Ragnar seated her on the deck beside him and talked with her, and his mood went well with her, and he was very pleased with her.
Hann kvað vísu:	He spoke a-verse:	He spoke a verse:
"Mundi víst, ef væri vörðr föður jarðar mætri mildri snótu, á mér taka höndum".	"Should-it-be certainly, if it-would-be Guardian father the-earth's Distinguished tender beauty, To mine take hand".	It should certainly be, if it would, The earths guardian father, Distinguished tender beauty, To take my hand".
Hún kvað:	She said:	She said:
"Vammlausa skalt, vísi, ef vilt griðum þyrma, heim höfum hilmi sóttan, heðan mik fara láta".	"Blemish-free shall, know, If will safe-conduct mercy, Home have prince sought, From-here my journey allow".	"Unblemished shall mark, If you will safe conduct mercy, Home, though prince I have sought, From here, my journey allow".

6

Nú segir hann, at honum líst vel á hana ok ætlar víst, at hún skyli með honum fara.	Now said he, that he beheld well of her and intended certainly, that she should-be with him travelling.	Now he said that he was very pleased with her, and that he certainly wanted her to travel with him.
Þá kvað hún eigi svá vera mega.	Then said she not so be-it may.	Then she said that it could not be.

Old Norse	Literal	English
Þá kvaðst hann vilja, at hún væri þar um nótt á skipi.	Then said he wished, that she would-be there about the-night in the-ship.	Then he said that he wished that she would stay the night on the ship.
Hún segir, at eigi skal þat vera, fyrr en hann kemr heim ór þeiri ferð, sem hann hafði ætlat, "ok má vera, at þá sýnist yðr annat".	She said, that not shall that be, before that he came home from their journey, which he had intended, "and may be, that there seems to-you something-else".	She said that could not be before he came home from their journey that he intended to go on, "and it may be that something else will seem better to you".
Þá kallar Ragnarr á féhirði sinn ok bað hann taka serk þann, er Þóra hefir átt ok var allr gullsaumaðr, ok færa sér.	Then called Ragnar to fee-servant his and asked him to-take shirt that, which Thora had owned and was all gold-embroidered, and brought to-see.	Then Ragnar called his treasurer and asked him to take a shirt that Thora had owned, which was embroidered with gold, and bring it to be seen.
Þá býðr Ragnarr Kráku á þá lund:	Then invited Ragnar Kraku in this manner:	Then Ragnar offered it to Kraka in this way:
"Viltu þenna þiggja, er Þóra hjörtr átti, serk við silfr of merkðan;	"Will-you this accept, Which Thora Hart had, Shirt with silver about marked	"Will you accept this, Which Thora Hart had, A shirt marked about with silver
sama allvel þér klæði;	Together all-well to-you clothing	It goes together with you well,
fóru hendr hvítar hennar um þessar gervar; sú var buðlungi bragna blíðum þekk til dauða".	Before hands white Hers about these skilled So was king hero Kind known until death".	Before, white hands Hers, over this skilled This king of heroes Was kind until death".
Kráka kvað á móti:	Kraka said in return:	Kraka said in return:
"Þorik eigi þann þiggja, er Þóra hjörtr átti, serk við silfd of merkðan; sama ælig mér klæði; því em ek Kráka kölluð, í kolsvörtum váðum, at ek hefi grjót of gengit ok geitr með sjá reknar".	"Greater-part not that accept, Which Thora Hart had, Shirt with silver of marked Together wretched to-me clothes Because am I Kraka called, In coal-black clothes, That I have gravel about gone And goats with so driven".	A greater part will not accept, That which Thora Hart had, The shirt marked with silver, Together with my wretched clothes, Because I am called Kraka, In coal black clothes, That have gone over gravel, And driven with goats".

Old Norse	Literal	English
"Ok vil ek víst eigi taka við serknum", segir hún.	"And will I certainly not take with the-shirt", said she.	"And I certainly don't want to take the shirt", she said.
"Vil ek ekki í skraut búast, meðan ek em hjá karli.	"Will I not about decoration prepare, as-long-as I am near the-old-man.	"I don't want to decorate myself as long as I live with the old man.
Kann vera, at yðr lítist betr á mik, ef ek búumst betr, ok vil ek nú fara heim.	Can it-be, that you look better to me, if I prepare better, and will I now travel home.	It may be that you look better upon me, if I am better prepared, and now I want to go home.
En þá máttu gera menn eptir mér, ef þér er þá samt í hug ok vilir þú, at ek fara með þér".	But then may send men after me, if you if then the-same in mind and will you, that I travel with you".	But you may send men after me, if you still have the same in mind and want me to travel with you".
Ragnarr segir, at eigi mun hugr hans skipast, ok ferr hún heim.	Ragnar answered, that not should mind his change, and travelled she home.	Ragnar answered that he would not change his mind, and she travelled home.
En þeir fóru, sem þeir höfðu ætlat, þegar þeim gaf byr, ok lý hann sínum erendum, eptir því sem hann hafði ætlat.	Then they went, as they had intended, as-soon-as they were-given fair-wind, and concluded he his errands, after accordingly as he had intended.	Then they travelled, as they had intended, as soon as they were given a fair wind, and he concluded his business as he intended.
Ok er hann ferr aptr, kemr hann sér í ina sömu höfn, sem hann hafði fyrr haft, þá er Kráka kom til hans.	And then he travelled back, came he himself to the same harbour, as he had before had, then when Kraka had-come to him.	And when he travelled back, he came to the same harbour as he had before, when Kraka came to him.
Ok þat it sama kveld sendir hann menn á fund hennar at segja orð Ragnars, at hún færi nú alfari.	And that the same evening sent his men to find her to say words Ragnar's, that she travel now for-good.	And that same evening, he sent his men to find her and give her Ragnar's message, that she should now travel for good.
En hún segir, at hún mun eigi fara fyrr en um morgininn.	But she said, that she could not travel before than about morning.	But she said that she could not travel before the morning.

Old Norse	Literal	English
Ríss Kráka upp snemma ok gengr til rekkju þeira karls ok kerlingar ok spyrr, hvárt þau vaki.	Rose Kraka up early and went to bed theirs the-old-man and the-old-woman and asked, if they-were awake.	Kraka rose up early and went to the old man and the old woman's bed, and asked if they were awake.
Þau kváðust vaka ok spurðu, hvat hún vildi.	They said-they awake and asked, what she wanted.	They said that they were awake, and asked what she wanted.
En hún segir, at hún ætlaði á brott ok vera þar ekki lengr.	Then she said, that she intended to away and be there no longer.	Then she said that she intended to go away and be there no longer.
"En ek veit, at þit drápuð Heimi, fóstra minn, ok á ek engum manni verra at launa en ykkr.	"And I know, that you killed Heimir, foster-father mine, and that I no person worse to repay than you.	"And I know that you killed Heimir, my foster father, and I want to pay back no one but you.
Ok fyrir þá sök vil ek ykkr ekki illt gera láta, at ek hefi lengi með ykkr verit, en nú vil ek þat um mæla, at annarr dagr sé ykkr öðrum verri, er yfir ykkr kemr, en inn síðasti verstr, ok munu vér nú skilja".	And for that sake will I to-you nothing ill be done, that I have long with you been, but now will I that about the-matter, that each day see you each worse, than over you came, then the next worse, and shall we now separate".	And for the sake of the long time that I have been with you, I do not want to do you any ill, but now I say that each day will be worse for you than those that came before, and your last day will be the worst, and we shall now separate".
Þá gengr hún leiðar sinnar til skipa, ok er þar vel við henni tekit.	Then went she way hers to ships, and was there well with her taken.	Then she went on her way to the ships, and she was well received.
Gefr þeim vel veðr.	Given were-they well weather.	They were given fair weather.
Þann aptan inn sama, er menn skulu rekkja undir sér, þá segir Ragnarr, at hann vill, at þau Kráka hvíli bæði saman.	Then evening the same, when men should-be covers under them, then said Ragnar, that he wished, that they Kraka rest both together.	Then the same evening, when men were to make their beds, Ragnar said that he wished that Kraka and he would rest both together.

Old Norse	Literal	English
Hún segir, at eigi mátti svá vera, "ok vil ek, at þú drekkir brúðlaup til mín, þá er þú kemr í ríki þitt, ok þykki mér þat mín virðing sem þín ok okkarrá erfingja, ef vit eigum nokkura".	She said, that not could so be, "and wish I, that you drink a-wedding-feast for me, then when you come to kingdom yours, and seems to-me that my honour as yours and our heirs, if sense to-have any".	She said that it could not be, "and I wish, that you drink a wedding feast for me, then when you come to your kingdom, that seems honourable to me as well as for you, and to our heirs, if we are to have any".
Hann veitti henni sína bæn, ok ferst þeim vel.	He granted to-her her bidding, and travelled they well.	He granted what she had asked, and they travelled well.
Kemr Ragnarr nú heim í land sitt, ok er dýrlig veisla búin í mót honum, ok nú er bæði drukkit fagnaðaröl í móti honum ok brúðlaup hans.	Came Ragnar now home to land his, and a dear feast prepared to meet him, and now were both drank-to toasts to meet him and wedding-feast his.	Ragnar now came to his land, and a dear feast was prepared to meet him, and now toasts were drunk to meet him, and for his wedding feast.
Ok inn fyrsta aptan, er þau koma í eina rekkju, vill Ragnarr eiga hjúskaparfar við konu sína, en hún biðst undan, því at hún segir, at á baki mundi bera nokkut, ef hún réði eigi.	And the first evening, when they came as one to-bed, willed Ragnar have marital-status with wife his, but she chose away-from, because that she said, that to back would carry something, if she ruled not.	And the first evening, when they came to bed together as one, Ragnar wished to have marital status with his wife, but she chose not to, because she said that she would carry a burden, if she did not get her way.
Ragnarr kvaðst ekki trúa mundu á þat, kvað þau ekki framvís karl ok kerlingu.	Ragnar said not believe would of that, said that not fore-knowing the-old-man and the-old-woman.	Ragnar said that he did not believe a word of it, and said that the old man and the old woman were not fore-knowing.
Hann spurði, hvé lengi svá skyldi vera.	He asked, how long so should-it be.	He asked how long it should be.
Þá kvað hún:	Then said she:	Then she said:
"Þrjár vit skulum þessar, ok þó saman, byggja	"Three we shall these, And though together, settle	"These three nights, we And though together be, sleep
hvárt sér nætr í höllu,	Each these nights in the-hall,	Each of these nights in the hall,
áðr heilug goð blótim;	About holy gods sacrifice	Rather sacrificing to holy gods,

Old Norse	Literal	English
þá munut mein á mínum megi til löng of verða; heldr ert bráðr at byrja þann, er bein hefir engi".	Than should harm to mine May to delay about be Behold your haste that brings-about then, which bones has none".	Than there would be my harm, This delay will not become Rather than your haste that brings Then, which has no bones".
Ok þó hún kvæði þetta, gaf Ragnarr at því engan gaum ok brá á sitt ráð.	And though she said this, gave Ragnar it since no heed and drew on his advice.	And although she had said this, Ragnar gave no heed, and drew on his own advice.
7	7	7
Nú líða stundir fram, ok var samför þeira góð ok miklar ástir.	Now passed awhile from, and was togetherness theirs good and much love.	Now a while passed, and their togetherness was good, and with much love.
En Kráka kennir sér sóttar ok verðr léttari ok elr sveinbarn, ok var sveinninn vatni ausinn ok nafn gefit ok kallaðr Ívarr.	Then Kraka knew herself symptoms and became lighter and raised a-baby-boy, and was the-boy water sprinkled and name given and called Ivar.	Then Kraka knew her symptoms and became with child, and raised a baby boy, and the boy was sprinkled with water and given the name Ivar.
En sá sveinn var beinlauss ok sem brjósk væri þar, sem bein skyldu vera.	But the boy was bone-less of which cartilage was there, where bone should be.	But the boy was boneless, as if there was cartilage where bone should be.
Ok þá er hann var ungr, var hann vexti svá mikill, at engir váru hans jafningjar.	And then as he was young, was he grown so much, that none was his equal.	And when he was young, he grew so large, that none was his equal.
Hann var allra manna fríðastr sýnum ok svá vitr, at eigi er víst, hverr meiri spekingr hefir verit en hann.	He was of-all men most-handsome thought and so wise, that none were certain, which more wise had been than he.	He was the most handsome of all men, and thought so wise, that none were certain if anyone had been wiser than him.
Þeim verðr enn fleiri barna auðit.	They became then more children fated.	They became fated to have more children.
Annarr sonr þeira hét Björn, inn þriði Hvítserkr, inn fjórði Rögnvaldr.	Another son theirs named Bjorn, the third Hvitserk, the fourth Rognvald.	Their second son was named Bjorn, the third Hvitserk, the fourth Rognvald.

Old Norse	Literal	English
Þeir váru miklir menn allir ok inir fræknustu, ok þegar þeir máttu nokkut at hafast, námu þeir alls konar íþróttir.	They were great men all and the bravest, and as-soon-as they could anything of have, took they all kinds sports.	They were all great men, and the bravest, and as soon as they could, they took up all kinds of sports.
Ok hvert sem þeir fóru, lét Ívarr bera sik á stöngum, því at hann mátti eigi ganga, ok skyldi hann hafa ráð fyrir þeim, hvat sem þeir höfðust at.	And wherever that they travelled, had Ivar bore himself upon poles, because that he may not walk, and should he have advice for them, whatever it-was they had to.	And wherever they travelled, Ivar had bore himself up on poles, because he could not walk, and he advised them on whatever they should do.
Nú eru þeir Eirekr ok Agnarr, synir Ragnars, miklir menn fyrir sér, svá at trautt finnast þeira jafningjar, ok búa þeir á herskipum hvert sumar ok eru ágætir af sínum hernaði.	Now were they Erik and Agnar, sons Ragnar's, great men for themselves, so that scarcely found they equal, and prepared they upon ships each summer and were-they renowned for their raiding.	Now Ragnar's sons Erik and Agnar, were such great mighty men, that their equal could not be found, they prepared their ships each summer and were renowned for their raiding.
Ok nú er þat einn dag, at Ívarr ræðir við bræðr sína, Hvítserk ok Björn, hvé lengi svá skal fram fara, at þeir skyli heima sitja ok leita sér engrar frægðar.	And now was it one day, that Ivar discussed with brothers his, Hvitserk and Bjorn, how long so shall forth travel, that they shall home sit and have themselves no-more fame.	And now it was one day, that Ivar discussed with his brothers, Hvitserk and Bjorn, how long it would be before they would travel forth, instead of sitting at home and not having any more fame for themselves.
En þeir segja, at þeir skyli hans ráðum fram fara um þat sem annat.	Then they said, that they should his advice forth go about it as other-things.	Then they said, that they should take his advice and go forth, as they did with other things.
"Nú vil ek", segir Ivarr, "at vér biðim, at oss sé fengin skip ok lið, svá at þau sé vel skipuð, ok síðan vil ek, at vér aflim oss fjár ok ágætis, ef svá vill upp takast".	"Now wish I", said Ivar, "that we wait, that we so get ship and crew, so that then be well equipped, and thereafter wish I, that we gain us wealth and greatness, if so will up take".	"Now I wish", said Ivar, "that we wait, so we get a ship and a crew, so that we will be well equipped, and afterwards I wish that we gain wealth and greatness for ourselves, if it will happen".

Old Norse	Literal	English
Ok er þeir höfðu þetta ráðit með sér, segja þeir Ragnari, at þeir vilja, at hann fái þeim skip ok skipi liði því, er reynt sé at herfangi ok búit vel fyrir alls sakir.	And when they had this discussed among themselves, told they Ragnar, what they wished, that he get them a-ship and equip a-crew accordingly, being experienced so as-to raiding and prepared well for all sake.	And when they had discussed this among themselves, they told Ragnar, that they wanted him to get them ships, and equip them with a crew accordingly, experienced in raiding and prepared for anything.
Ok gerir hann þat eptir því, sem þeir beiddu.	And did he that afterwards accordingly, as they asked.	And afterwards he did according to what they asked.
Ok nú er þetta lið er búit, fara þeir ór landi.	And now when that crew was prepared, travelled they over lands.	And now that the crew was prepared, they travelled over lands.
En þar sem þeir berjast við menn, fá þeir meira hlut ok fá sér nú bæði mikit lið ok fé.	And then as they fought with men, got they more loot and got themselves now both great men and wealth.	And then as they fought with men, they got more loot, and won for themselves both great men and wealth.
Ok nú segir Ívarr, at hann vildi, at þeir heldi þar til, er meira ofrefli er fyrir, ok reyndi svá sinn hraustleik.	And now said Ivar, that he wished, that they rather there until, that a-more overwhelming-force was present, and test so their bravery.	And now Ivar said that he wished for them to head for where a more overwhelming force was, so as to test their bravery.
Ok nú spyrja þeir, hvar hann vissi þess ván.	And now asked they, where he knew this hope.	And now they asked where he knew this hope.
Ok nú nefnir hann einn stað, þann er heitir Hvítabær, en þar höfðu verit blót, "ok margir hafa til leitat at vinna, ok hafa engir sigrast", ok hafði Ragnarr komit þar ok varð frá at hverfa ok fekk ekki at gert.	And now named he one place, that he named Hvitabaer, where they have made sacrifices, "and many have until sought to win, and have none conquered", and had Ragnar come there and was away-from to disappear and got nothing of done.	And now he named a place called Hvitabaer, where they made sacrifices, "and many have sought to win, and none have conquered", and Ragnar had gone there, but had been turned back and achieved nothing.
"Hvárt er þat lið svá mikit", segja þeir, "ok svá harðfengt, eða eru þar önnur torveldi?"	"Either is that company so great", said they, "and so tough, or are there other difficulties?"	"Is the company so great", they said, "or so tough, or are there other difficulties?"

Old Norse	Literal	English
Ívarr segir, at bæði var fjölmenni mikit ok blótstaðr mikill ok þat hafði öllum fyrir komit ok engir höfðu staðist.	Ivar said, that both were followers great and sacrificial-places great and that had all before come and none had withstood.	Ivar said, that they were great in followers and sacrificial places that of all that had come before them, none had withstood.
Ok nú mæla þeir, at hann skyldi fyrir ráða, hvárt þeir skyldu þangat halda eða eigi.	And now spoke they, that he should for decide, if they should from-there hold or not.	And now they spoke, that he should decide for them, if they should head there or not.
En hann segir, at hann vill heldr hætta á, hvárt meira má þeim harðfengi eða blótskapr landsmanna.	Then he said, that he willed-to behold the-danger of, whether more may-be their toughness or sorcery countrymen.	Then he said, that he wanted to see which was of more danger, their toughness, or the sorcery of the countrymen.
8	8	8
Nú halda þeir þangat, ok er þeir koma þar í land, búast þeir til uppgöngu.	Now held they from-there, and as they came there to land, prepared they to up-going.	Now they headed away from there, and as they came to land, they prepared to go on to land.
Ok nú þykkir þeim þurfa, at liðit gæti sumt skipanna.	And now thought they needed, a group to-guard some of-the-ships.	And now they thought that they needed a group fo guard some of the ships.
En Rögnvaldr, bróðir þeira, var þá ungr, at þeim þótti hann eigi til færr vera í svá mikilli mannraun at vera sem þeim þótti líkligt, at vera mundi, ok láta hann gæta skipa með sumu liði.	Then Rognvald, brother theirs, was then young, that they thought he was-not to capable was of so much trial as being which they thought likely, that being would, and had him guard the-ships with some men.	Then Rognvald, their brother, was young, so they thought he was not capable of such a trial that they thought there likely to be, and they had him guard the ships with some men.
En áðr þeir færi frá skipum, segir Ívarr, at þeir borgarmenn eigu naut tvau, ok eru þat kvígendi, ok menn höfðu því frá horfit, at eigi mátti standast lát þeira ok tröllskap.	And before they went from the-ships, said Ivar, that the townspeople owned bulls two, and are they bullocks, and men have before from turned, that none may withstand bellowing theirs and magic like.	And before they went from the ships, Ivar said, that the townspeople owned two bulls, and they are bullocks, and men have turned away from them, as no one may withstand their magical bellowing.

Old Norse	Literal	English
Þá mælti Ívarr: "Verðið við sem best, þótt yðr bjóði nokkurn ótta, því at eigi mun til saka".	Then spoke Ivar: "Become with as best, though you offer some fear, because that no-one should-be to blame".	Then Ivar spoke: "Become the best you can, even though you may feel fear, because nothing will be able to harm you".
Nú fylkja þeir liði sínu.	Now rallied they forces theirs.	Now they rallied their forces.
Ok er þeir nálgast borgina, verða þeir varir við, er byggja staðinn, taka nú at leysa út naut þessi, er þeir trúðu á.	And as they approached the-city, became they aware with, that settlement there, took now to releasing out the-bulls these, which they believed in.	As they approached the city, they became aware that the settlement there were about to release the bulls that they worshipped.
Ok er kvígendin eru laus látin, hlaupa þau hart ok láta illa.	And as the-bullocks were loose let, ran they roughly and bellowed wickedly.	As the bullocks were let loose, they ran roughly and bellowed wickedly.
Nú sér Ívarr þetta, þar sem hann er borinn á skildi, ok biðr fá sér boga, ok svá var gert.	Now saw Ivar this, there since he was carried a shield, and asked get his bow, and so was done.	Now Ivar saw this, since he was carried on a shield, and he asked them to get his bow, and so it was done.
Nú skýtr hann þessi in illu kvígendi, svá at hvárttveggja fekk bana, ok var nú af hendi leystr þessi ófriðr, er mönnum þótti mestr ótti at.	Now shot he these the evil bullocks, so that either got death, and was now of his-hand released this terror, that men thought the-greatest fear was.	Now he shot these evil bullocks, so that either of them were killed, and now this terror that the greatest fear to the men, was released by his hand.
Nú tekr Rögnvaldr til orða at skipum ok mælti við lið sitt, at þeir menn væri sælir, er slíka skemmtan skyldu hafa sem þeir bræðr hans hafa.	Now took Rognvald to words at the-ships and spoke with crew his, that they the-men would-be lucky, of such amusement should have as they brothers his had.	Now Rognvald at the ships took to words and spoke with his crew, saying that the men would be lucky if they should have such amusement as his brothers had.
"Ok gengr þeim ekki annat til, er ek skylda eptir vera, en þeir einir vilja hafa virðing af.	"And went they not any-other to, that I should behind be, but they only willed to-have honour of.	"And they went in no other way, that I stay behind, but they win all the honour.
Nú skulu vér ganga upp gervallir".	Now shall we go up all".	Now we shall all go up".
Ok nú gera þeir svá.	And now did they so.	And now they did so.

Old Norse	Literal	English
Ok þá er þeir koma eptir liðinu, gengr Rögnvaldr hart fram í bardagann, ok lýkr svá, at hann fellr.	And then as they came after the-forces, went Rognvald roughly forwards to battle, and ended so, that he fell.	And when they came upon the armies, then Rognvald went so roughly into battle, and it ended so, that he fell.
En þeir komast í borgina bræðr, ok tekst nú bardagi af nýju, ok lýkr svá, at borgarmenn komast á flótta, en þeir reka flóttann.	But then came into the-city brothers, and took now battle of new, and ended so, that the-townspeople came to flee, as they drove to-escape.	But the brothers came into the city, and the battle began again, and ended so that the townspeople came to flee, as they drove to escape.
Ok er þeir hverfa aptr til borgarinnar, kveðr Björn vísu:	And as they turned back to the-townspeople, said Bjorn a-verse:	And as they turned the townspeople back, Bjorn said a verse:
"Upp hrundu vér ópi, ór bitu meira en þeira,	"Up raised our battle-cry, Out-of bit more than they,	"Our battle cry was raised up, Our blades bit more than theirs,
satt mun ek til þess segja, sverð, í Gnípafirði; knátti hverr, er vildi,	Truth should I to this say, Swords, in Gnipafjord Should every-man, that wills,	I should say this truly, Swords, in Gnipafjord, Should every man, who wishes,
fyr Hvítabæ útan, né sitt spari sveinar sverð, mannsbani verða".	Before Hvitabaer out-of, Nor long save lads Swords, man-slayer become".	Become, out of Hvitabaer, Nor long sparing the lands, Swords, become slayers of men".
Ok er þeir koma aptr í borgina, taka þeir allt lausafé, en brenna hvert hús, er í var borginni, ok brjóta alla borgarveggi.	And when they came back to city, took they altogether wealth, and burned each house, that in was the-city, and broke all city-walls.	And when they came back to the city, they took their wealth all together, and burned each house that was in the city, and broke all the city walls.
Ok nú halda þeir skipum sínum þaðan.	And now held they ship theirs from-there.	Then their ship headed away from there.
9	9	9
Eysteinn hefir konungr heitit, er réð fyrir Svíþjóðu.	Eystein had king the-name, that ruled for Sweden.	There was a king who was named Eystein, that ruled Sweden.
Hann var kvángaðr ok átti eina dóttur.	He was married and had one daughter.	He was married and had one daughter.
Sú hét Ingibjörg.	So named Ingibjorg.	She was so named Ingibjorg.

Old Norse	Literal	English
Hún var allra kvenna fríðust ok vænst sýnum.	She was of-all women the-most-beautiful and fair seen.	She was one of the fairest and most beautiful women of all ever seen.
Eysteinn konungr var ríkr ok fjölmennr, illgjarn ok þó vitr.	Eystein king was powerful and many-men, ill-tempered and though wise.	King Eystein was powerful with many followers, ill tempered but wise.
Hann hafði atsetu at Uppsölum.	He had a-seat at Uppsala.	He had his royal seat at Uppsala.
Hann var blótmaðr mikill, ok at Uppsölum váru blót svá mikil í þann tíma, at hvergi hafa verit meiri á Norðrlöndum.	He was a-sacrificing-man great, and at Uppsala were sacrifices so much in that time, that nowhere had been more in the-North-Lands.	He was a great sacrificer, and at Uppsala the sacrifices were so much in that time, that there had never been more in the north lands.
Þeir höfðu átrúnað mikinn á einni kú, ok kölluðu þeir hana Síbilju.	They had belief great in one cow, and called they her Sibilja.	They had belief in a great cow, and they called her Sibilja.
Hún var svá mjök blótin, at menn máttu eigi standast lát hennar.	She was so much sacrificed-to, that men could not withstand bellowing hers.	She was so sacrificed to, that men would not withstand her bellowing.
Ok því var konungr vanr, þá er hers var ván, at þessi kýr in sama var fyrir fylkingum, ok svá mikill djöfuls kraptr fylgdi henni, at óvinir hans urðu svá ærir, þegar þeir heyrðu til hennar, at þeir börðust sjálfir ok gáðu sín eigi, ok fyrir þá sök var óherskátt á Svíþjóð, at menn treystust eigi við slíkt ofrefli at etja.	And accordingly it-was the-King's custom, then when war was expected, that this cow the same was before the-King, and so much devil's strength followed her, that enemies his became so insane, as-soon-as they heard of her, that they thought themselves and heeded themselves not, and for that reason was un-invaded all Sweden, that men trusted not with such overwheming-force to provoke.	And so it was the king's custom, when war was expected, that this same cow was before the king, and so much devil's strength followed her, that enemies became insane as soon as they heard her, and took no heed for themselves, and for that reason, Sweden was remained un-invaded, for men did not dare to provoke such an overwhelming force.

Old Norse	Literal	English
Eysteinn konungr átti vingott við marga menn ok höfðingja, ok er þat sagt, at í þann tíma var vinátta mikil með þeim Ragnari ok Eysteini konungi ok þeir váru því vanir, at sitt sumar skyldi sækja veislu hvárr þeira til annars.	Eystein the-King had friends-good with many men and chieftains, and was it said, that in those times was friendship great with them Ragnar and Eystein the-King and they were therefore friends, that they summer would seek-to feast each they at the-other's.	King Eystein had a good many friends among men and chieftans, and it was said, that in those times, there was great friendship with Ragnar and King Eystein, and they were great friends that would seek to feast with each other in the summer.
Nú kemr at því, at Ragnarr skal sækja veislu til Eysteins konungs.	Now came that therefore, that Ragnar would seek a-feast to Eystein the-King.	Now it came to be that Ragnar would seek to feast with Eysten the king.
Ok er hann kemr til Uppsala, var honum vel fagnat ok liði hans.	And as he came to Uppsala, was he well welcomed and company his.	And as he came to Uppsala, he was well welcomed and his company.
Ok þá er þeir drekka inn fyrsta aptan, lætr konungr dóttur sína byrla sér ok Ragnari.	And then as they drank the first evening, had the-King daughter his pour for-him and Ragnar.	And as they drank the first evening, the king had his daughter pour for him and Ragnar.
Ok þat mæltu menn Ragnars með sér, at engi væri annarr til en hann bæði dóttur Eysteins konungs, en hann ætti eigi lengr karlsdóttur.	And so spoke men Ragnar's among themselves, that nothing should-be otherwise to than he choose daughter Eystein's the-King, that he have no longer a-peasant's-daughter.	And Ragnar's men spoke among themselves that it should be no other way that he should choose King Eystein's daughter, and no longer have a peasant's daughter.
Ok nú verðr til einnhverr hans manna at tjá þetta fyrir honum, ok því lýkr svá, at honum er heitit konunni, ok skyldi hún þó sitja í festum mjök lengi.	And now became that one-of his men had expressed this before him, and therefore concluded so, that she was called the-woman, and should she though sit as promised-for very long.	And so it became that one of his men had expressed this to him, and so it concluded that the woman was promised to him, and she would stay betrothed to him for a very long time.
En þá er þeiri veislu var lokit, býst Ragnarr heim, ok ferst honum vel, ok er ekki sagt frá ferð hans, fyrr en hann á skammt til borgarinnar, ok liggr leið hans um skóg einn.	When then as there the-feast was ended, prepared Ragnar home, and left he well, and was nothing said from journey his, for that he then shortly-distance to the-city, and made way his about the-forest one.	When the feast was ended, Ragnar prepared for home, and he left well, and nothing was said about his journey, except when he was a short distance from the city, and made his way about the forest.

Old Norse	Literal	English
Þeir koma í eitt rjóðr, er var í skóginum.	They came to a clearing, and were in the-forest.	They came to a clearing, and were in the forest.
Þá lætr Ragnarr nema staðar lið sitt ok kvaddi sér hljóðs ok biðr þá menn alla, er í hans ferð höfðu verit til Svíþjóðar, at engi skyldi segja hans fyrirætlan, er stofnuð var um ráðahag við dóttur Eysteins konungs.	Then had Ragnar take places company his and called he be-heard and asked then men all, that of his journey had been to Sweden, that none should say his before-intentions, as established where about marriage-proposal with daughter Eystein's king.	Then Ragnar had his company take places and called to be heard, and he asked them all, that had been on his journey to Sweden, that there should be no discussion of his intentions regarding the marriage proposal with King Eystein's daughter.
Nú leggr hann svá ríkt við þetta, ef sá er nokkurr, er of þetta geti, at hann skal engu fyrir týna nema lífinu.	Now had he so ruled with this, if so that anything, that of this mentioned, that he shall nothing ahead-of lose except his-life.	Now he ruled along with this, that if anything of this was mentioned, that he shall have nothing ahead except losing his life.
En nú er hann hafði talað slíkt er hann vildi, fór hann heim til bæjarins.	When now had he had told such as he willed, travelled he home to the-estate.	When now he had told them such as he willed, he travelled home to the estate.
Ok nú verða menn fegnir, er hann kemr aptr, ok þá var drukkit fagnaðaröl í móti honum.	And now became men celebrated, that he came back, and then were drunk celebrations to meet him.	Men came to celebrate that he had come back, and then celebrations were drunk to meet him.
Ok er hann kemr í hásætit ok hefir setit eigi lengi, áðr Kráka kemr í höllina fyrir Ragnar ok sest í kné honum ok leggr hendr um háls honum ok spyrr: "Hvat er tíðenda?"	And when he came to high-seat and had sat not long, back Kraka came to the-hall before Ragnar and sat on knee his and laid hand about neck his and asked: "What is the-news?"	And when he came to his high seat and had not long sat, Kraka came to the hall before Ragnar and sat on his knee, and laid her hand about his neck, and asked: "What is the news?"
En hann kveðst engi kunna at segja.	But he said not knowing to tell.	But he said he knew of nothing to tell.
Ok er á leið kveldit, taka menn til drykkju, ok síðan fara menn til svefns.	And when about way evening, took men to drinking, and afterwards went men to sleep.	And so it went that evening, men took to drinking, and afterwards the men went to sleep.

Old Norse	Literal	English
Ok er þau koma í eina rekkju Ragnarr ok Kráka, spyrr hún hann enn tíðenda, en hann kveðst engi vita.	And when they came to as-one in-bed Ragnar and Kraka, asked she him yet news, but he said not knowing.	And when Ragnar and Krara came together in bed, she asked him the news, but he said he knew of nothing.
Nú vill hún hjala margt, en hann kveðst vera syfjaðr mjök ok farmóðr.	Now willed she to-talk many, but he said being sleepy much and travel-weary.	Now she wanted to talk more, but he said he was sleepy and very weary from his travels.
"Nú mun ek segja þér tíðendi", segir hún, "ef þú vilt mér engi segja".	"Now shall I say to-you news", said she, "if you will to-me not say".	"Now I shall tell you the news", she said, "if you will not say to me".
Hann spyrr, hver þau væri.	He asked, what that would-be.	He asked what that would be.
"Þat kalla ek tíðendi", segir hún, "ef konungi er heitit konu, en þat er þó sumra manna mál, at hann eigi sér aðra áðr".	"That call I news", said she, "if the-King has promised a-woman, but it is though some men say, that he not himself another before".	"That I would call news", she said, "If the king has promised a woman, but yet some men are saying, has he not another already".
"Hverr sagði þér þetta?" segir Ragnarr.	"Who said to-you this?" said Ragnar.	"Who said this to you?" said Ragnar.
"Halda skulu menn þínir lífi ok limum, því at engi sagði mér þinna manna", segir hún.	"Keep shall men yours lives and limbs, because that none told me your men", said she.	"Your men shall keep their lives and limbs, because none of your men told me", she said.
"Þér munduð sjá, at fuglar þrír sátu í trénu hjá yðr.	"You must-have seen, that birds three sat about the-tree beside you.	"You must have seen, that three birds sat about the tree beside you.
Þeir sögðu mér þessi tíðendi.	They told me this news.	They told me this news.
Þess bið ek, at þú vitir eigi ráða þessa, sem ætlat er.	This ask I, that you know not decision this, which intended is.	I ask you not to take this decision which you intend.

Old Norse	Literal	English
Nú mun ek segja þér, at ek em konungs dóttir, en eigi karls, ok faðir minn var svá ágætr maðr, at eigi fekkst hans jafningi, en mín móðir var allra kvenna fríðust ok vitrust, ok hennar nafn mun uppi, meðan veröldin stendr".	Now must I say to-you, that I am a-king's daughter, but not peasant's, and father mine was so great a-man, that not found-is his equal, but my mother was of-all woman the-most-beautiful and wise, and her name shall up, while the-world stands".	Now I must say to you, that I am a king's daughter, not a peasent's, and my father was so great a man, that his equal is not found, and my mother was the most beautiful and wise of all women, and her name will be remembered while the world stands".
Nú spyrr hann, hverr faðir hennar var, ef hún væri eigi dóttir þess ins fátæka karls, er á Spangarheiði var.	Now asked he, who father hers was, if she was not the-daughter this the poor man's, which at Spangarheid was.	Now he asked who her father was, if she was not the daughter of a poor man who was at Spangarheid.
Hún segir, at hún var dóttir Sigurðar Fáfnisbana ok Brynhildar Buðladóttur.	She said, that she was the-daughter-of Sigurd Slayer-of-Fafnir and Brynhild Daughter-of-Budla.	She said that she was the daughter of Sigurd, the slayer of Fafnir, and Brynhild, the daughter of Budla.
"Þat þykki mér allólíkligt, at þeira dóttir mundi Kráka heita eða þeira barn mundi í slíku fátæki upp vaxa sem á Spangarheiði var".	"That seems-to me all-unlikely, that their daughter would Kraka be-named or they child would of such poverty up grow as in Spangarheid was".	"That seems unlikely to me, that they would have a daughter named Kraka, or a child who would grow up in such poverty as there was in Spangarheid".
Þá svarar hún: "Saga er til þess", ok nú segir hún ok hefr þar upp sögu, sem þau hittust á fjallinu Sigurðr ok Brynhildr ok hún var byrjuð.	Then answered she: "The-story is to this", and now said she and had there up the-saga, how they met on a-mountain Sigurd and Brynhild and she was brought.	Then she answered: "The story is this", and now she said the saga of what had happened, how they met on a mountain, Sigurd and Brynhild, and she was born.
"Ok er Brynhildr varð léttari, var mér nafn gefit, ok var ek kölluð Áslaug".	"And that Brynhild became lighter, was to-me a-name given, and was I called Aslaug".	"And that Brynhild became with child, and I was given a name and called Aslaug".
Ok nú segir hún allt, sem farit hafði frá því, er þau karl hittust.	And now said she all, that went had from before, that then old-man met.	And now she said all that had gone before, when the old man was met.
Þá svarar Ragnarr: "Þessum mun ek við bregða Áslaugar órunum, er þú mælir".	Then answered Ragnar: "This will I with unbelievable Aslaug tales, of-which you speak".	Then Ragnar answered: "I am amazed at these unbelievable tales of which you speak".

Old Norse	Literal	English
Hún svarar: "Þú veist, at ek em eigi heill maðr, ok mun þat vera sveinbarn, er ek geng með, en á þeim sveini mun vera þat mark, at svá mun þykkja sem ormr liggi um auga sveininum.	She answered: "you know, that I am not a-whole person, and should it be a-baby-boy, am I walking with, but about that boy shall be this mark, that so should seem as a-serpent lying in the-eyes the-boy's.	She answered: "You know that I am with child, and if it should be a baby boy I am walking with, there shall be a mark about his head, that shall look like a serpent lying in the boy's eyes.
Ok ef þetta gengr eptir, bið ek þess, at þú komir eigi til Svíþjóðar þeirar tíðar, at þú fáir dóttur Eysteins konungs.	And if this happens after, ask I this, that you come not to Sweden there this-time, that you marry daughter Eystein king's.	And if this happens after, I ask this, that you do not go to Sweden or marry King Eystein's daughter.
En ef þetta rýfst, far þú með sem þú vilt.	But if this fails, go you with as you wish.	But if this fails, go along with whatever you wish.
En ek vil, at sjá sveinn sé heitinn eptir feðr mínum, ef í hans auga er þetta frægðarmark, sem ek ætla, at vera muni".	But I wish, that so the-boy he-be named after father mine, if in his eyes is that birth-mark, as I suppose, that be shall".	But I wish that the boy be named after my father, if he has the birth mark in his eyes, as I suppose he will".
Nú kemr at þeiri stundu, er hún kennir sér sóttar ok verðr léttari ok elr sveinbarn.	Now came that they while, that she knew herself symptoms and was lighter and gave-birth-to a-baby-boy.	Now came the time when she knew her symptoms, and gave birth to a baby boy.
Nú tóku þjónustukonur sveininn ok sýndu henni.	Now took servant-maids the-boy and showed him.	Now the servant maids took the boy and showed him.
Þá mælti hún, at bera skyldi til Ragnars ok láta hann sjá.	Then said she, that bear should to Ragnar and let him see.	Then she spoke and said that they should bear him to Ragnar and let him see.
Ok nú er svá gert, at sá inn ungi maðr var borinn í höllina ok lagðr í skikkjuskaut Ragnars.	And now was so done, that so the young person was brought into the-hall and laid in the-lap-of-cloak Ragnar's.	And now it was done, so that the young person was brought into the hall and laig in the lap of Ragnar's cloak.
En er hann sér sveininn, var hann spurðr, hvat heita skyldi.	And when he saw the-boy, was he asked, what named should-be.	And they he saw the boy, he was asked what he should be named.
Hann kvað vísu:	He spoke a-verse:	He spoke a verse:

Old Norse	Literal	English
"Sigurðr mun sveinn of heitinn, sá mun orrostur heyja, mjök líkr vera móður ok mögr föður kallaðr; sá mun Óðins ættar yfirbátr vera heitinn, þeim er ormr í auga, er annan lét svelta".	"Sigurd should the-boy of be-called, So shall battles fight, Much like being mother And sons father called So shall Odin's lineage Above be named, Those which snakes in eyes, That others had slain".	Sigurd, the boy should be called, So shall battles fight, Much like his own mother, And son's father called, So shall be Odin's lineage, Above be named, Those which snakes in eyes, That others had slain.
Nú dregr hann gull af hendi sér ok gefr sveininum at nafnfesti.	Now drew he gold of hand his and gave the-boy that name-fastening.	Now he drew gold from his hand and gave the boy a name gift.
Ok þá er hann réttir höndina með gullinu, kemr við bak sveininum, en þat virðir Ragnarr svá sem hann vildi hata gullinu.	And then when he right hand with gold, came to back the-boy's, and that valued Ragnar so that he would hate gold.	And then when he held out the gold in his right hand, he touched his back, and Ragnar valued that he would hate gold.
Ok nú kvað hann vísu:	And now spoke he a-verse:	And now he spoke this verse:
"Brynhildar líst brögnum brúnstein hafa fránan dóttur mögr inn dýri ok dyggligast hjarta; sjá berr alla ýta undleygs boði magni, Buðla niðr, er baugi bráðgerr, hatar rauðum".	"Brynhild behold trickery, Brow-stones have from, Daughter sons the dear And most-virtuous heart Seen bears all out-to Wound-flame bringer strength, Budli descendant, of rings Disdains, hates red".	Brynhild, behold trickery, Brow-stones have from, Daughter dear to sons, And most virtuous heart, Seen borne out all to, Wound flame bringer of strength, Budli descendant of rings, Disdains the red gold".
Ok enn kvað hann:.	And then said he:	And then he said:
"Sá ek engum sveini nema Sigurði einum í brúnsteinum brúna barðhjarls tauma lagða; sjá hefir dagrýrir dýja, dælt er hann at því kenna, hvass í hvarmatúni	"See I none in-the-boy Except Sigurd alone In brow-stones brown Land-snakes bridle enriched So has day-diminishing beast, Dealt is he that therefore known, Sharp about eyelids-enclosure	"I see in no young boy, Except Sigurd alone, In brow stones brown, Land snakes bridle enriched, The beast's day diminisher, Dealt is he that is therefore known, Sharp in the eyelids enclosure,

Old Norse	Literal	English
hring myrkviðar fengit".	Ring dark-forests found".	Ring dark forests found".
Nú mælti hann, at þann svein skyldi bera í skemmu út.	Now said he, that the boy should carry to storehouse out.	Now he said that the boy should be carried out to the storehouse.
En þá var því lokit, at hann mundi til Svíþjóðar fara.	And then was therefore ended, that he would to Sweden travel.	And it was therefore ended, that he would travel to Sweden.
Ok nú kemr upp ætt Áslaugar, svá at þat veit hverr maðr, at hún er dóttir Sigurðar Fáfnisbana ok Brynhildar Buðladóttur.	And now came up the-lineage Auslag's, so that it-was known to-each man, that she was the-daughter-of Sigurd Slayer-of-Fafnir and Brynhild Daughter-of-Budla.	And the lineage of Auslag's was brought up, so that it was known to every man, that she was the daughter of Sigurd the slayer of Fafnir, and Brynhild, the daughter of Budla.

10

Old Norse	Literal	English
Nú er sú stund var liðin, er á var kveðit, at Ragnarr skyldi veisluna sækja til Uppsala ok kom hann eigi, þótti Eysteini konungi ger til sín svívirðing ok dóttur sinnar, ok nú var lokit vinfengi þeira konunganna.	Now as that time was passed, when it was declared, that Ragnar should feast seek at Uppsala and came he not, thought Eystein the-King had-done to him a-disgrace and daughter his, and now was ended friendship theirs the-King's.	Now the time had passed, when it was declared that Ragnar should seek a feast at Uppsala, and he did not come, and King Eystein thought that he had disgraced him and his daughter, and now the king ended their friendship.
Ok þá er þeir Eirekr ok Agnarr, synir Ragnars, spyrja þetta, þá ræddu þeir með sér, at þeir mundu fá sér lið mikit, sem þeir mætti mest, ok mundu herja á Svíþjóð.	And then were they Erik and Agnar, sons Ragnar's, learned of-this, then decided they with themselves, that they would get themselves a-company great, as they might most, and would wage-war in Sweden.	And then when Ragnar's sons Erik and Agnar learned of this, they decided among themselves that they would get themselves the greatest company that they could, and they would wage war in Sweden.
Ok nú draga þeir saman lið mikit ok búa skip sín, en þótti mikit undir, at vel tækist til, þá er skip skyldi fram setja.	And now drew they together a-group great and prepared ships theirs, but thought much depended, that well took to, then as ship should forwards set-out.	And now they drew together a great company and prepared their ships, but they thought that much would depend on their success when the ship set out.

Old Norse	Literal	English
Nú verðr þat, at skip Agnars skaust af hlunni, ok varð þar maðr fyrir, ok fær sá bana, ok kölluðu þeir þat hlunnroð.	Now was it, the ship Agnar's launched of the-rollers, and came there a-man in-front-of, and went so to-death, and called they that rollers-red.	Now it was that Agnar's ship was launched off its rollers, and there was a man in front of it, and he was killed, and they called that roller-red.
Nú þótti þeim eigi vel til takast í fyrstu ok vildu ekki láta standa þat fyrir ferð sinni.	Now seemed to-them not well to take at first and willed not-to let stand it before journey theirs.	Now it seemed to them that things had not got off to a good start, but they did not want to let it stand in the way of their journey.
Ok þá er lið þeira var búit, fara þeir með lið sitt til Svíþjóðar, ok þar, er þeir koma fyrst í ríki Eysteins konungs, fóru þeir herskildi yfir.	And then when crew theirs was ready, travelled they with the-crew this to Sweden, and there, as they came first to the-Kingdom-of Eystein the-King, travelled they war-shields up.	And then when their crew were ready, they travelled with this crew to Sweden, and as they came to the kingdom of King Eystein they bore up their war shields.
En landsmenn urðu varir við ok fóru til Uppsala ok segja Eysteini konungi, at herr var kominn í landit.	Then landsmen became aware of and travelled to Uppsala and told Eystein the-King, that a-war-band was coming to land.	Then landsmen became aware of this and travelled to Uppsala and told King Eystein, that a war band was coming to land.
En konungrinn lætr fara örvarboð um ríki sitt ok dregr svá mikinn her saman, at furða var at.	Then the-King had go arrow-summons about the-Kingdom his and drew so a-great war-band together, that a-wonder was to.	Then the king had the war arrow sent throughout his kingdom, and summoned such a large war band together, that it was a wonder.
Ok þann her flytr hann, þar til er hann kemr í skóg einn, ok setr þar sínar herbúðir, ok hefir hann nú með sér kúna Síbilju, ok mjök er hún nú blótin, áðr en hún vildi fara.	And then the-forces advanced his, then until that he came to forest one, and set there his war-camp, and had he now with him a-cow Sibilja, and much was she now sacrificed-to, before that she would travel.	And then he advanced his forces until he came to the forest, and he set his war camp there, and he now had the cow Sibilja with him, and many sacrifices were made to her, before she would travel.

Old Norse	Literal	English
Ok er þeir eru í skóginum, mælti Eysteinn konungr: "Frétt hefi ek til", segir hann, "at synir Ragnars eru á völlunum fyrir framan skóginn, en þat er mér sannliga sagt, at þeir hafi eigi einn þriðjung liðs við oss.	And when they were in the-forest, spoke Eystein the-King: "News have I of", said he, "that sons Ragnar's are about the-fields before in-front-of the-forest, which that was to-me truly said, that they have not one third-of force as us.	And when they were in the forest, King Eystein spoke: "I have news", he said, "that Ragnar's sons are in the fields before in front of the forest, and I have been truly told, that they do not have one third of our forces.
Nú skulu vér skipa várar fylkingar til at berjast, ok skal þriðjungr liðs várs fara í mót þeim, ok eru þeir svá harðfengnir, at þeir munu þykkjast hafa ráð várt í hendi, ok þegar eptir skulum vér öllum megin koma at þeim, ok kýrin skal fara fyrir liðinu, ok væntir mik, at eigi skuli þeir haldast við fyrir lát hennar".	Now shall we divide our ranks to then battle, and shall a-third-of forces ours go to meet them, and are they so war-taken, that they should seem-to have the-business ours in hand, and straight-away after shall we all may come to them, and the-cow shall go before the-men, and expect me, that none shall there hold with before bellowing hers".	Now we shall divide our ranks then to battle, and a third of our forces shall go out to meet them, and when battle begins, they shall seem to have the matter in hand, and straight away we shall all come at them, and the cow shall go before the men, and I expect, that no one there will hold against her bellowing".
Ok nú er svá gert.	And now was so done.	And now it was done.
Ok þegar er þeir bræðr sjá lið Eysteins konungs, þótti þeim sér ekki ofrefli við at eiga ok ætla eigi meira liðit vera munu.	And as-soon as the brothers saw forces Eystein the-King's, thought they themselves nothing overwhelming with that had and supposed not more forces being would.	And as soon as the brothers saw King Eystein's forces, they thought that it was nothing overwhelming, and they did not suppose that there would be more forces.
Ok þegar hér eptir kemr allt liðit ór skóginum, ok kýrin er laus látin, ok hleypr hún fyrir liðinu ok lætr grimmliga, ok varð svá mikill gnýr at þeim hermönnum, er heyrðu, at þeir börðust sjálfir, nema þeir bræðr tveir fengu staðist.	And then forces after came altogether company from-out-of forest, and the-cow was loose let, and ran she before the-forces and bellowed fiercely, and was so much a-din that the forces, who heard, that they battled themselves, except the brothers two held steadfast.	And then the forces came together from out of the forest, and the cow was let loose, and she ran before the forces and bellowed fiercely, and there was so much din, that the forces who heard it battled with themselves, except for the two brothers who held steadfast.
En sú in illa vættr vá með hornum sínum margan mann þann dag.	And so the evil gored slew with horns hers many men that day.	And so the evil creature gored many men with her horns that day.

Old Norse	Literal	English
Ok þótt synir Ragnars væri miklir fyrir sér, þá máttu þeir eigi bæði standast ofrefli fjölmennis ok blótskap, ok þó veittu þeir harða viðtöku ok vörðust vel ok drengiliga ok af mikilli frægð.	And though sons Ragnar's were great for them, then could they not both withstand overwhelming the-crowd and sorcery, and though had they hard resistance and guarded well and bravely and of much fame.	And though Ragnar's sons were mighty, they could not withstand both the overwhelming crowd and the sorcery, although they put up stiff resistance and guarded themselves well and bravely with great fame.
Þeir Eirekr ok Agnarr váru í öndverðri fylkingu þann dag, ok opt gengu þeir í gegnum fylkingar Eysteins konungs.	They Erik and Agnar were in at-the-front the-ranks that day, and often went they among through the-ranks Eystein king's.	Erik and Agnar were in at the front of the ranks that day, and they often went among and through King Eystein's ranks.
Ok nú fell Agnarr.	And now fell Agnar.	And now Agnar fell.
Nú sér Eirekr þat ok berst nú allra fræknligast ok hirðir nú eigi, hvárt hann kemst í brott eða eigi.	Now saw Erik that and bore now all the-braver and cared now not, whether he came to away or not.	Now Erik saw that and bore himself all the braver, and did not care whether he would come away or not.
Ok nú verðr hann ofrliði borinn ok handtekinn.	And now became he outnumbered carried and captured.	And now he became outnumbered and was captured and carried.
Ok nú mælti Eysteinn, at stöðva skyldi bardagann, ok bauð Eireki grið.	And now spoke Eystein, that stop should battle, and offered Erik mercy.	And now King Eystein spoke and said that the battle should stop, and he offered Erik mercy.
"Ok þat mun ek til leggja", segir hann, "við þik, at ek mun gifta þér dóttur mína".	"And that should I to grant", said he, "with you, that I should give to-you daughter mine".	"And I shall grant you this as well", he said, "that I will offer you my daughter's hand".
Eirekr segir ok kvað vísu:	Erik answered and spoke a-verse:	Erik answeredd and spoke a verse:
"Vilkat boð fyr bróður né baugum mey kaupa, Eystein kveða orðinn Agnars bana, heyra; grætr eigi mik móðir,	"Which bid before brother Nor ring maid buy, Eystein it-is-said became Agnar's bane, hear Weep not my mother,	"Which offer before my brother, Nor buy a maid with rings, Eystein, it is said, became Agnar's bane, hear, Weep not, my mother,

Old Norse	Literal	English
munk efstr of val deyja,	Remember uppermost of foe dead,	Remember above the slain,
ok geirtré í gögnum gerr, látið mik standa".	And spear-tree to use willing, have me standing".	Let the ravenous spear tree, willing, have me standing".
Nú segir hann, at hann vill, at þeir menn hafi grið ok fari hvert er þeir vilja, er þeim hafa fylgt.	Now said he, that he willed, that they men have mercy and travel each as they will, that they have followed.	Now he said that he wanted those men who had followed him to have mercy and safe travel as the wished.
"En ek vil, at spjót sé tekin sem flest ok sé stungit spjótunum í völl niðr, ok þar vil ek mik láta hefja á upp, ok þar vil ek láta lífit".	"But I will, of spears be taken as most and be pierced spears in the-field down, and there will I me lay begin on up, and there will I lay my-life".	"But I want as many spears as possible to be placed down in the field, and there I want to be laid upon, and there I will lay down my life".
Nú segir Eysteinn konungr, at eptir því skal gera, sem hann beiðir, þótt hann kjósi þat, er verr gegnir hvárumtveggjum.	Now said Eystein the-King, that after accordingly would be-done, as he asked, though he chose that, was the-worst served either-way.	Now King Eystein said that would be done according to his wishes, though he had made the worst choice for both of them.
Nú eru spjótin niðr sett, ok kvað Eirekr vísu:	Now were the-spears down set, and spoke Erik a-verse:	Now the spears were set down, and Erik spoke a verse:
"Munat eins konungs efni, svát ek vita dæmi, á dýrra beð deyja, til dögurðar hrafni; mun blóði þá bráðir ok brátt yfir gjalla bræðra beggja slíta blár, þótt illa launi".	"Remember one's king's prospect, So I knowing deem, A dearer bed to-die, To day's-meal raven's Will blood than prey And soon over scream Brothers both tear blue, though ill reward".	Remember one king's son, So I know deemed, Die on a dearer bed, A day's mean for the raven, Will blood then pray, And soon over scream, Brothers both tear, Blue, though ill-reward".
Ok nú gengr hann þar til, er spjótin eru niðr sett, ok tekr hring af hendi sér ok kastar til þeira, er honum höfðu fylgt ok þá váru grið gefin, ok sendir þá til Áslaugar ok kvað vísu:	And now went he there to, as spears were down set, and took ring off hand his and cast to them, who him had followed and there was mercy given, and sent then to Aslaug and spoke a-verse:	And now he went to the place where the spears were set down, and he took a ring off his hand, and cast it to those men who had followed him and had been granted mercy, and he sent them to Aslaug and spoke a verse:

Old Norse	Literal	English
"Þau berið orð it efra,	"There bear words these ever,	"There bear these final words,
eru austrfarar liðnar,	Are eastern-journeys passed,	That the eastern journeys are passed,
at mær hafi mína	That maiden have mine	That the maiden will have mine,
mjó, Áslaugu, bauga;	Slender, Aslaug, rings	Slender Aslaug, rings,
þá mun mest af móði,	Then shall most of mother,	Them shall most of mother,
er mik spyrja dauðan,	Of me learn-of death,	Learn of my death,
mín stjúpmóðir mildum	My step-mother mild	My stepmother mild,
mögum sínum til segja".	Sons hers to tell".	Sons hers to tell".
Ok nú er hann hafinn upp á spjótin.	And now as he started up upon spears.	And now as he was lifted upon the spears.
Þá sér hann, hvar hrafn flýgr, ok enn kvað hann:	Then saw he, where raven flew, and then spoke he:	Then he saw, a raven flying, and then he spoke:
"Hlakkar már of höfði	"Screaming gull about head	"Screaming gull about my head,
hér mínu nú sára,	Here my now wound,	Here now my wound,
krefr unda valr augna	Craves beneath slain eyes	Craves beneath slain eyes,
ósýnna hér minna;	Unseeing here mine	Mine unseeing here,
veist, ef hrafn ór höfði	Know, if raven from head	Know, if the raven from my head,
höggr brúnsteina mína,	Hews brow-stones mine,	Hews my brow stones,
launar unda valr Ekkils	Repaid under slain Ekkil	The raven, for Ekkil's bounty
illa marga fylli".	Bad many fill".	Repays me badly".
Nú lætr hann líf sitt með mikilli hreysti.	Now laid he life his with much valour.	Now he laid his lie with much valour.
En sendimenn hans fóru heim ok létta eigi fyrr en þeir koma þar, er Ragnarr átti atsetu.	Then messengers his travelled home and laid not before that they came there, where Ragnar had a-seat.	Then his messengers travelled home, and did not stop until they had come to where Ragnar had his royal seat.
Ok þá var hann farinn í konungastefnu.	And there was he travelled to king's-assembly.	And then he had travelled to a king's assembly.
Þeir váru ok eigi heim komnir synir Ragnars ór hernaði.	They were also not home come sons Ragnar's from raiding.	Ragnar's sons also had not come home from raiding.

Old Norse	Literal	English
Nú eru þeir þar þrjár nætr, áðr þeir gangi til fundar við Áslaugu.	Now were they there three nights, before they went to meet with Aslaug.	Now they were there for three nights before they went to meet with Aslaug.
Ok þá er þeir koma fyrir hásætit Áslaugar, kveðja þeir hana virðuliga, ok tekr hún kveðju þeira, ok hafði hún einn líndúk fyrir knjám sér ok ætlaði at kemba sér, ok hárit hafði hún leyst.	And then when they came before the-high-seat Auslag's, greeted they her worthily, and took she greetings theirs, and had she one linen for knees hers and intended to comb herself, and hair had she let-down.	And then when they came before Aslaug's high seat, they greeted her worthily, and she took their greeting, and she had a linen on her knees as she had intended to comb her hair, which she had let down.
Nú spyrr hún, hverir þeir væri, fyrir því at hún hafði þá eigi fyrr sét.	Now asked she, who they were, for because that she had them not before seen.	Now she asked who they were, because she had not seen them before.
Sá, er orð hafði fyrir þeim, sagði, at þeir höfðu verit liðsmenn þeira Eireks ok Agnars, sona Ragnars.	So, as word had for them, said, that they had been company-men they Erik's and Agnar's, sons Ragnar's.	So, the one who had words for them, said, that they had been warriors of Ragnar's sons Erik and Agnar.
Þá kvað hún vísu:	Then spoke she a-verse:	Then she spoke a verse:
"Hvat segið ér ór yðru, eru Svíar í landi eða elligar úti, allnýs konungs spjalli? Fregit hefk hitt, at fóru, en fremr vitum eigi, ok hildingar höfðu hlunnroð, Danir sunnan".	"What telling is of yours, Are Swedes about land Either or out, All-Prying king's friends News have found, that travelling, But from knowing not, And princes had rollers-red, Danes from-the-south".	What telling is yours, Are Swedes about the land, Or are they outed? All prying king's friends, News has been found, that travelling, But knowing no further, The princes had, Rollers red, Danes from the south".
Hann kvað vísu í mót:	He spoke verse in reply:	He spoke a verse in reply:
"Þér segjum vér, þínum, þat er nauð, kona, dauða, ill eru einkar manni, örlög, sonu Þóru; þung spjöll vitum önnur eigi nýjari en þessi;	"To-you say we, your, That a distressing, lady, death, Ill are very men, Fate, sons Thora's Heavier to-tell we-know other Not new than this	To you we say, yours, That a distressing, lady, death, Ill they are very men, Fate, Thora's sons, Heavier to tell what we know, other, None new than this,

Old Norse	Literal	English
nú hefk fram komit fréttum,	Now have from coming news,	Now come from hearing the news,
flaug örn of ná dauðan".	Flown eagle about reaching death".	Flown an eagle about reached death".
Nú spyrr hún, hvé farit hafði.	Now asked she, how fared had.	Now she asked how it had fared.
Ok nú kvað hann þá vísu, er Eirekr hafði kveðit, er hann sendi henni hringinn.	And now said he then a-verse, which Erik had spoken, as he sent her the-ring.	And now he said a verse, which Erik had spoken as he sent her the ring.
Nú sjá þeir, at hún felldi tár, en þat var sem blóð væri álits, en hart sem haglkorn.	Now saw they, that she fell tears, but that was as blood was thought, and rough as hailstone.	Now they saw, that she fell tears, but they were as blood, and was rough as a hailstone.
Þat hafði engi maðr sét, at hún hefði tár fellt, hvárki áðr né síðan.	That had no man seen, that she had tears fell, neither before nor since.	That no man had seen, that she had tears fallen, neither before nor since.
Nú segir hún, at hún má ekki til hefnda sýsla, fyrr en heim koma aðrir hvárir, Ragnarr eða synir hans.	Now said she, that she may not to revenge pursue, before that home came others each, Ragnar or sons his.	Now she said that she may not pursue revenge, before the others, Ragnar or his sons, each came home.
"En þér skuluð vera hér þar til, en ekki skal af spara at eggja til hefnda, jafnt sem þeir væri mínir synir".	"But you should be here then until, that none shall of spare that encouragement to revenge, equally as they were my sons".	"But you should be here until then, so that none shall be spared of encouragement to revenge, equally as if they were my sons".
Nú eru þeir þar.	Now were they there.	Now they were there.
En svá gefr til, at þeir Ívarr koma fyrri heim en Ragnarr, ok eru þeir eigi lengi heima, áðr Áslaug ferr at finna sonu sína, en Sigurðr var þá þrévetr.	And so given until, that they Ivar came before home than Ragnar, and were they not long home, back Aslaug went to find sons hers, as Sigurd was then three-winters.	And it was so given, that Ivar and his brothers came home before Ragnar, and the were not long home, before Aslaug went to meet her sons, as Sigurd was then three winters old.
Hann ferr með móður sinni.	He went with mother his.	He went with his mother.

Old Norse	Literal	English
Ok þá er hún kemr í höll þá, er þeir réðu fyrir bræðr, fagna þeir henni vel, ok spyrja hvárir aðra tíðenda, ok segja þeir fyrri fall Rögnvalds, sonar hennar, ok frá þeim atburðum, er þar höfðu orðit.	And then as she came to hall then, as they discussed before brothers, welcomed they her well, and asked each other news, and said they before fall Rognvald's, son hers, and from those events, that there had become.	And then as she came to the hall, where the brothers were having their discussion, they welcomed her well, and they asked each other for news, and they said what had happened of the fall of her son Rognvald, and the events that come afterwards.
En ekki fær henni þat mikils ok kvað:	But not affected her that much and said:	But this did not afect her that much, and she said:
"Kaga létu mik mínir mávangs synir löngum, ér eruð heim ok heiman	"Staring had me my Seagull's sons long, That are home and from-home	"Staring had me my, at the seagull's long, sons, That are home and from home,
húsgangs meðalfærir;	House-going between-faring	House going between travelling,
Rögnvaldr tók at rjóða rönd í gumna blóði; hann kom yngstr til Óðins ógndjarfr sona minna.	Rognvald took to redden Shield of men's blood He came young to Odin Unafraid son mine.	Rognvald took to redden The shield of men's blood, He came to Odin young, Unafraid my son".
Ek kann eigi þat at sjá", segir hún, "at hann mundi til meiri frægðar lifa".	I can not so that see, said she, "that he would to greater fame live".	"I cannot see", she said, "How he would have lived for greater fame".
Nú spyrja þeir, hvat hún segi tíðenda.	Now asked they, what she said of-news.	Now they asked, what she had of news.
Hún svarar: "Fall þeira Eireks ok Agnars, bræðra yðarra, en stjúpsona minna, þeira manna, er ek ætla, at inir bestu drengir hafi verit.	She answered: "Fallen are-they Erik and Agnar, brothers yours, but stepsons mine, those men, that I suppose, that the best warriors had been.	She answered: "Erik and Agnar, they are fallen, your brothers, my stepsons, those men, as I suppose, the best warriors that have ever been".
Ok er þat ókynligt, at þér þolið slíkt eigi ok hefnið miklu.	And as that not-strange, that you enduring such not also revenge great.	It will not be strange, that you do not endure such a thing, and do great revenge".
Ok þess vil ek biðja yðr ok í öllum atbeina vera með yðr, at þessa verði meir hefnt en miðr".	And this will I propose to-you and in all assistance be with you, that this will-be more revenge than less".	And I propose this to you, that I will be of every assistance to you, and this revenge ill be more rather than less".

Old Norse	Literal	English
Nú segir Ívarr, at "þat er víst, at til Svíþjóðar kem ek aldri þeirar tíðar, at ek berjumst við Eystein konung ok þann blótskap, er þar er".	Now said Ivar, that "It is certain, that to Sweden come I never there visit, that I fight with Eystein the-King and this sorcery, that there is".	Now Ivar said: "It is certain, that I did not come to Sweden in order to fight King Eystein and his sorcery that is there".
Hún fylgir þessu vel, en Ívarr hefir orð fyrir þeim ok synjar ávallt fararinnar.	She followed this well, but Ivar had words for them and refused always of-the-journey.	She followed this well, but Ivar spoke for them and always refused to make the journey.
Ok nú kvað hún vísu:	And now said she a-verse:	And now she said a verse:
"Eigi mundi yðar óhefnt vera bræðra	"Not would you Without-vengeance being brothers	"You would not, Without vengeance brothers be,
eitt misseri eptir, ef ér dæið fyrri;	One season after, If were dead before	One season after, If you were dead before,
lítt hirðik því leyna,	Little wearing therefore concealing,	Little wearing therefore concealing,
ef líf hafa knætti Eirekr sitt ok Agnarr, óbornir mér niðjar".	If live have could Erik theirs and Agnar, Unborn of-me descendants".	If live could have, Theirs, Erik and Agnar, Descendants unborn of me".
"Eigi er víst", segir Ívarr, "hvárt þat stoðar nakkvat, þótt þú kveðir aðra vísu at annarri, eða hvé gerla veistu, hverr fastgarðr þar er fyrir?"	"Not is certain", said Ivar, "whether that supports somewhat, though you say another verse to another, but how completely know-you, what stronghold there is before?"	"It is not certain", said Ivar, "whether that supports somewhat, though you speak one verse after another, but how completely do you know, what defences are there before us?"
"Eigi veit ek þat víst", segir hún, "eða hvat kanntu at segja, hver torveldi þar er á?"	"Not know I that certainly", said she, "or what obstacles to say, how difficult there is about?"	"I do not know that certainly", she said, "but what can you say about the obstacles that are there?"
Ívarr segir, at þar er blótskapr svá mikill, at hvergi kvaðst hann spurdaga hafa, at þvílíkr mundi vera.	Ivar said, that there are sorcery so great, that nowhere said he news had, about how-like could be.	Ivar said that there was such sorcery, that nowhere had he heard news about how its like could be.
"Ok sá konungr er bæði ríkr ok illgjarn".	"And so the-King is both powerful and ill-doing".	"And so the king is both powerful and wicked".

Old Norse	Literal	English
"Hvat er þat, er hann trúir mest á í blótum?"	"What is it, that he believes most at this sacrifice?"	"What is it that he worships most at this sacrifice?"
Hann segir: "Þat er kýr ein mikil, ok er hún kölluð Síbilja.	He said: "There is cow one great, and was she called Sibilja.	He said: "There is one great cow, and she was called Sibilja.
Hún er svá mjök mögnuð, at þegar er menn heyra lát hennar, hafa óvinir hans engir staðist, ok er trautt sem berjast skuli við menn at eins, heldr má til þess ætla, at fyrri skal tröllskapnum mæta en konunginum, ok vil ek hvárki hætta þar til mér né liði mínu".	She is so much mighty, that there when men hear bellowing hers, have enemies his none withstood, and is scarcely as-if fight shall with men at alone, rather may to this suppose, that before shall sorcery meet than the-King, and will I neither danger there to me nor men mine".	She is so mighty, that when men hear her bellowing, none of their enemies can withstand, and it is scarcely as if we shall be fighting with men alone, rather I suppose, that we shall first meet sorcery before we shall meet the king, and I do not want to risk danger to me or my men".
Hún segir: "Á hitt máttu líta, at þú munt eigi bæði mega heita mestr maðr ok vinna ekki til".	She said: "Out-of meeting could look, that you shall not both be called greatest man and win nothing to".	She said: "If you avoid meeting this, it will look like you shall not be called the greatest of men or win anything".
Ok nú er henni þykkir fyrir ván komit, ætlar hún í brott; þótti henni þeir eigi mikils meta sín orð.	And now that she thought therefore in-vain came, supposed she that to-away; thought she they not much appreciated her words.	And now it seemed to her that it was in vain, the supposed that they did not appreciate her words much.
Þá mælti Sigurðr ormr í auga: "Segja má ek þér, móðir", segir hann, "hvat mér er í hug, en eigi má ek ráða þeira svörum".	Then spoke Sigurd Snake-in-the-eye: "Say may I to-you, mother", said he, "what for-me is in mind, but not may I plans theirs answer".	Then Sigurd Snake-in-the-eye spoke: "I must say to you mother", he said, "what is in my mind, though it not go against their answer".
"Heyra vil ek þat", segir hún.	"Hear will I that", said she.	"I want to hear it", she said.
Nú kvað hann vísu:	Now spoke he a-verse:	Now he spoke a verse:
"Þat skal þriggja nátta, ef þik tregar, móðir, leið eigu vér langa, leiðangr búinn verða; skal Uppsölum eigi,	"It shall-be three nights, If you troubled, mother, Journey our-own we long, Journeying prepared be Shall Uppsala not,	"It shall be three nights, If you are troubled, mother, Our journey must be long, For our forces to be ready, Uppsala shall not,

Old Norse	Literal	English

Þótt ófafé bjóði,
ef oss duga eggjar,
Eysteinn konungr ráða".

Though wealth offer,
If we aided edges,
Eystein king's rule".

Though wealth offered,
If blade edges aid us,
King Eystein rule".

Ok er hann hafði þessa vísu kveðit, skipast nokkut hugr þeira bræðra.

And when he had this verse spoken, changed somewhat minds they brothers.

And when he had spoken this verse, the brothers changed their mind somewhat.

Ok nú mælti Áslaug: "Yfir lýsir þú nú, sonr minn, at þú vilt gera minn vilja.

And now spoke Aslaug: "Over declare you now, son mine, that you will do my will.

And now Aslaug spoke: "Now you have declared that you will do my will, my son.

En þó má ek eigi yfir sjá, at vit komim þessu á leið, ef vit höfum eigi fullting bræðra þinna, en þat mætti svá verða, at mér mætti best þykkja, at þessa yrði hefnt, ok vel þykki mér þér fara, sonr minn".

But though may I not over see, that we come this to pass, if we have not help brothers yours, but it may so be, that to-me may best think, that this should-be revenge, and well think me to-you to-go, son mine".

But I cannot see how we two will go on this journey, if we do not have the help of your brothers, but it may be that this deed shall be avenged, as it seems best to me, I think it is good that you go, my son".

Ok nú kvað Björn vísu:

And now said Bjorn a-verse:

And now Bjorn spoke a verse:

"Duga mun hugr ok hjarta
í hauksnöru brjósti,
þótt minnr um þat mæli,
manni innan rifja;
eigi er oss í augum
ormr né fránir snákar,
bræðr glöddu mik mínir,
mank stjúpsonu þína".

"Help must mind and heart
The hawk-snare breast,
Though less about it speaks,
Men inside review
Not are ours in eyes
Serpents nor flashing snakes,
Brothers glad to-me mine,
Remember stepsons yours".

"Heart and mind must help,
The hawk snare breast,
But little spoken about it,
Men review inside,
Not are in our eyes,
Serpents or flashing snakes,
My brothers merry to me,
I remember your stepsons".

Ok nú kvað Hvítserkr vísu:

And now spoke Hvitserk verse:

And now Hvitserk spoke a verse:

"Hyggjum at, áðr heitim,
at hefnt megi verða,
látum ýmsa illu,
Agnars bana, fagna;
skjótum húf á hrannir,
höggum ís fyr barði,
sjám á hitt, hvé snekkjur

"Let-us-think about, before promising,
That revenge may be,
Let-us various evil,
Agnar's bane, rejoice
Early hull to waves,
Blows ice before bow,
Let-us-see to meet, how-to sailboats

"Let us plan before we promise,
That revenge may be,
Must bear various evils,
Agnar's banesman, be glad,
Shoot the hull to the waves,
Shatter ice before the bow,
Let us see how soon to sailboats,

Old Norse	Literal	English
snemmst vér fáim búnar".	Soonest we get prepared".	The soonest we can get prepared".
En Hvítserkr ræddi því um þat, at ís skyldi höggva, at frost váru á mikil, ok váru skip þeira inni frerin.	Then Hvitserk advised therefore about that, the ice should break, that frosted was the-river much, and was ship theirs in frozen.	Then Hvitserk advised about how they should break the ice, because the river was much frosted, and their ship was frozen in.
Ok nú tók Ívarr til orða ok segir, at þá var þar komit, er hann mundi nokkurn hlut í eiga, ok nú kvað hann vísu:	And now took Ivar to words and said, that then was there coming, that he would somehow share in own, and now said he verse:	And now Ivar took to words and said, that things had come to the point that he must somehow share in it, and now he said a verse:
"Hafið ofrhuga ærinn ok áræði bæði, þess mundi þá þurfa, at þrá mikit fylgdi; bera mun mik fyr bragna beinlausan fram verða, þó gatk hönd til hefnda, at hváriga nýtak".	"Have courage boundless And daring both, This would then need, To desire much follow Bore-up should-be me above heroes Boneless from being, Though get hand to revenge, That whichever new-take".	"Having courage boundless, And daring both, This would then need, To desire much to follow, Bore up should I be above heroes, From being boneless, I'll have a hand in revenge, Whichever I may take".
"Ok er hitt nú til", segir Ívarr, "at vér leggjum á slíkan hug sem vér megum of skipabúnað ok um samdrátt herliðs, því at vér munum þess við þurfa at spara ekki af, ef vér skulum sigrast".	"And is meeting now to", said Ivar, "that we let-us-lay to such mind which we may of ship-preparing and about gathering a-war-band, because that we shall this with need to spare not of, if we shall be-victorious".	"And now is the time", said Ivar, "that we lay our minds to how to prepare our ship, and gather a warband, because we shall spare not, if we shall be victorious".
Nú gengr Áslaug í brott.	Now went Aslaug to away.	Now Aslaug went away.
11	11	11
Sigurðr hefir átt sér einn fóstra, ok annast sá fyrir hans hönd bæði skip at búa ok lið til at fá, svá at þau væri öll skipuð.	Sigurd had had himself a foster-father, and took-care-of he for his hand both ships to prepare and a-crew to about get, so that they were all arranged.	Sigurd had a foster father, and he took care of both preparing the ships, and getting a crew, so that they were all arranged.

Old Norse	Literal	English
Ok nú gengr þeim svá skjótt, at þat lið, er Sigurðr skyldi búit hafa, var búit, er þrjár nætr váru liðnar, ok hafði hann fimm skip ok öll vel skipuð.	And now went they so swiftly, that this crew, when Sigurd should be-prepared to-sea, was ready, when three nights were passed, and had he five ships and all well prepared.	And now they went so swiftly, that this crew, when Sigurd was prepared to go to sea, was ready when three nights had passed, and he had five ships all well prepared.
Ok þá er fimm nætr váru liðnar, hafði Hvítserkr ok Björn búin fjórtán skip, en Ívarr hafði tíu skip ok Áslaug önnur tíu, þá er sjau nætr váru liðnar frá því, er þau höfðu við ræðst ok þeir höfðu heitit ferðinni.	And then when five nights were passed, had Hvitserk and Bjorn readied fourteen ships, and Ivar had ten ships and Aslaug another ten, then as seven nights were passed from since, was they had therefore decided and they had called to-travel.	And then when five nights were passed, Hvitserk and Bjorn had fourteen ships ready, and Ivar had ten ships, then as seven nights passed after they had decided that they were going to travel, Aslaug had another ten.
Nú hittast þau öll saman, ok segir hvárt þeira öðru, hvé mikit lið hvert hafði fengit.	Now met they all together, and said each they to-the-other, how much company each had got.	Now they all met together, and each said to the other, how much company they had.
Ok nú segir Ívarr, at hann hafði sent landveg riddaralið.	And now said Ivar, that he had sent land-ways riding-men.	And now Ivar said that he had sent riding men across the land.
Áslaug segir: "Ef ek vissa, at þat lið mætti til gagns komast, er land færi, þá mætta ek mikit lið hafa sent".	Aslaug said: "If I knew, that the crew may to need coming, were land going, there might I much company have sent".	Aslaug said: "If I'd have known that there was need for land men, I might have sent much company".
"Ekki skal nú at því dveljast", segir Ívarr, "með þetta lið skal nú fara, sem vér höfum saman dregit".	"Not shall now that because-of dwell", said Ivar, "with this company shall now travel, as we have together drawn".	"We shall not now dwell on that", said Ivar, "we shall travel now with this company as we are drawn together".
Nú segir Áslaug, at hún vill fara með þeim, "ok veit ek þá gerst, hver stund á er lögð at hefna þeira bræðra".	Now said Aslaug, that she wished-to travel with them, "and know I then to-do, each while it is had to revenge they the-brothers".	Now Aslaug said that she wished to travel with them, "and I know then what is to be done in order to avenge the brothers".
"Þat er víst", segir Ívarr, "at þú kemr eigi á vár skip.	"That is certain", said Ivar, "that you come not on our ships.	"That is certain", said Ivar, "that you will not come on our ships.

Old Norse	Literal	English
Hitt skal vera, ef þú vill, at þú ráðir fyrir því liði, er landveg ferr".	Meeting shall be, if you will, that you command for the company, which land-way journeys".	If it be found, if you wish to command the company that travels on the land".
Hún kvað svá vera skulu.	She said so be should.	She said that it would be so.
Nú er breytt nafni hennar ok er nú kölluð Randalín.	Now was changed name hers and was now called Randalin.	Now her name was changed and she was called Randalin.
Nú ferr liðit hvárttveggja, ok kvað Ívarr á áðr, hvar þau skyldu finnast.	Now travelled company each-way, and said Ivar to return, where they should meet-up.	Now the company travelled each way, and Ivar said where they should return to and meet up.
Nú ferst þeim vel hvárumtveggjum ok hittast þar, sem ákveðit er.	Now travelled they well each-way and met there, as decided was.	Now they travelled well each way, and they met where they had decided.
Ok hvar sem þau koma við Svíþjóð í ríki Eysteins konungs, fara þeir herskildi yfir, svá at þeir brenndu allt þat, er fyrir varð, drápu hvert mannsbarn, ok því jóku þeir við, at þeir drápu allt þat, er kvikt var.	And where as they came to Sweden in kingdom Eystein the-King, travelled they separately across, so as they burned all that, which before-them was, killed each man's-son, and then increased they with, that they killed all that, which alive was.	And when they came to Sweden in the kingdom of Eystein, they travelled separately across, and they burned everything which was before them, killed each man's son, and even more, they killed every living thing.

12 12 12

Nú er þat eitthvert sinn, at menn komast undan á fund Eysteins konungs ok segja honum, at í ríki hans var kominn mikill herr ok svá illr viðskiptis, at þeir létu ekki ógert ok þeir höfðu eytt allt þar, er þeir höfðu yfir farit, ok ekki hús stóð upp.	Now was that some-time that, the men came out-from to find Eystein the-King and said to-him, that in the-Kingdom his was coming a-great army and so ill business, that they let nothing undone and they had devastated all there, as they had across travelled, and no house stood up.	It happened that some men escaped and found King Eystein and said to him that in his kingdom there was a great army coming, with such wicked business, that they left nothing undamaged, and devastated all that was there, as they travelled across, and no house remained standing.
Nú er Eysteinn konungr heyrir þessi tíðendi, þykkist hann vita, hverir þeir víkingar munu vera.	Now when Eystein the-King heard this news, thought he knew, who these vikings would be.	Now when King Eystein heard this news, he thought he knew, who these vikings would be.

Old Norse	Literal	English
Ok nú lætr hann fara örvarboð um allt sitt ríki ok stefnir öllum til, þeim er hans menn eru ok honum vilja lið veita ok skildi megu valda.	And now had he sent arrow-messages about all his kingdom and summoned all to, they who his men were and to-him willed company grant and shields may wield.	And now he had the war arrow sent about all of his kingdom and summoned everyone of his men who would grant their company and wield shields.
"Vér skulum hafa með oss kúna Síbilju, goð várt, ok láta hana hlaupa fyrir liðinu, ok væntir mik, at enn fari sem fyrr, at þeir megu eigi standast lát hennar.	"We shall have with us the-cow Sibilja, god ours, and have her run before the-forces, and expect me, that it goes as before, that they may not withstand bellowing hers.	"We shall have the cow Sibilja with us, our god, and we shall have her running before the forces, and I expect that it will go as before, that they may not withstand her bellowing.
Vil ek allt lið mitt þess eggja, at sem best dugi, ok rekum af oss þenna inn mikla her ok inn illa".	Wish I all forces mine these encourage, that as best enough, and drive off us these the great army and this evil".	I will encourage all my forces to do the best they can, and we shall drive off this heathen army and this evil".
Ok nú er svá gert, at Síbilja er laus látin.	And now was so done, that Sibilja was loose let.	And now it was done, and Sibilja was let loose.
Ok nú sér Ívarr för hennar ok heyrir þau in grimmligu læti, er ór henni váru.	And now saw Ivar going her and heard they the fearful bellowing, that from her was.	And now Ivar saw her going and they heard the fearful bellowing that came from her.
Mælir hann, at allt liðit skyldi gera óhljóð mikit, bæði af vápnum ok herópi, at þeir heyri sem síst rödd hennar, þess ins illa kykvendis, er fór í móti þeim.	Spoke he, that all company should do loudly great, both of weapons and war-cry, that they hear as none voice hers, this the evil creature, that comes to meet them.	He spoke, that all the company should make a great loud noise, with their weapons and their war cries, so that no one may hear her voice, this evil creature that comes to meet them.
Ívarr mælti við sína burðarmenn, at þeir skyldu bera hann á móti, svá sem þeir mætti framast.	Ivar said that his bearer-men, that they should bear him to meet, so as they may foremost.	Ivar said to his bearers that they should bear him up to meet, as far forward as they may.
"Ok þá er sjá kýr kemr at oss, kastið mér at henni, ok mun þá vera annathvárt, er ek skal láta mitt líf, eða hún skal fá bana.	"And then when seeing the-cow coming that we, cast me at her, and shall then be either, that I shall lay my life, or she shall get death.	"And then when we see the cow coming, cast me at her, and it shall be either that I lay my life, or she shall get her death.

Old Norse	Literal	English
Nú skulu þér taka eitt tré mikit ok telgja á bogamynd ok skeyti með".	Now shall you take a tree great and carve a bow-shape and arrows with".	Now you shall take a great tree and carve a bow-shape and arrows with it".
Ok nú er honum færðr sjá bogi inn sterki ok þau in miklu skeyti, er hann hafði gera látit, en engum þótti sér vápnhæft annarra.	And now was he brought to-see bow the strong and then the great arrows, that he had made had, but none thought themselves weapon-handy each-other.	And now he was brought to see the strong bow and the great arrows, that he'd had made, but no one thought to themselves that they would be useful as weapons.
Nú eggjar Ívarr hvern mann, at dugi sem best.	Now encouraged Ivar each man, that could as best.	Now Ivar encouraged each man to do his best.
Nú ferr lið þeira með miklum geysingi ok gný, en Ívarr var borinn fyrir fylkingum þeira.	Now went forces they with much forcefulness and rage, and Ivar was carried before ranks theirs.	Now their forces went with much forcefulness and rage, and Ivar was carried before their ranks.
Nú verðr svá mikill gnýr, er Síbilja beljar, at þeir heyrðu jafngerla sem þeir þegði ok stæði kyrrir.	Now became so great the-noise, as Sibilja bellowed, that they heard equally as-if they-were silent and stood still.	Now the noise became so great, as Sibilja bellowed, that they heard it just as clearly as if they were silent and stood still.
Nú bregðr þeim svá við þetta, at lið þeira vill berjast allt nema þeir bræðr.	Now shocked were-they so with this, that forces they wanted-to fight altogether except they the-brothers.	Now they were so shocked with this, that the forces wanted to fight one another, except for the brothers.
Ok er þessi endemi verða, sjá þeir þat, er Ívar báru, at hann dregr svá boga sinn sem hann hefði einn álmsveig veikan, ok við því þótti þeim búit, at hann drægi fyrir odd örvar sínar.	But as this unheard-of was, saw they that, then Ivar bore, that he drew so bow his as it would-have-been an elm-twig weak, and with therefore thought they prepared, that he drew before point arrow his.	But when this unheard of thing happened, they saw that Ivar bore and drew his bow as if it had been a weak elm twig, and they thought that he had readied, and drawn the arrows with the points behind the bow.
Nú heyra þeir, at strengr gellr hans svá hátt, at hann heyrðu þeir aldrigi svá fyrri.	Now heard they, that string bowstring his so loudly, that it heard they never so before.	Now they heard that the bowstring twanged so loudly, that they had never heard anything like it before.

Old Norse	Literal	English
Ok nú sjá þeir, at hans örvar flugu svá snart sem hann hefði skotit af inum sterkasta lásboga ok svá gegnt, at í sitt auga kom hvár örin Síbilju.	And now saw they, that his arrows flew so fast as-if he had shot of the strongest lock-bow and so straight, that about her eyes came each arrow Sibilja.	And now they saw, that his arrows flew so fast as if he had shot the strongest lock bow, and so straight, that each arrow came to Sibilja's eyes.
Ok nú fellr hún, ok eptir þat ferr hún höfuðsteypu, ok nú eru læti hennar miklu verri en fyrri.	And now fell she, as after that went she head-tumbled, and now was bellowing hers much worse than before.	And now she fell, and then fell head over heels, and now her bellowing was much worse than before.
Ok er hún kemr at þeim, biðr hann kasta sér at henni, ok verðr þeim hann svá léttr sem þeir kasti barni litlu, því at þeir váru eigi allnær kúnni, þá er þeir köstuðu honum.	And as she came at them, asked he to-cast him at her, and became to-them he so light as they cast a-child little, because that they were not all-near the-cow, then when they threw him.	And as she came at them, he asked them to cast him at her, and he then appeared so light to them, as if he was a little child, because they were not at all near the cow, where they threw him.
Ok þá kom hann á hrygg kúnni Síbilju, ok varð hann þá svá þungr sem bjarg eitt felli á hana, ok hvert bein brotnar í henni, ok fær hún af því bana.	And then came he upon the-spine the-cow Sibilja's, and became he then so heavy as boulder one fell on her, and each bone broken of hers, and got she of this death.	And then he came upon the spine of Sibilja the cow, and then he became as heavy as a boulder that had fallen upon her, and each of her bones was broken, and with that she got her death.
Nú biðr hann menn sik upp taka sem skjótast.	Now asked he men him up take as soonest.	Now he asked his men to take him up as quickly as possible.
Ok nú er hann upp tekinn, ok nú er rödd hans svá hvell, at svá þótti öllum herinum, er hann mælti, sem við sjálft væri, þótt fjarri væri staddir, ok it besta hljóð væri til gefit hans erendis.	And now was he up taken, and now was voice his so sharp, that so thought all the-forces, that he speaking, as with himself was, though far-away was present, and the best silence was to give his errands.	And now he was taken up, and now his voice was so sharp, that all of the forces thought that he was speaking as with himself, though he was far away, he gave his orders in silence.
Ok svá lýkr hann sinni tölu, at ófriðr sjá, nemst þegar af allr, er yfir þá hafði komit, ok þá sakaði ekki, því at lið þeira hafði skamma stund barist.	And so ended he his speech, that hostility seen, taken already of all, was over then had come, and then hurt not, because the forces they had short awhile bore.	And he ended his speech in this way, that the hostility of which they had already taken, was going to be overcome, and nothing would hurt them, because their forces had bore a short while.

Old Norse	Literal	English
Nú eggjar Ívarr, at þeir skyli vinna sem verst verk á þeim.	Now encouraged Ivar, that they should win as worst work to them.	Now Ivar encouraged that they should do their worst work to them.
"Ok nú þykki mér af inn ólmasti, er kýrin er drepin".	"And now thought for-me of the wildest, the cow is killed".	"And now I think that the wildest of them, the cow is killed".
Ok nú hafa hvárirtveggju fylkt liði sínu, ok sígr saman orrostan, ok er bardagi svá harðr, at þat mæltu allir Svíar, at þeir hefði aldri í slíkri mannraun verit.	And now had either-side mustered company theirs, and victory together battle, and was the-battle so hard, then it was-said all Swedes, that they had never of such trial been.	And now either side had mustered their company, and they were victorious in a battle that was so hard, then all the Swedes said that they had never had such a trial.
Nú ganga þeir svá hart fram bræðr, Hvítserkr ok Björn, at engi fylking stendr við.	Now went they so roughly forwards the-brothers, Hvitserk and Bjorn, that none-of the-ranks stood with.	Now the brothers Hvitserk and Bjorn went forwards so roughly, that none of the ranks could withstand them.
Ok nú fellr svá mjök lið Eysteins konungs, at minna stendr upp, en sumt kemr á flótta.	And now fell so many forces Eystein the-King's, that less stood up, then some came to flee.	And now so many of King Eystein's forces fell, that few were left standing, and some came to flee.
Ok nú lýkr svá þeira bardaga, at Eysteinn konungr fellr, en þeir bræðr hafa sigr.	And now ended so they the-battle, that Eystein the-King fell, and they the-brothers had success.	And now they ended the battle, as King Eystein fell, and the brothers had success.
Ok nú gefa þeir þeim grið, sem eptir váru.	And now gave they them mercy, as after was.	And now they gave mercy to all those afterwards.
Ok nú segir Ívarr, at hann vildi eigi herja lengr í því landi, því at þat land var nú höfðingjalaust.	And now said Ivar, that he willed not harrying longer about that land, because that the land was now leader-less.	And now Ivar said that he did not want to go harrying any longer in that land, because the land was now without a leader.
"Ok vil ek heldr, at vit haldim þar til, er meira ofrefli er fyrir".	"And wish I rather, to with head there to, where more greater-force is before-us".	"And I wish to head to where there is a greater force ahead of us".
En Randalín fór heim með sumt liðit.	Then Randalin travelled home with some-of the-men.	Then Randalin travelled home with some of the men.

Old Norse	Literal	English
13	*13*	*13*
Nú ráða þeir þat með sér, at þeir skulu herja í Suðrríki.	Now decided they that with themselves, that they should harry in the-southern-kingdom.	Now they decided among themselves, that they would be harrying in the southern kingdom.
En Sigurðr ormr-í-auga, sonr hennar, fór með bræðrum sínum í hverja herför síðan.	Then Sigurd Snake-in-the-eye, son hers, travelled with the-brothers his to every raiding since.	Then Sigurd Snake-in-the-eye, Randalin's son, travelled with the brothers on every raiding journey since.
Í þessi för leggja þeir til hverrar borgar, er mikil er, ok unnu svá, at ekki stóð við.	On this voyage laid they to each city, which great was, and won so, that none stood with.	On this journey they headed for every sizeable town, and conquered it, so that none withstood them.
Ok nú spyrja þeir til einnar borgar þeirar, at bæði var mikil ok fjölmenn ok harðger.	And now learned they about one city there, that both was great and populous and strongly-built.	And now they learned about one city there, that was both great, and populous, and strongly built.
Ok nú segir Ívarr, at hann vill þar til stefna.	And now said Ivar, that he wished there to direct.	Now Ivar said that he wished to direct there.
Ok þat var ok sagt, hvat sú borg hét ok hverr fyrir ræðr.	And it was also said, what the city called and who for ruled.	And it was also said about how the city was named, and who ruled it.
En sá höfðingi var kallaðr Vífill.	Then so the-chief was called Vifil.	The chieftan was called Vifil.
Af hans nafni var borgin kölluð Vífilsborg.	Of his namesake was the-city called Vifilsborg.	And from his name, the city was called Vifilsborg.
Nú fara þeir svá herskildi yfir, at þeir eyða allar borgir, er fyrir urðu, þar til er þeir kómu til Vífilsborgar.	Now travelled they so separated across, that they devastated all cities, that they came, there to until they came to Vifilsborg.	Now they travelled separately across, that they devastated all cities that they came to, until they came to Vifilsborg.
Höfðinginn var eigi heima í borg sinni ok mikit lið með honum.	The-chieftain was not home in city his and much company with him.	The chieftan was not home in his city, and many of his men had gone with him.

Old Norse	Literal	English
Nú setja þeir upp búðir sínar á völlum þeim, er hjá borginni váru, ok eru í kyrrðum þann dag, er þeir kómu til borgarinnar, ok höfðu mál af borgarmönnum.	Now set they up booths theirs in fields they, as beside the-city being, and they with peaceful that day, when they came to the-city, and had-they conversations of townspeople.	Now they set up their booths in their fields, being beside the city, and they went peacefully that day, when they came to the city, and they had conversations with the townspeople.
Þeir buðu þeim, hvárt þeir vildu heldr gefa upp borgina, ok mundi þá friðr gefinn öllum mönnum, eða þeir ynni af sínu ofrefli ok harðfengi, ok munu þá engum mönnum grið gefin.	They offered them, either they would rather give up the-city, and would they peace be-given all people, or they won of their overwhelming and toughness, and would then no people mercy be-given.	They offered them, either to give up the city, and they would all be given peace, or they would be overwhelmed with their toughness and then people would be given no mercy.
En þeir leystu skjótt ór ok sögðu, at þá borg fengi þeir aldrigi unnit, svá at þeir gefi hana upp.	But they dismissed quickly out and said, that the city got they never won, so-as that they gave her up.	But they dismissed them quickly out, and said that their city had never been conquered, and so they would never give it up.
"Ok munu þér verða fyrr at reyna yðr ok sýna oss yðvarn fræknleik ok kapp".	"And should you be before this tested yours and show us your bravery and eagerness".	"And you must first be tested for your bravery and eagerness".
Líðr nú sú nótt.	Passed now the night.	The night now passed.
Ok inn næsta dag eptir leita þeir til at vinna borgina ok fá ekki at gert.	And the next day after sought they to then win the-city and got nothing to-be done.	And the next day after they then sought to win the city and achieved nothing.
Sitja þeir um þá borg hálfan mánuð ok leita til hvern dag, at þeir geti þá borg unnit, ok með ýmsum brögðum.	Set they about the city half month and sought to each day, that they could then city win, and with various tricks.	They set themselves around the city for half a month and tried every day to conquer it, trying various tricks.
En þat ferr því firr sem þeir hafa lengr við leitat, ok ætluðu nú frá at hverfa.	Then so went therefore forwards which they had longer with seeking, and intended now from to turn-back.	But the longer they kept trying, the longer they sought, and now they intended to turn back.

Old Norse	Literal	English
Ok þá er borgarmenn verða við þat varir, at þeir ætla frá at hverfa, þá ganga þeir út á borgarveggi ok breiða guðvefjarpell of alla borgarveggina ok öll klæði þau, er fegrst váru í borginni, ok törruðu fyrir þeim gulli ok gersimum þeim, er mestar váru í borginni.	And then when townspeople became with that aware, that they intended away to turn, then went they out onto the-city-walls and spread fine-cloth about all the-city-walls and all cloth there, the finest that-was in the-city, and arranged before them gold and jewels they, that most were in the-city.	And then when the townspeople became aware that they intended to turn back, they went out onto the city walls and spread fine cloth about the city walls, all the cloth that was the finest in the city, arranged before them with gold and jewels, the greatest treasures of the town.
Ok nú tekr einn til orða af liði þeira ok mælti: "Vér hugðum, at þessir menn, synir Ragnars, ok lið þeira væri harðfengnir menn, en vér megum þat segja, at þeim hefir eigi nær farit en öðrum".	And now took one to words of company theirs and spoke: "We thought, that these men, sons Ragnar's, and company theirs were brave men, but we may so say, that they have not nearer fared than others".	And then one of their company took to words and spoke: "We thought that these men, Ragnar's sons, and their company were brave men, but we may say that they have done no better than the others".
Nú eptir þetta æptu þeir á þá ok börðu á skjölduna ok eggjuðu at sér sem þeir máttu mest.	Now after that shouted they at them and beat at shields and egged at them as they might most.	Now after they had shouted that at them, they beat their shields and egged them on as much as they could.
Ok er Ívarr heyrir þetta, brá honum við mjök, svá at hann fær af þessu sótt mikla, svá at hann má hvergi hræra, ok verða þeir at bíða, at annathvárt batni honum ella hafi hann bana.	And when Ivar heard that, startled him by much, so that he got of this sickness much, so that he may neither move, and became they to wait, that either-way better himself or have he death.	And when Ivar heard that, it startled him so much, that he became ill, so that he could not move, and they had to wait until he either got better or died.
Hann liggr þenna dag allan til kvelds, svá at hann mælti ekki orð.	He lay then day all until evening, so that he spoke not words.	He lay all that day until evening, and he spoke not a word.
Ok þá mælti hann við þá menn, er hjá honum váru, at þeir skyldu segja þeim Birni, Hvítserki ok Sigurði, at hann vildi þeira fund hafa ok allra inna vitrustu manna.	And then spoke he with the men, that beside him were, that they should say to-them Bjorn, Hvitserk and Sigurd, that he willed they find have and all the wisest men.	And then he spoke with the men that were beside him, that they should tell Bjorn, Hvitserk, and Sigurd, that he wanted to find all the wisest men.

Old Norse	Literal	English
Ok nú er þeir koma allir í einn stað, er mestir höfðingjar eru í þeira liði, þá spyrr Ívarr þá eptir, ef þeir hefði nokkur ráð sét, þau er líkari væri til at sigrast en þau, er þeir höfðu fyrr haft.	And now when they came all to one place, the greatest chieftains they of their company, then asked Ivar they after, if they had any advice seen, they that likened would-be to that victory that they, who they had before had.	And now when they all came to one place, the greatest chieftans of their company, and then Ivar asked them if they had any plan that would be more likely to give them victory than before.
En þeir svara allir, at þeir hefði eigi vit til þess at sjá þau brögð, er þeim væri sigr í.	But they answered all, that they had not wit about this to say they tricks, that they would-be successful with.	But they all answered that the did not have the wit to say of any tricks that they would be successful with.
"Er nú sem optar, at þinna ráða mun njóta verða".	"But now as often, that your advice would useful be".	"But now, as often before, your plan will be useful".
Þá svarar Ívarr: "Mér hefir eitt ráð í hug komit, þat er vér höfum eigi freistat.	Then answered Ivar: "To me has a plan I think comes, that as we have not tried.	Then Ivar answered: "A plan comes to me that I think we have not tried".
Hér er skógr mikill eigi langt í brott, ok nú, er náttar, skulu vér fara ór tjöldum várum leyniliga til skógar, en herbúðir várar skulu standa eptir, ok er vér komum í mörkina, skal hverr maðr binda sér byrði.	Here is a-forest great not long to away, and now, when night, shall we travel from tents ours secretly to woods, but war-booths ours shall stand after, and when we come to the-trees, shall each man tie himself a-bundle.	Here is a great forest not a long way away, and now at night, we shall travel from our tents secretly to the woods, but our war booths shall remain standing, and when we come to the trees, each man shall tie himself a bundle.
Ok er því er lokit, skulu vér fara at borginni öllum megin ok slá eldi í viðinn, ok mun þá gerast bál mikit, ok borgarveggir þeira munu þá láta lím sitt fyrir þeim eldi, ok skulu vér þá bera at valslöngur ok reyna, hvé harðger hún er".	And when that is done, shall we travel to the-city all ways and strike fire about wood, and should then be fire great, and city-walls they shall then lose mortar theirs because their fire, and shall we then bear to war-slings and test, how hardy she is".	And when that is done, we shall travel to all sides of the city wall and strike a fire in the wood, and then the fire should be great, and they shall lose their mortar because of the fire, then we shall bring catapults to bear and test how hardy the walls are".
Ok nú er svá gert, at þeir fara til skógar, eru þar slíka hríð sem Ívari sýndist.	And now was so done, that they travelled to the-woods, were they so awhile as Ivar thought-fit.	And now it was done, they travelled to the woods, and they were there as long as Ivar thought fit.

Old Norse	Literal	English
Nú fara þeir at borginni eptir tilskipun hans, ok þá er þeir lustu eldi í viðinn inn mikla, varð bál svá mikit, at veggirnir megu eigi standast ok láta lím sitt, ok bera þeir þá valslöngur at borginni ok brjóta á hlið mörg, ok tekst nú bardagi.	Now travelled they to the-city-walls after directions his, and then as they struck fire among the-wood the greatest, became the-fire so much, to the-walls may none withstand and burned mortar theirs, and bore they then war-slings to the-city and broke about the-sides many, and took now battle.	Now they travelled to the city walls as he directed, and then as they struck a great fire with the wood, and the fire became so much, that the walls could not withstand it and their mortar burned, and then they bore catapults to the city, and many of the sides were broken, and they took to battle.
Ok þegar er þeir standa jafnt at vígi, þá fellr lið borgarmanna, en sumt flýr undan, ok svá lýkr þeira skiptum, at þeir drepa hvert mannsbarn, er í var borginni, ok taka brott allt fé, en brenna borgina, áðr þeir fari á brott.	And as-soon as they stood equal at the-fort, then fell the-company-of townspeople, but some fled away, and so ended their exchange, that they killed each man's-child, who in was the-city, and took away all wealth, but burned the-city, after they went to away.	And as soon as they faced each other at the fort, the townspeople fell, but some fled. And so ended their exchange, that they had killed every man's child, who was in the city, and took away all the wealth, but burned the city after they went away.
14	14	14
Nú halda þeir í brott þaðan, þar til er þeir koma í þá borg, er Lúna hét.	Now held they to away from-there, then until that they came to then the-city, that-was Luna named.	Now they set off from there, until they came to the city that was named Luna.
Þá höfðu þeir hverja borg ok hvern kastala brotit náliga í öllu Suðríki, ok nú eru þeir svá frægir of allan heim, at ekki var svá lítit barn, at eigi kynni nafn þeira.	Then had they each city and each castle burned down in all the-southern-kingdom, and now were they so famous of all households, that not was so a-little child, that did-not know name theirs.	Then they had burned each city and castle in all of the southern kingdom, and now they were so famous that in all the households, there was not a single child, no matter how little, who did not know their names.
Nú ætla þeir at létta eigi fyrr en þeir koma til Rómaborgar, af því at sú borg var þeim bæði sögð mikil ok fjölmenn ok ágæt ok auðig.	Now intended they that rest not before that they came to Rome-city, for accordingly was this city were they both told great and populous and famous and wealthy.	They intended not to rest until they came to the city of Rome, for they were told that this city was great, and populous, and famous, and wealthy.

Old Norse	Literal	English
En þat vissu þeir eigi gerla, hvé löng leið þangat er, en þeir höfðu svá mikit lið, at eigi fengust vistir.	But this knew they not completely, how long a-journey from-there it-was, and they had so many men, that not got-they provisions.	But they did not know completely, how long the journey was from there, and they had so many men, that provisions could not be obtained.
Ok nú eru þeir í þeiri borg Lúna ok ræða með sér of ferð sína.	And now were they in there the-city Luna and discussing with themselves of journey theirs.	And now they were in the city of Luna and discussing their journey among themselves.
Nú kemr þar maðr einn, gamall ok geðsligr.	Now came there man one, old and engaging.	A man came along, old and good natured.
Þeir spyrja, hvat manna hann væri, en hann segir, at hann sé einn stafkarl ok hafi alla ævi farit yfir land.	They asked, what man he was, then he said, that he be a poor-beggar and had all life travelled across land.	They asked what man he was, then he said that he was a poor beggar, and he had travelled across lands all his life.
"Þú munt margt kunna tíðenda at segja oss, þat er vér viljum vita".	"You must many know tidings to say-to us, that which we wish-to know".	"You must know many news to tell us, that we wish to know".
Inn gamli maðr svarar: "Eigi veit ek þat víst, af hverjum löndum þér vilið spyrja, þess er ek veit eigi at segja yðr".	The old man answered: "Not know I that-which-is known, of any land you will ask, that which I know not to answer you".	The old man answered: "I do not know that which is known, of any land that you might ask, that I will not know how to answer you".
"Þat viljum vér, at þú segir oss, hvé löng leið er heðan til Rómaborgar".	"That wish we, that you tell us, how long journey is from-here to Rome-city".	"That we wish you to tell us, how long is the journey from here to the city of Rome".
Hann svarar: "Ek kann segja yðr nokkut til merkja.	He answered: "I can say-to you something to sign.	He answered: "I can say to you something of a sign.
Þér meguð hér sjá þessa járnskó, er ek hefi á fótum mér, þeir eru nú fornir, ok þá aðra, er ek hefi á baki mér, þeir eru nú ok slitnir.	You may here see these iron-shoes, that I have on feet mine, they are now old, and the others, that I have on back mine, they are now also broken.	You may see here these iron shoes, that I have on my feet, they are now old, and the others, that I have on my back, they are now also broken.

Old Norse	Literal	English
En þá er ek fór þaðan, batt ek þessa á fætr mér ina slitnu, er ek hefi nú á baki mér, ok váru þá nýir báðir, ok á þeiri leið hefi ek verit ávallt síðan".	About then when I travelled from-there, bought I these for feet mine these broken, that I have now about back mine, also were they new both, and from there journey have I been always since".	About the time when I travelled from there, I bought these for my feet which are broken now on my back, they were both new, and I have been on that journey ever since".
En er inn gamli maðr hafði þetta mælt, þykkjast þeir sjá, at þeir megu eigi þessu á leið koma, er þeir hafa fyrir sér ætlat, til Róms at fara.	Then as the old man had this said, thought they it-seemed, that they may not this to journey come, that they have before themselves intended, to Rome to travel.	Then as the old man had said this, they thought it seemed that they may not journey as they had intended before, to Rome.
Ok nú snúa þeir frá með her sinn ok unnu margar borgir, þær er aldri höfðu unnar verit fyrr, ok þess jarteinir sjást enn í dag.	And now turned they away with war-band theirs and won many cities, there that never had won been before, and this tokens seen still this day.	And now they turned away with their war band and won many cities, that had never been won before, and there are tokens of this seen still to this day.
15	15	15
Nú er þar til máls at taka, er Ragnarr sitr heima í ríki sínu ok hann veit eigi, hvar synir hans eru né Randalín, kona hans.	Now is there to matter to take, that Ragnar sits home in kingdom his and he knew not, where sons his were nor Randalin, wife his.	Now there is the matter to take, that Ragnar sat home in his kingdom and he did not know where his sons or Randalin his wife were.
Ok þat heyrði hann hvern tala af sínum mönnum, at engir mætti jafnast við sonu hans, ok hugðist honum svá at, at engir væri jafnfrægir þeim.	And that heard he each speak of his men, that none may equal with sons his, and thought he so then, that none were equal-famous they.	And he heard each of his men say that no one was the equal of his sons, and so he thought that none were equal in their fame.
Nú hyggr hann at því, hverrar frægðar hann mætti þess leita, er eigi væri skemmr uppi.	Now thought he about so, how-so fame he might this seek, that not would short stand-up.	So now he thought about how he might seek fame that would be long standing.

Old Norse	Literal	English
Nú hyggr hann ráð sitt ok fær sér smiða ok lætr fella mörk til tveggja skipa mikilla, ok þat skildu menn, at þat váru knerrir tveir svá miklir, at engir höfðu slíkir verit gervir á Norðrlöndum, ok þar með lætr hann hafa of allt sitt ríki mikinn vápnabúnað.	Now considered he plan his and got himself smiths and had felled timber to two ships great, and that understood men, that there were knorrs two so great, that none had such been made in the-Northern-Lands, and there with let him have of all the kingdom many weapons-prepared.	Now he considered his plan and got himself smiths, and had timber felled to make two great ships, and people understood, that there were two knorrs that were so great, that nothing like them had been made in all the northern lands, and there with them he had weapons prepared from all the kingdom.
Ok með þessi breytni skilja menn þat, at hann mun ætla nokkura herferð fyrir sér ór landinu.	And with this conduct understood men that, that he should intend some war-voyage for himself out-from lands.	And with this conduct people understood, that he intended to go on some war voyage for himself in other lands.
Þetta spyrst víða á lönd þau, er næst varu.	This heard-of widely the lands that, the nearest were.	This was heard of widely in the lands that were nearest.
Ok nú ugga menn þat ok allir konungar, er fyrir landi réðu, at þeir mundu eigi í löndum sínum eða ríkjum vera mega.	And now feared men that and all kings, that for lands ruled, that they would not in land theirs or rule being may.	And now men and all the kings who ruled the lands feared that they would not be able to remain in their land.
Ok nú lætr hverr þeira vera varðhöld um lönd sín, ef nokkur beri hann at.	And now had each of-them be a-watch about lands his, if any bore he to.	And now each of them had watch persons placed about their lands, if he bore any.
Þat er eitt sinn, er Randalín spurði Ragnar, hverja för hann aætlaði fyrir sér.	There was one occasion, that Randalin asked Ragnar, what journey he intended for himself.	There was one occasion, that Randalin asked Ragnar, what journey he intended for himself.
Hann segir henni, at hann ætlaði til Englands ok hafa eigi fleiri skip en tvá knörru ok þat lið, sem á þeim má fara.	He said to-her, that he intended towards England and had not more ships than two knorrs and that crew, which that they may travel.	He said to her, that he intended to go to England and had no more ships than two knorrs, and the crew that they may travel with.
Þá segir Randalín: "Sú för líst mér óvarlig, er nú ætlar þú.	Then said Randalin: "This journey behold I un-careful, that now intend you.	Then Randalin said: "This journey looks careless to me, that you now intend.

Old Norse	Literal	English
Mér þætti þér ráðligra at hafa fleiri skip ok smæri".	To-me seems to-you more-advisable to have more ships and smaller".	It seems to me that it would be more advisable for you to have more ships, and smaller".
"Þat er ekki ágæti".	"That has no glory".	"There is no glory in that".
segir hann, "þótt menn fái unnit land með mörgum skipum.	Said he, "though men get winning land with many ships.	He said: "though men conquer lands with many ships.
En til þessa eru eigi dæmi, at með tveimr skipum hafi unnit verit slíkt land sem England er.	But to this are no examples, that with two ships had won been such land as England then.	But there are no examples where two ships have won such a land as England.
En ef ek fæ ósigr, þess betr sem ek hefi færi skip ór landi".	But if I get defeat, this-is better that I have brought ships out-of land".	But if I am defeated, it is better that I have fewer ships taken away from my land".
Þá svarar Randalín: "Mér sýnist sjá eigi minni fékostnaðr, áðr þessi skip sé búin, en þótt þú hefðir langskip mörg til þessarar ferðar.	Then answered Randalin: "To-me seems so not less fee-costly, after these ships so prepared, but though you have longships many to that-kind-of journey.	Then Randalin answered: "It seems to me no less expensive, instead of building these ships, for you to have many longships for that kind of journey.
En þú veist þat, at illt er skipum at halda at Englandi, ok ef svá verðr, at skip þín týndist, þótt menn komist á land, þá eru þeir þegar upp gefnir, ef landherr kemr at, en betra er at halda langskipum til hafna en knörrum".	But you know that, to ill that ships to hold to England, and if so becomes, if ship yours lost, though many come to land, then are they straightaway up given, if lord-of-the-land comes to, then better that to have longships to harbour than knorrs".	But you know that it is bad for ships to sail for England, and if it happens that your ship is wrecked, though many come to land, then they must surrender straight away, if the lord of the land comes, then it is better to have longships in the harbour than knorrs".
Nú kveðr Ragnarr vísu:	Now said Ragnar a-verse:	Now Ragnar said a verse:
"Spari manngi röf Rínar,	"Spare no-man amber Rhine's,	"Let no man spare the Rhine's amber,
ef röskva vill hermenn,	If seasoned wills war-men,	If seasoned he wants war men,
verr samir horskum hilmi	Worse so the-wise helm	Harmful for the helm wise,
hringa fjöld en drengja;	Rings full-many than fellows	To hoard rings rather than troops,
illt er í borghlið baugi	Ill is to city-side rings	Hard it is to fortress gates,

Old Norse	Literal	English
brandrauðum fram standa; allmarga veit ek jöfra, þá er auðr lifir, dauða".	Fiery-Red from withstand All-many knowing I ruler, When that wealth outlives, the-dead".	From fiery red withstanding, Many rulers I know, When the wealth outlives the dead".
Nú lætr hann skip sín búa ok fær sér lið, svá at þeir knerrir eru mjök skipaðir.	Now had he ships his prepared and got himself a-crew, so that the knorrs were much fully-loaded.	Now he had his ships prepared and got himself a crew, so that the knorrs were very much fully loaded.
Nú er fjölrætt um hans fyrirætlan.	Now was discussed of his for-intentions.	Now there was a discussion about his intentions.
Ok enn kvað hann vísu:	And then spoke he a-verse:	And then he spoke a verse:
"Hvat er þats baugs ór björgum brjótr heyrir nú þjóta, at muni mundelds meiðir mars sviðr ófni hafna? Þó skal þeira ráða, þorn-Bil, ef goð vilja, ægir alnar leygjar ókvíðandi bíða".	"What is that ring from rocks Breaks heard now howling, That shall hand-fire injure Steed rapid sea-serpents forsake Though shall they plan, Brooch-Bil, if gods will, The-ocean measure of-the-flame Bravely bid".	"What does the ring from rocks, Breaker hear now howling, That the injury of hand fire, Must forsake his sea serpents? Though they shall plan, Brooch-Bul, if the gods will, The ocean measure of the flame, Bravely bid".
Ok er skip hans eru búin ok þat lið, er honum skyldi fylgja, ok þá er þat veðr kemr, er honum þótti sér vel koma, segir Ragnarr, at þá mundi hann fara til skipa.	And when ships his were prepared and the crew, that he wished follow, and then when that wind came, that to-him seemed so well came, said Ragnar, that then should he travel to ships.	And when his ships were prepared and the crew that he wished to follow him, and then when the wind came, that seemed favourable to him, Ragnar said, that the the ships should travel.
Ok er hann var búinn, leiddi hún hann til skipa.	And when he was prepared, led her he to the-ships.	And when he was prepared, he led her to the ships.
Ok áðr þau skiljast, kjeðst hún mundu launa honum serk þann, er hann hafði gefit henni.	And before they parted, said she would repay him shirt that, which he had given her.	And before they parted, she said she would reward him for the shirt that he had given to her.
Hann spyrr, með hverjum hætti þat væri.	He asked, with which way that would-be.	He asked what that reward would be.

Old Norse	Literal	English
En hún kvað vísu:	Then she spoke a-verse:	Then she spoke a verse:
"Þér annk serk inn síða ok saumaðan hvergi, við heilan hug ofnu ór hársíma gránu; mun eigi ben blæða, né bíta þik eggjar í heilagri hjúpu, var hún goðum signuð".	"To-your purpose shirt the improved And sewn-and-stitched nowhere, With healing thoughts woven From hair-strands grey Will no wound bleed, Nor bite you edges This hallowed covering, Was she the-gods signed".	"To your purpose the shirt is improved, And sewn and stitched nowhere, With healing thoughts woven, From grey hair strands, Will no wound bleed, Nor edges bite you, This hallowed covering, Was she by the gods signed".
Hann segir, at hann vill þessi ráð þiggja.	He said, that he would this advice accept.	He said that he would accept this advice.
En þá er þau skildust, var auðsætt, at henni þótti mikit fyrir þeira skilnaði.	And when that they parted, it-was obvious, that she thought much because-of their separation.	And when they parted, it was obvious, that their separation affected her very much.
Nú heldr Ragnarr skipum sínum til Englands, sem hann hafði ætlat.	Now headed Ragnar ships his to England, as he had intended.	Now Ragnar headed his ships to England, as he had intended.
Honum gaf byri hvassa, svá at við England brýtr hann báða knörru sína, en á land komst allt lið hans, ok heldu klæðum sínum ok vápnum.	He was-given wind harsh, so that with England broke he both knorrs his, about the land came all crew his, and held clothing theirs and weapons.	He was given a harsh wind, so that when he arrived in England, both his ships were broken, all of his crew made it to land, and held their clothing and weapons.
Ok þar, sem hann kemr við þorp ok borgir ok kastala, þá vinnr hann.	And there, as he came to villages and cities and castles, then won he.	And there as he came to villages and cities and castles, then he conquered.
En konungr sá hét Ella, er þá réð Englandi.	The king so named Ælla, was then ruling England.	The king who was so named Aella, was then ruling England.
Hann hafði haft fréttir til Ragnars, er hann fór ór landi.	He had had news about Ragnar, as he travelled out-from the-land.	He had received news about Ragnar, that he travelled out of his lands.

Old Norse	Literal	English
Hann hafði sett menn fyrir, at hann skyldi þegar vita, er herrinn kæmi við land.	He had set men therefore, that he should straight-away know, when harrying came to land.	He had therefore set men so that he should know straight away, when they came harrying to land.
Nú fóru þeir menn til fundar við Ellu konung ok segja honum hersögu.	Now travelled they men to meet with Ælla the-King and said-to him war-declaration.	Now men travelled to meet with King Aella and give him talk of war.
Nú lætr hann senda boð um allt sitt ríki ok bað til sín koma hvern mann, er skildi má valda ok hesti ríða ok þori at berjast, ok dregr hann saman svá mikinn her, at furða var at.	Now had he sent invitation about all his kingdom and invited to they come each man, that shield may wield and horse ride and greater-part to fight, and drew he together so great an-army, that a-wonder was it.	Now he had a summons sent throughout all his kingdom and invited each man to come who may wield a shield, ride a horse, and more importantly fight, and he drew together so great an army, that it was a wonder.
Nú búast þeir til bardaga Ella konungr.	Now prepared they to battle Ælla the-King.	Now King Aella prepared himself for battle.
Þá mælti Ella konungr við lið sitt: "Ef vér sigrumst í bardaga þessum ok verði þér við þat varir, at Ragnarr er kominn, þá skulu þér eigi bera vápn á hann, því at hann á þá sonu eptir, er aldri munu af oss ganga, ef hann fellr".	Then spoke Ælla the-King with company his: "If we gain-victory in battle this and become you with it aware, that Ragnar has come, then shall you not bear weapons to him, because that he has there sons after, which never shall of us go, if he falls".	Then King Aella spoke with his company: "If we gain victory in battle, and if you become aware that Ragnar has come, then you shall not bear weapons to him, because he has left sons behind, which shall never leave us alone if he falls".
Ragnarr býst nú til bardaga, ok hann hafði þat klæði, er Randalín hafði gefit honum at skilnaði, fyrir brynju ok þat spjót í hendi, er hann vann at orminum, er lá um sal Þóru, ok engi þorði annarra, ok hann hafði enga hlíf nema hjálm.	Ragnar prepared now to battle, and he had this clothing, that Randalin had given him when parted, for armour and the spear in hand, that he won the serpent, which laid about hall Thora's, and none dared another, and he had none protection except helmet.	Ragnar now prepared to go to battle, and he had this clothing, that Randalin had given him when they parted, for armour, and the spear in hand which he had defeated the serpent with, that had laid around Thora's hall, when no one else dared, and he had no other protection apart from a helmet.
En þá er þeir hittast tókst bardagi.	And then when they met took battle.	And then when they met the battle began.
Ragnarr hafði miklu minna lið.	Ragnar had much less forces.	Ragnar had much less forces.

Old Norse	Literal	English
Bardaginn hafði eigi lengi verit, áðr lið Ragnars fell mjök.	The-battle had not long been, before forces Ragnar's fell many.	The battle had not been going long before many of Ragnar's forces fell.
En þar, sem hann fór, varð rýrt fyrir, ok gekk hann í gegnum fylkingar þann dag, ok þar, sem hann hjó eða lagði í skjöldu, brynjur eða hjálma, þá váru svá stór högg hans, at ekki vetta stóð við, en aldri var svá til hans höggvit eða skotit, at né eitt vápn yrði honum at meini, ok fekk hann aldri sár, en hann drap mikinn fjölda af liði Ellu konungs.	But there, as he went, became reduced before, and got he in through the-ranks that day, and there, as he struck or laid to shields, armour or helms, then was so great striking his, that not blade stood with, but never was so to him struck or shot, that not one weapon became him to harm, and got he never wounded, but he killed a-great many of forces Ælla the-King.	But wherever he went, the company fell before him, he broke through the ranks that day, and wherever he hewed or struck shield, armour, or helms, his blows were so strong that no one withstood them, but he was never struck or shot, and not one weapon did harm to him, and he never got wounded, but he killed a great many of King Aella's forces.
En þó lauk svá bardaga þeira, at allt lið Ragnars fell, en at honum váru bornir skildir ok svá handtekinn.	But though concluded so the-battle theirs, that all forces Ragnar's fell, but to him was borne shields and so hand-taken.	But though ended their battle, that all of Ragnar's forces fell, but he was pressed under shields, and so captured.
Nú var hann spurðr, hvat manna hann var, en hann þagði við ok svaraði engu.	Now was he asked, what man he was, but he silent with and answered not.	Now he was asked what man he was, but he was silent and did not answer.
Þá mælti Ella konungr: "Sjá maðr mun verða at koma í meiri mannraun, ef hann vill eigi segja oss, hverr hann er.	Then spoke Ælla king: "See-this man should be to come to more trial, if he will not say-to us, who he is.	Then King Aella spoke: "This man should be put to more trial, if he will not say to us, who he is.
Nú skal kasta honum í einn ormgarð ok láta hann þar sitja mjök lengi, ok ef hann mælir nakkvat þat, er vér megim skilja, at hann sé Ragnarr, þá skal hann í brott taka sem skjótast".	Now shall cast him in a snake-pit and have him there sit very long, and if he speaks not-any this, that we may know, that he is Ragnar, then shall he to away be-taken as quickest".	I will cast him into a pit of snakes and have him sit there for a very long time, and if he speaks of anything, so that we may know, that he is Ragnar, then he shall be taken away as quick as possible".

Old Norse	Literal	English
Nú er honum þangat fylgt, ok hann sitr þar mjök lengi, svá at hvergi festast ormar við hann.	Now was he from-there followed, and he sat there very long, so that nowhere fastened serpents to him.	Now he was followed from there, and he sat there for a very long time, and so nowhere serpents fastened themselves to him.
Þá mæltu menn: "Þessi maðr er mikill fyrir sér; hann bitu eigi vápn í dag, en nú granda honum eigi ormar".	Then spoke men: "This man is mighty therefore himself; he-was bitten not weapons all day, and now injure him no serpents".	Then men spoke: "This man is mighty, he was not bitten by weapons all day, and now no serpents injure him".
Þá mælti Ella konungr, at hann væri flettr af klæði því, er hann hafði yst, ok nú var svá gert, ok hengu ormar öllum megin á honum.	Then spoke Ælla the-King, that he would-be stripped of clothes that, which he has outer, and now was so done, and hung serpents all most of him.	Then King Aella spoke, that he should be stripped of the clothes which he had on his outer, and now it was done, and serpents hung on almost all of him.
Þá mælti Ragnarr: "Gnyðja mundu nú grísir, ef þeir vissi, hvat inn gamli þyldi".	Then spoke Ragnar: "Grumble would now piglets, if they knew, how the old suffered".	Then Ragnar spoke: "The piglets would grumble now, if they knew how the old suffered".
Ok þótt hann mælti slíkt, þá vissu þeir eigi at gerr, at Ragnarr væri þat heldr en annarr konungr.	And though he spoke such, then knew they not was done, that Ragnar it-was that rather than another king.	And although he said as such, they knew that it was not done, that it was Ragnar rather than another king.
Nú kvað hann vísu:	Now spoke he a-verse:	Now he spoke a verse:
"Orrostur hefk áttar, þærs ágætar þóttu, gerða ek mörgum mönnum mein, fimm ok eina; eigi hugðak orma at aldrlagi mínu; verðr mjök mörgu sinni, þats minnst varir sjálfan".	"Battles have born, Of-that great thought, Made I many men Harm, fifty and one Not thought serpent To never me Become much many this, That least foreseen himself".	Battles I have born, Though of that great, I have made many men, Harm, fiftyone, Not thought that a serpent, To me never, Become to so much this, Which men themselves least forsee".
Ok enn kvað hann:	And still spoke he:	And he spoke again:
"Gnyðja mundu grísir, ef galtar hag vissi,	"Grumble would piglets, If boar circumstances knew,	"The piglets would grumble, If they knew the circumstances of the boar,

Old Norse	Literal	English
mér er gnótt at grandi,	To-me is abundance of injury,	To-me is an abundance of injury,
grafa inn rönum sínum ok harðliga hváta, hafa mik sogit, ormar; nú munk nár af bragði	Engrave in peace theirs And hard urge, Have me sucked-at, serpents Now remember corpse of looking	Engrave in their peace, And hard urge, Have sucked my life out, Now remember I will be a corpse,
ok nær dýrum deyja".	And near wild-animals die".	Beside the beasts, I will die".
Nú lætr hann líf sitt, ok er hann nú færðr á brott þaðan.	Now laid he life his, and was he now brought to away from-there.	Now he had laid his life, and he was now brougt away from there.
En Ella konungr þykkist vita, at Ragnarr hefir líf sitt látit.	Then Ælla the-King seemed to-know, that Ragnar had life his laid.	Then King Aella seemed to know that Ragnar had laid down his life.
Nú hyggr hann fyrir sér, hvé hann skyldi þess verða varr eða með fara, at hann mætti halda ríki sínu eða vita, hvé þeim brygði við sonum Ragnars, er þeir spyrja.	Now thought he therefore himself, how he should this be wary or with going, that he might hold kingdom his or know, how they react with sons Ragnar's, when they heard.	Now he thought about himself, how he should be wary and going forward, how he might hold on to his kingdom, and how Ragnar's sons would react then they heard.
Hann tekr þat til ráðs, at hann lætr búa skip eitt ok fær þann mann til fyrir at ráða, er bæði var vitr ok harðfengr, ok þar fær hann menn til, svá at þat skip var vel skipat, ok segir, at hann vill þá senda á fund Ívars ok þeira bræðra ok segja þeim fall föður þeira.	He took it to plan, that he had he ship one and got then a-man to for that plan, who both was wise and hardy, and there got he men to, so that the ship was well prepared, and said, that he wished then send to find Ivar and they brothers and tell them fall father theirs.	He took upon a plan, he had a ship prepared and got a man to carry out his plan, who was both wise and hardy, and he got men so that the ship was well prepared, he said that he wanted to send them to find Ivar and his brothers and tell them about their father.
En sjá för líst flestum óvænlig, svá at fáir vildu fara.	But looked journey like most unlikely, so that few willed to-go.	But the journey looked most unlikely to succeed, so few wanted to go.
Þá mælti konungr: "At því skulu þér vandliga hyggja, hversu hverjum þeira bræðra bregðr við þessi tíðendi.	Then said king: "That accordingly shall you closely think, how-so each they brothers react with this news.	Then the king said: "Accordingly you shall closely observe how each of the brothers react with this news".

Old Norse	Literal	English
"Farit þá leiðar yðarrar síðan, er yðr gefr veðr".	"Fare then route yours afterwards, as you are-given wind".	"Travel on your route afterwards, when you are given fair wind".
Svá lætr hann búa ferð þeira, at þeir þurftu at engu annarra.	So had he prepared journey theirs, that they needed of nothing else.	So had he prepared their journey, that they needed nothing else.
Ok nú fara þeir, ok ferst þeim vel.	And now went they, and travelled they well.	And now they travelled, and travelled well.
En synir Ragnars höfðu herjat of Suðrríki.	Then sons Ragnar's had harried about southern-lands.	Then Ragnar's sons had harried about the southern lands.
Þá sneru þeir á Norðrlönd ok ætluðu at vitja ríkis síns, þess er Ragnarr réð fyrir.	Then turned they to north-lands and intended to visit kingdoms theirs, these that Ragnar ruled for.	Then they turned to the north lands and intended to visit their kingdoms, which Ragnar ruled.
En þeir vissu eigi herför hans, hversu hún hafði orðit, ok þó er þeim mikil forvitni á, hversu hún hafði orðit.	But they knew not warfare his, how it had become, and though were they much curious about, how-so it had become.	But they did not know how his warfare had gone, and they were very curious to know how what had become of it.
Nú fara þeir sunnan of land.	Now travelled they south about the-land.	Now they travelled south about the land.
En hvarvetna, er menn frétta til fara þeira bræðra, eyddu menn borgir sínar ok færðu fé sitt á brott ok flýðu undan, svá at trautt fengu þeir liði sínu mat.	And everywhere, where men heard-news of journey they the-brothers, devastated men cities theirs and carried wealth theirs to away and fled away, so that scarcely gathered their company themselves food.	And everywhere where men heard news of the journey of these brothers, men devastated their cities and carried their wealth away and fled away, so that their company could scarcely gather themselves food.
Þat er einn morgin, at Björn járnsíða vaknar ok kvað vísu:	It was one morning, that Bjorn Ironside awoke and said a-verse:	It was one morning that Bjorn Ironside awoke and said a verse:
"Hér flýgr hverjan morgin hress of borgir þessar, læst heill munu af hungri, heiðir vals, of deyja;	"Here flies each morning Well about city this, Locked hail shall of hunger, High roller, about die	"Here flies each morning, Well about these fortresses, Locked shall the hail of hunger, High roller, of death,

Old Norse	Literal	English
hann fari suðr um sanda,	He travel south about sands,	He shall travel south about the sands,
sára hvar vér létum,	Wounds where we made,	Where wounds we have made,
þar fær dauðs manns dreyra,	There goes dead man's blood,	There goes the dead man's blood,
dögg ór skýlihöggum".	Dew of axe-cuts".	Dew of axe cuts".
Ok enn kvað hann:	And still spoke he:	And then he spoke:
"Þat var fyrst, er fórum,	"That when first, where travelled,	"That when first we travelled,
Freys leika tókk heyja,	Frey's games took conducted,	Frey's games were taken up,
þars andvíga áttum	There opposition had	There had opposition,
öld, í Rómaveldi;	age, of Roman-world	In the age, of the Roman world,
þar létk of grön grána,	There let of moustache grey,	There had the grey moustached ones,
gall örn of valfalli,	Bellowed eagle about slain-fall,	Eagle screamed over the slain fallen,
at mannskæðu morði	That man's-damage murder	That man's damage murder,
mitt sverð dregit verða".	My sword drawn became".	My sword became drawn.

16

Nú berr svá til, at þeir koma fyrri í Danaveldi en sendimenn Ellu konungs ok sitja nú kyrrir með lið sitt.	Now bore so until, that they came for to Denmark when messengers Ælla the-King's and sat now still with men his.	Now it happened that they came travelling to Denmark, when the messengers of King Aella sat quietly with his men.
En sendimenn koma með lið sitt til þeirar borgar, er synir Ragnars þiggja veislu, ok ganga í þá höll, er þeir drekka, ok fyrir hásætit, er Ívarr liggr í.	When messengers came among men his to their city, were sons Ragnar's accepted a-feast, and went among then hall, where they drank, and before the-high-seat, where Ivar lay at.	When the messengers came among his men to their city, Ragnar's sons accepted a feast, and they went among the hall where they drank, and before the high seat, where Ivar lay at.
Sigurðr ormr í auga ok Hvítserkr hvati sitja at hneftafli, en Björn járnsíða skefr spjótskepti á hallargólfinu.	Sigurd Snake-in-the-eye and Hvitserk the-Swift sat at a-gaming-table, but Bjorn Ironside planed a-spear-shaft on the-hall-floor.	Sigurd Snake-in-the-eye and Hvitserk the Swift sat at a gaming table, but Bjorn Ironside planed a spear shaft on the hall floor.

Old Norse	Literal	English
Ok er sendimenn Ellu konungs koma fyrir Ívar, kveðja þeir hann virðuliga.	And when messengers Ælla the-King's came before Ivar, greeted them he worthily.	And when King Aella's messengers came before Ivar, he greeted them worthily.
En hann tekr kveðju þeira ok spyrr, hvaðan þeir sé eða hvat þeir segja tíðenda.	Then he took greeting theirs and asked, from-where they be or what they said of-news.	Then he took their greeting and asked where they were from, and what news they had.
Ok sá, er fyrir þeim var, segir, at þeir váru enskir menn ok þá hefir Ella konungr þangat senda með þau tíðendi at segja fall Ragnars, föður þeira.	And then, were before them who, said, that they were English men and that had Ælla the-King from-there sent with them news to say-of fall Ragnar's, father theirs.	And then, those who were before them, said that they were English men, and that King Aella had sent them with news to say of the fall of Ragnar their father.
Hvítserkr ok Sigurðr láta þegar falla niðr taflit ok hyggja at vandliga þessi tíðenda sögn.	Hvitserk and Sigurd let they fall down game-pieces and observed that closely this news said.	Hvitserk and Sigurd let the game pieces fall down and they observed this news closely.
Björn stendr á hallargólfinu ok studdist við spjótskepti sitt.	Bjorn stood on the-hall-floor and stood with spear-shaft his.	Bjorn stood on the hall floor and stood with his spear shaft.
En Ívarr spurði þá vandliga, með hverjum atburð líflát hans hafði verit.	Then Ivar asked then closely, about each events death his that-had been.	Then Ivar asked closely, about each of the events of his death.
En þeir sögðu allt sem farit hafði þaðan frá, er hann kom við England ok til þess, er hann lét líf sitt.	When they said all which gone had there from, when he came to England and until this, that he laid life his.	When they had said all of what had gone before, when he came to England until this, when he laid his life.
Ok nú er þessi sögu var þar komit, er hann hafði þetta mælt: "Gnyðja mundu grísir", þokar Björn höndum sínum á spjótskaptinu, ok svá hafði hann tekit fast, at handastaðinn sá á eptir.	And now when this story was then come-to, that he had this said: "Grumble will the-piglets", shook Bjorn hand his in spear-shaft, and so had he taken close, that hand-print was-seen on afterwards.	And now when the story had come to where he said: "The piglets would grumble", Bjorn clenched the spear shaft so hard that his hand print could be seen on it afterwards.

Old Norse	Literal	English
Þá er sendimenn luku frásögn þessi, hristir Björn spjótit í sundr, svá at stökk í tvá hluti.	Then as the-messengers finished from-saying this, shook Bjorn spear to asunder, so that split in two parts.	Then as the messengers finished saying this, Bjorn shook the spear apart so that it split into two pieces.
En Hvítserkr hélt töfl einni, er hann hafði drepit, ok hann kreisti hana svá fast, at blóð stökk undan hverjum nagli.	Then Hvitserk held a-game-piece one, in he had taken, and he crushed it so tightly, that blood emanated from each nail.	Then Hvitserk held a game piece in his hand, and he crushed it so tightly that blood emanated from each nail.
En Sigurðr ormr í auga hafði haldit á knífi einum ok skóf nagl sinn, er þessi tíðendi váru sögð, ok hugði svá vandliga at þessum tíðendum, at hann kenndi eigi fyrr en knífrinn stóð í beini, ok brást hann ekki við.	Then Sigurd Snake-in-the-eye had held a knife one and scraped nail his, as this news was said, and thought so closely at this news, that he knew not for that the-knife stood in bone, and startled he not with.	Then Sigurd Snake-in-the-eye held a knife, and scraped his nail, as the news was said, he observed this news so closely, that he did not know that his knife stood in bone, and he did not startle.
En Ívarr spyrr at öllu sem gerst, en litr hans var stundum rauðr, en stundum blár, en lotum var hann bleikr, ok hann var svá þrútinn, at hans hörund var allt blásit af þeim grimmleik, er í brjósti hans var.	Then Ivar asked of all which done, then colour his was awhile red, and awhile blue, about sometimes was he pale, and he was so swollen, that his skin was all blown of the savagery, that in breast his was.	Then Ivar asked all the details of what had been done, and his colour was red for a while, then blue for a while, and sometimes he went pale, and he was so swollen, that his skin was swollen from all the savagery in his breast.
Nú tekr Hvítserkr til orða ok sagði, at svá mætti hefndina bráðast upp hefja at drepa sendimenn Ellu konungs.	Now took Hvitserk to words and said, that so may revenge quickly up have to kill messengers Ælla the-King's.	Now Hvitserk took to words and said that they may have revenge quickest by killing King Aella's messengers.
Ívarr segir: "Þat skal eigi vera.	Ivar said: "That shall not be.	Ivar said: "That shall not be.
Þeir skulu fara í friði, hvert er þeir vilja, ok ef nokkurr hlutr er sá, at þá skorti, skulu þeir mér til segja, ok skal ek fá þeim".	They should travel in peace, wherever that they wish, and if any part is so, that they shortage-of, shall they to-me to say, and shall I get-for them".	They should travel in peace, wherever they wish, and if in any part they have a shortage, they shall tell me, and I shall get it for them".

Old Norse	Literal	English
Ok nú er þeir hafa lokit erendi sínu, snúa þeir utar eptir höllunni ok til skips síns.	And now as they had ended errands theirs, turned they out after the-hall and to ships theirs.	And now as they had ended their errand, they turned and walked out of the hall, and to their ships.
Ok er þeim gefr byr, láta þeir í haf, ok ferst þeim vel, þar til er þeir koma á fund Ellu konungs, ok segja honum frá, hversu hverjum þeira hefir við brugðit þessa tíðenda sögn.	And when they were-given fair-wind, lay-out they to sea, and travelled they well, then until that they came to find Ælla the-King, and said-to him from, how each they had with appeared this news said.	And when they were given fair wind, they set out to sea, and they travelled well, until they came to King Aella, and said to him how each of them had appeared with the news.
Ok er Ella konungr heyrir þetta, þá mælti hann: "Þess er ván, at annathvárt munu vér Ívar þurfa at óttast eða engan ella, at því er þér segið frá honum, ok mundi þeim gott innan rifja, ok haldit munu vér fá ríki váru fyrir þeim".	And when Ælla the-King heard this, then spoke he: "This-is as expected, that either-way should we Ivar need to fear or none other, that because-of what you say of him, and would-be of-them good to consider, and hold shall we have kingdom ours before them".	And when King Aella heard this, then he spoke: "This is as expected, that either we must fear Ivar or no one, because of what you say of him, and it would be good to consider the others, and we shall have hold of our kingdom before them".
Nú lætr hann varðhöld hafa um allt sitt ríki, svá at eigi mátti herr komast á óvart honum.	Now had he watch-holders at-sea about all his kingdom, so that none may army come to un-warned him.	Now he had watchmen set at sea all along his kingdom, so that no army may come to him without warning.
En er sendimenn Ellu konungs váru brott farnir, ganga þeir bræðr á málstefnu, hversu þeir skyldu með fara of hefnd eptir Ragnar, föður sinn.	When the messengers Ælla the-King's were away travelled, went they brothers to council, how-so they should with travel about revenge after Ragnar, father theirs.	When King Aella's messengers had travelled away, the brothers held a council, how they should travel to gain revenge for their father Ragnar.
Þá mælti Ívarr: "Engan hlut mun ek í eiga ok eigi fá lið til, því at Ragnarr fór sem mik varði.	Then spoke Ivar: "No part shall I in have and none get crew to, therefore as Ragnar fared as my expectation.	Then Ivar spoke: "I shall have no part in it, and I shall summon no men, because Ragnar did as I expected he would.
Hann bjó illa sína sök til í upphafi.	He prepared badly his fault to this the-beginning.	He prepared badly to a fault from the beginning.

Old Norse	Literal	English
Hann átti engar sakir við Ellu konung, ok hefir þat opt orðit, ef maðr ætlar ofrkapp fyrir sér með rangendum, at hann hefir því óvirðuligar niðr komit.	He had no sake with Ælla king, and has it often become, if men intend overkill for himself with wrong-doing, that he had therefore unworthy down come.	He had no quarrel with King Aella, and it has often happened, if men intend overkill for themselves unjustly, they are therefore unworthy and laid low.
Ok vil ek þiggja fébætr af Ellu konungi, ef hann vill til leggja við mik".	And will I accept compensation of Ælla the-King, if he will to place with me".	And I will accept compensation from King Aella, if he will grant it to me".
En er þeir heyra þetta bræðr hans, verða þeir reiðir mjök ok segja, at aldri skyldu þeir svá at klækjum verða, þótt hann vildi svá.	When that they heard this brothers his, became they angry much and said, that never should they so to shame become, though he willed-it so.	When his brothers heard this, they became very angry, and said that never should they come to such shame, as he willed it.
"Munu þat margir mæla, at oss sé mislagðar hendr í kné, ef vér skulum eigi hefna föður várs, en vér höfum víða farit um heim með herskildi ok drepit margan mann saklausan.	"Would this many say, that us be mislaid hands in allegiance, if we shall not avenge father ours, though we have widely travelled about home with raiding and killed many men innocent.	"Many will say that our hands would be misguided in alliegance, if we shall not avenge our father, though we have travelled widely in our home lands, raided and killed many innocent men".
Ok enn skal eigi þat verða, heldr skal búa hvert skip, er sæfært er í Danaveldi.	And then shall not that be, rather shall prepare each ship, that seaworthy is in Denmark.	That shall not happen, rather we shall prepare each ship that is seaworthy in Denmark.
Skal svá gersamliga safna liði, at hverr maðr, er skjöld má bera í mót Ellu konungi, skal fara".	Shall so altogether raise company, that every man, that shields may bear to against Ælla the-King, shall travel".	We shall all together raise a company, that every man that may bear a shield against King Aella shall travel".
En Ívarr segir, at hann mundi eptir sitja ok þau skip, er hann á fyrir at ráða, "nema þat eitt, er ek á sjálfr".	But Ivar said, that he would behind sit and his ships, which he that before had planned, "Except that one, which I have myself".	But Ivar said that he would leave his ships behind, "Except for the one which I have myself".

Old Norse	Literal	English
Ok er þetta spyrst, at Ívarr leggr enga stund á, fá þeir miklu minna lið ok fara þó eigi at síðr.	And when this learned, that Ivar had no time to, got they much less company and travelled though none the less.	And when this was learned, that Ivar would not have part in it, they got much less of a company, but they travelled nonetheless.
Ok þegar er þeir kómu við England, verðr Ella konungr varr við ok lætr þegar lúðr sinn við gjalla ok býðr til sín öllum mönnum, er honum vilja fylgja.	And as-soon as they came to England, became Ælla the-King aware by and had straightaway trumpets his with sounded and invited to his all men, who he willed to-follow.	And as soon as they came to England, King Aella became aware, and straightaway had trumpets sounded, and invited all men who wished to follow.
Ok nú fær hann svá mikit lið, at engi maðr mátti tölu á koma, ok ferr í mót þeim bræðrum.	And now got he so many men, that no man could count that came, and travelled to meet they the-brothers.	And now he got so many men, that no man could count who had come, and they travelled to meet the brothers.
Ok er þeir finnast, var Ívarr ekki í þeim bardaga.	And when they found, was Ivar not with them to-battle.	And when they found them, Ivar was not with them at the battle.
Ok svá lýkr þeira bardaga, at synir Ragnars koma á flótta, en Ella konungr hefir sigr.	And so concluded their battle, that sons Ragnar's came to flee, and Ælla the-King had success.	And so concluded their battle, that Ragnar's sons came to flee, and King Aella had success.
Ok er hann var at at reka flóttann, segir Ívarr, at hann ætlar ekki aptr at hverfa til lands síns, "ok vil ek reyna, hvárt Ella konungr vill mér nokkurrar sæmdar unna eða engrar, ok þykki mér sá betri at þiggja yfirbót af honum en fara slíkar ófarar fleiri sem nú fóru vér".	And when he was towards the expelled fleeing, said Ivar, that he intended not back to turn to land his, "And will I test, whether Ælla the-King will to-me some honour grant or not, and think to-me so better to accept redress of him than travel such impossible more as now travelled we".	And when he was pursuing the fleeing company, Ivar said that he did not intend to return to his homeland, "And I will test, whether King Aella will grant me some honour or not, and I think it will be better to accept compensation from him than to travel such unlucky voyages, such as we have now gone on".
Hvítserkr segir, at eigi mátti hlut í eiga með honum ok hann yrði at fara með sín efni sem hann vill, "en aldri skulu vér fé taka eptir föður várn".	Hvitserk said, that not may share in owning with him and he could to go with his matter as he willed, "But never shall we wealth take after father ours".	Hvitserk said, that he would have no part in this with him, and he could continue with this matter as he wished, "But never shall we take wealth for our father".

Old Norse	Literal	English
Ívarr segir, at þar mundi skilja með þeim, ok bað þá ráða ríki því, er þeir áttu allir saman, "en þér skuluð senda mér lausafé, sem ek kveð á".	Ivar said, that there would-be a-part with them, and asked then to-rule kingdom as, which they had all together, "But you should send me loose-fee, when I ask for".	Ivar said, that he would part with them there, and asked them to rule the kingdom which they all had in common, "but you must send me money when I ask for it".
En er hann hafði mælt, bað hann þá vel fara.	Then when he had spoken, bid he them well faring.	Then when they had spoken, he bid them farewell.
En hann snýr aptr sinni ferð á fund Ellu konungs.	Then he turned back his journey to find Ælla the-King.	Then he turned back on his journey to find King Aella.
Ok er hann kemr fyrir hann, kveðr hann konunginn virðuliga ok hefr svá mál sitt: "Ek em kominn á fund yðarn, ok vil ek mæla til sætta við þik ok slíkrar sæmdar sem þú vilt gert hafa til mín.	And when he came before him, greeted he the-King worthily and had so the-matter his: "I am come to meet you, and wish I matter to settle with you and such honour as you will done have to me.	And when he came before him, he greeted the king worthily, and began to state his matter: "I have come to meet you, and I wish to settle with you with such honour that you have shown me.
Ok nú sé ek þat, at ek hefi ekki við þér, ok þykki mér þat betra at þiggja af yðr slíka sæmd sem þú vilt mér veita en láta mína menn fleiri fyrir yðr eða sjálfan mik".	And now see I this, that I have nothing against you, and think me that-it-is better to accept from you such honour as you will to-me grant than leave my men more to you or self mine".	And now I see that, I have nothing against you, and I think it is better to accept from you such honour as you will grant to me, than to surrender my men or myself to you".
Þá svarar Ella konungr: "Þat kalla sumir menn, at eigi sé hægt at trúa þér ok þú mælir þá opt fagrt, er þú hyggr flátt, ok mun oss vera vant at sjá við þér eða bræðrum þínum".	Then answered Ælla king: "That call some men, that not so possible to trust you and you speak then often fairly, when you think craftily, and should we come-to difficulty to see about you or brothers yours".	Then King Aella answered: "Some men say that it is not possible to trust you, and that you speak fairly, when you think craftily, and it will be difficult to keep an eye on you or your brothers".
"Ek mun til lítils mæla við þik, ef þú lætr þat til.	"I would to little matter from you, if you allow that to.	"I will ask for little from you, if you will grant it.
Skal ek þat sverja þér á mót, at ek skal aldri vera í mót þér".	Shall I that swear to-you in return, that I shall never be of against you".	I shall swear to you in return, that I shall never be against you".

Old Norse	Literal	English
Nú spyrr konungr, til hvers hann mælti of yfirbætr.	Now asked the-King, about how he might about compensate.	Now the king asked how he might compensate.
"Ek vil", segir Ívarr, "at þú gefir mér þat af landi þínu, er uxahúð tekr yfir, en þar utan um skal grundvöll gera, ok mun ek eigi til meira mæla við þik, ok þat sé ek, at þú vilt mér engrar sæmdar unna, ef þú vilt eigi þetta".	"I wish", said Ivar, "that you give to-me that of land yours, that an-ox-hide takes over, but there out-of about shall foundations make, and shall I not to more matters with you, and this know I, that you will to-me not honour grant, if you will not this".	"I wish", said Ivar, "for you to give me land of yours, that an ox hide may span over, and around that I shall build foundations, and I will not ask any more of you than this, and this I know, you will not grant me any honour, if you will not do this".
"Eigi veit ek", segir konungr, "at oss megi þetta at meini verða, þótt þú hafir þetta ór mínu landi, ok at vísu mun ek fá þér þetta, ef þú vilt þat sverja mér at berjast eigi í mót mér, ok eigi uggi ek bræðr þína, ef þú ert mér trúr".	"Not know I", said the-King, "that we may this to harm become, though you have this of my land, and that certainly will I give you this, if you will that swear to-me to fight not to against me, and not fear I brothers yours, if you are to-me true".	"I do not know", said the king, "how this could do us any harm to give you this piece of my land, and I will certainly give you this, if you will swear to me that you will not fight against me, and I do not fear your brothers if you are true to me".
17	17	17
Nú ráða þeir þetta með sér, at Ívarr sverr honum eiða, at hann skyldi eigi skjóta í mót honum ok eigi ráð leggja til meins honum, en hann skal eignast af Englandi þat, sem uxahúð tekr yfir, er hann fengi mesta til.	Now discussed they this with themselves, that Ivar swore to-him oath, that he should not launch to against him and not plans make to harm him, and he shall own of England that, which an-ox-hide takes over, which he got the-most to.	Now they discussed the matter between themselves, that Ivar had sworn an oath to him, that he should not launch an attack against him, and not make plans to harm him, and he shall own land of England which the largest hide that he could get, would span over.
Nú fær Ívarr sér öldungshúð eina, ok nú lætr hann hana bleyta, ok þrisvar lætr hann hana þenja.	Now got Ivar himself old-bull one, and now had he it softened, and three-times had he it stretched.	Now Ivar got himself an old bull hide, and he had it softened, and he had it stretched three times.
Nú lætr hann rista hana sem mjóst alla í sundr, ok þá lætr hann renna sér hvárt, háram eða holdrosu.	Now had he carved it as thin all to distribute, and then had it split to each, the-hairy-side or the-fleshy-side.	Now he had it carved as thin as it could possibly be, and he had the hairy side split from the fleshy side.

Old Norse	Literal	English
Ok er þessu var lokit, var þvengr sjá svá langr, at furða var at, ok engum kom í hug, at svá mætti verða.	And when this was concluded, was thong seen so long, that a-wonder was it, and none came to think, that so it-might become.	And when this was done, there was a thong that was so long, that it was a wonder, and no one thought that it would become so long.
Ok þá lætr hann breiða á einum velli, en þat var svá vítt land, at þat var mikil borgarvídd, ok þar fyrir utan lætr hann marka grundvöll sem til mikilla borgarveggja.	And then laid he widely in a field, then it was so wide land, that it was a-great city-wide, and there before out laid he marks foundations as to great city-walls.	And then he laid it widely in a field, and it was so wide, that it was as great as a city, and outside of it, he laid the marks for the foundations of great city walls.
Ok þá fær hann sér smiði marga ok lætr reisa hús mörg á þeim velli, ok þar lætr hann gera borg eina mikla, ok er sú kölluð Lundúnaborg.	And then got he himself smiths many and had raised houses many about the fields, and there had he made city one so-great, and was so called London-city.	And then he got himself many smiths, and had many houses raised on that field, and there he had built a great city, and it was called the City of London.
Hún er allra borga mest ok ágæst of öll Norðrlönd.	She is altogether city the-most and the-greatest about all The-Northern-Lands.	She is altogether the most and greatest city in all of the northern lands.
Ok nú er hann hafði borg þessa látit gera, hafði hann lausafé upp gefit.	And now that he had city his made done, had he treasure up given.	And now that he had this city built, he gave treasure.
En hann var svá örr, at hann gaf á tvær hendr, ok þótti svá mikit um speki hans, at allir sóttu hann at sínum ráðum ok vandamálum.	Then he was so open-handed, that he gave with two hands, and was-thought so much about wisdom his, that all sought to-him of his advice and problems.	Then he was so generous, that he gave with two hands, and much was thought about his wisdom, so that everyone sought his advice with their problems.
Ok svá skipaði hann öllum málum sem hverjum þótti sér best gegna, ok gerist hann vinsæll, svá at hann á undir hverjum manni vin, ok er Ellu konungi mikit lið at honum fyrir landráða sakir, svá at konungr lætr hann mörgum ráðum ok málum skipa ok þarf eigi til at koma sjálfr.	And so directed he all matters as each as-seemed to-him best going, and was he popular, so that he about to every man a-friend, and was Ælla the-King great help of him for land-ruling's sake, so that the-King let him many advice and matters command and needed not to that come himself.	And he directed all matters as he thought best, and he was popular, so that to every man he was a friend, and King Aella has great help from him in ruling the land, so the king let him advise and command in many matters that he need not come to himself.

Old Norse	Literal	English
Ok er Ívarr hafði svá komit ráði sínu, at þar þykkir til allrar spektar at sjá, sendir hann menn á fund bræðra sinna þess erendis, at þeir sendi honum gull ok silfr svá mikit sem hann kvað á.	And when Ivar had so come plan his, that there seemed to all peaceful to see, sent he man to meet brothers his this errand, that they sent him gold and silver so much that he asked for.	And when Ivar had come this far with his plans, his intentions seemed peaceful to everyone, he sent men to meet his brothers, with a request that they send him as much gold and silver as he asked for.
En er þessir menn koma á fund þeira bræðra, segja þeir sín erendi ok svá, hvar þá var komit hans ráð, því at menn þóttust þat eigi vita, yfir hverjum brögðum hann bjó.	When that these men came to meet they the-brothers, told them his errands and so, where then were coming his plans, because that men thought that none knew, about which strategy he prepared.	When these men came to meet the brothers, they told them his business, and where his plans were coming from, because no one knew, what he was planning.
Ok svá skildu þeir bræðr, at hann hafði ekki skapsmuni eptir því, sem hann var vanr.	And so knew they the-brothers, that he had not temperament after before, which he was lacking.	And so the brothers knew that he was not in the same state of mind as before.
Nú senda þeir slíkt fé sem hann á kvæði.	Now sent they such wealth as he had asked.	Now they sent as much wealth as he had asked for.
Ok er þeir koma til Ívars, gefr hann þau öll fé inum stærstum mönnum í landinu ok dregr svá lið undan Ellu konungi, ok allir hétu því, at kyrrir mundu sitja, þótt hann gerði þangat herför.	And as they came to Ivar, gave him then all wealth in greatest people in the-land and drew so company from-under Ælla the-King, and all pledged that, to still would-be sat, though he went from-there war-going.	And when they came to Ivar, he then gave all his wealth to the greatest people in the land, and lured the men from under King Aella, and they pledged that they would stay still, even if there was going to be war.
Ok er Ívarr hefir svá lið dregit undir sik, þá sendir hann menn á fund bræðra sinna at segja þeim, at vildi hann, at þeir byði út leiðangri of þau lönd öll, er þeira ríki stóð yfir, ok þeir skoraði hverjum manni, er þeir fengi.	And when Ivar had so company drawn behind him, then sent he men to find brothers his to say to-them, that willed he, that they invite out expedition about the land all, that they kingdom stood over, and they summoned each man, that they got.	And when Ivar had such a company gathered behind him, then he sent men to find his brothers to say to them, that he wanted to raise the levy from all the lands that they ruled over, and summoned each man that they had.

Old Norse	Literal	English
Ok þá er þessi orðsending kom til þeira bræðra, kennast þeir við skjótt, skilja, at nú mundi honum þykkja mjök vænligt um, at nú mundi þeir fá sigr.	And then were these messages came to they the-brothers, knew they therefore quickly, understood, about now could he think much promisingly about, that now would they get success.	And then when these messages came to the brothers, they therefore quickly understood that now he thought they had the most promising chance of success.
Nú safna þeir liði um alla Danmörk ok Gautland ok öll þau ríki, er þeira völd váru yfir, ok draga óvígan her saman ok hafa almenning úti.	Now raised they company from all Denmark and Götaland and all the kingdom, that they powerful were over, and drew unconquerable war-band together and have all-men about.	Now they raised their men from all of Denmark and Götaland, and all the kingdom, that they ruled over, and gathered the unconquerable war band together all about.
Þá halda þeir skipum sínum til Englands bæði nótt ok dag ok vildu nú sem síst láta fara njósn fyrir þeim.	Then held they ships theirs to England both night and day and willed not as little-as-possible let travel spying before them.	They headed their ships to England both night and day, and they wanted as little news as possible of their travel spied before them.
Nú er sjá hersaga sögð Ellu konungi.	Now was so news-of-war told-to Ælla the-King.	Now was this news of war told to King Aella.
Nú safnar hann sér liði ok fær lítit, fyrir því at Ívarr hafði mikit lið undan honum dregit.	Now collected he his men and got little, for because that Ivar had many men from-under him drawn.	Now he collected his men, and only got a little, because Ivar had lured many men from under him.
Nú ferr Ívarr í mót Ellu konungi ok segir, at hann mundi enda þat, er hann hafði svarit.	Now travelled Ivar to meet Ælla the-King and said, that he would conclude that, which he had sworn.	Now Ivar travelled to meet King Aella, and said that he would conclude what he had sworn.
"En eigi má ek ráða tiltekju bræðra minna, en því má ek ráða at finna þá ok vita, ef þeir vili stöðva her sinn ok gera eigi meira illt en þeir hafa áðr gert".	"But not may I plans change brothers mine, but therefore may I plan to find them and know, if they will stop war theirs and do no more harm than they had before done".	"But I may not change my brothers' plans, but I plan to find them and know if they will stop their war and do no more harm than they have already done".

Old Norse	Literal	English
Nú ferr Ívarr á fund bræðra sinna ok eggjar þá nú mjök, at þeir skyldi sem best fram ganga ok sem bráðast láta bardaga verða, "því at konungr hefir miklu minna lið".	Now went Ivar to meet brothers his and encouraged then now much, that they should as best from go and as quickly lay battle be, "Because that the-King has many less men".	Now Ivar went to meet his brothers and then encouraged them, to advance as best they could, and begin the battle as quickly as possible, "Because the king has many less men".
En þeir svara, at eigi mundi hann þurfa at eggja þá ok þeim var it sama í hug sem fyrr.	But they answered, that not would he need to encourage them and they were the same in thought as before.	But they answered that they would not need encouragement, and they thought the same as before.
Nú ferr Ívarr ok hittir Ellu konung ok segir honum, at miklu váru þeir ákafari ok óðari en þeir vildi á hans orð hlýða.	Now went Ivar and met Ælla the-King and told him, that greater were they eager and mad than they willed to his words listen.	Now Ivar went and met King Aella and told him that they were too eager and mad, and they did not want to listen to his words.
"Ok þá er ek vilda um grið leita yðar í milli, æptu þeir í gegn.	"And then when I willed about mercy seek yours in among, shouted they to against.	"And then I tried to seek your mercy, but they shouted against this.
Nú mun ek enda mína svardaga, at ek mun eigi berjast í móti þér, ok mun ek vera kyrr hjá ok mitt lið, en bardagi gengr með yðr sem verða má".	Now must I complete my oath, that I will not fight with against you, and will I be still nearby and my men, and battle goes with you as being may".	Now I must complete my oath, that I will not fight against you, and I will stay still nearby with my men, and the battle shall go with you as it may".
Nú sjá þeir Ella konungr lið þeira bræðra, ok ferr svá geyst, at furða var at.	Now saw they Ælla the-King men theirs brothers, and went so rushed, at fury was from.	Now King Aella saw the brothers' forces, and they advanced with such fury.
Þá mælti Ívarr: "Þat er nú til, Ella konungr, at þú fylkir liði þínu, en ek get þess, at þeir veiti þér harða atsókn nokkura hríð".	Then spoke Ivar: "It is now to, Ælla the-King, that you command men yours, and I guess this, that they will to-you roughly attack some while".	Then Ivar spoke: "Now it's time, King Aella, for you to command your men, and I guess that they will attack you roughly for some while".

Old Norse	Literal	English
En þegar þeira lið hittist, verðr bardagi mikill, ok ganga þeir hart fram synir Ragnars í gegnum fylkingar Ellu konungs, ok svá eru þeir ákafir, at þeir hyggja at því einu at gera at verkum sem mest, ok sú orrosta var bæði löng ok hörð.	And when their forces met, became the-battle great, and went they roughly ahead sons Ragnar's to through flanks Ælla the-King's, and so were they eager, that they thought of for only to do as actions which most, and so battle was both long and hard.	And when their forces met, the battle became great, and Ragnar's sons went roughly ahead through King Aella's flanks, and they were so eager, that they thought only of doing as much damage as possible, and the battle was both long and hard.
Ok hér lauk svá, at Ella konungr ok lið hans kom á flótta ok hann varð handtekinn.	And here concluded so, that Ælla the-King and forces his came to flee and he became hand-taken.	And here it concluded that King Aella and his forces came to flee, and he became captured.
Ok þá var Ívarr þar í nánd ok mælti, at svá skyldi breyta um líflát hans: "Er nú þat ráð", segir hann, "at minnast, hvern dauðdaga hann valdi föður várum.	And then was Ivar there about close-by and spoke, that so should bring about life-loss his: "Is now the plan", said he, "that remember, each death-day he chose father ours".	And then Ivar was close by, and spoke that so his death should be brought about: "Now is the plan", he said, "that we each remember the death day he chose for our father".
Nú skal sá maðr, er oddhagastr er, marka örn á baki honum sem inniligast, ok þann örn skal rjóða með blóði hans".	Now shall so man, that carving is, mark eagle in back his as deepest, and then the-eagle shall redden with blood his".	Now the man who is the most skilled at carving, shall mark an eagle deep into his back, and the eagle shall redden with his blood".
En sá maðr, er kvaddr var til þessarar sýslu, gerir sem Ívarr bauð honum, en Ella konungr var mjök sárr, áðr þessi sýslu lýkr.	Then so man, was called was to this work, did as Ivar bid him, then Ælla the-King was much wounded, after this work was-concluded.	Then such a man, was called to this work, and he did as Ivar bid him, then King Aella was wounder greatly, after this work was concluded.
Lætr hann nú líf sitt, ok þykkjast þeir nú hefnt hafa föður síns, Ragnars.	Laid he now life his, and thought they now revenge had father theirs, Ragnar's.	He now laid down his life, and they now thought that they had revenge for Ragnar, their father.
Ívarr segir, at hann vill þeim gefa ríki þat, er þeir áttu allir saman, en hann kveðst ráða vilja fyrir Englandi.	Ivar said, that he willed to-them give kingdom that, which they had all together, but he said plans wished for England.	Ivar said, that he wanted to give them all the kingdom which they all had together, but he said he planned to rule over England.

Old Norse	Literal	English
18	*18*	*18*
Eptir þetta fara þeir Hvítserkr ok Björn heim til ríkis síns ok Sigurðr, en Ívarr er eptir ok ræðr Englandi.	After that travelled they Hvitserk and Bjorn home to kingdom theirs and Sigurd, but Ivar was back and ruling England.	After that Hvitserk and Bjorn travelled home to their kingdoms, and Sigurd as well, but Ivar was back and ruling England.
Þaðan frá halda þeir miðr saman liði sínu ok herjuðu á ýmsi lönd.	There from headed they between together forces theirs and raided about various lands.	From there they headed with their forces joined raiding about various lands.
En Randalín, móðir þeira, varð gömul kona.	Then Randalin, mother theirs, was an-old woman.	Then Randalin, their mother, was an old woman.
En Hvítserkr, sonr hennar, hafði herjat eitthvert sinn í Austrveg, ok kom svá mikit ofrefli í mót honum, at hann mátti eigi rönd við reisa, ok varð hann handtekinn.	Then Hvitserk, son hers, had raided some then in eastern-lands, and came so great overwhelming to meet him, that he could not against with rise, and was he hand-taken.	Then Hvitserk, her son, had raided some eastern lands, and such overwhelming forces came against him, that he would not withstand then, and he was captured.
En hann kaus sér þann dauðdaga, at bál skyldi gera af mannahöfðum; þar skyldi hann brenna, ok svá lét hann líf sitt.	But he chose his then death-day, that fire should be-made of men's-heads there should he burn, and so lay his life there.	But he chose his own death day, that a fire should be made of men's heads burning, and so he lay down his life there.
Ok er Randalín spyrr þetta, þá kvað hún vísu:	And when Randalin learned this, then spoke she a-verse:	And when Randalin learned of this, she spoke a verse:
"Sonr beið einn, sás áttak, í Austrvegi dauða, Hvítserkr var sá heitinn, hvergi gjarn at flýja; hitnaði hann af höfðum höggvins vals at rómu, kaus þann bana þengill þróttarsnjallr, áðr felli".	"Son sought one, this-who fed, In eastern-lands death, Hvitserk was so named, Neither willing to flee Heated he from heads Struck-off rolled in battle, Chose he death prince Bold-and-brave, before falling".	"One son, who I fed, In eastern lands, death, Hvitserk was he named, Neither willing to flee, Heated was he from heads, Struck off rolled in battle, Chose he the price of death, Bold and brave, before falling".
Ok enn kvað hún:	And yet said she:	And then she said:
"Höfðum létu of hrundit	"Heads laid about heaped	"Heads laid about heaped,

Old Norse	Literal	English
hundmörgum gram undir, at feigum bör folka fingi eldr yfir syngja; hvat skyldi beð inn betra böðheggr und sik leggja; olli, deyr við orðstír allvaldr, jöfurr falli".	Countless warriors under, To doomed bore folk Getting flame over song What should bed the better Offered-tree under himself laying How-much, dies with fame All-wielding, ruler fell".	Countless warriors under, To doomed bore folk, Getting flame over song, What bed should be better, Offered-tree under himself laying How much dies with fame, All wielding, ruler fell".
En frá Sigurði orm í auga er mikill ættbogi kominn.	And from Sigurd Snake-in-the-eye are great descendents come.	And many great descendents came from Sigurd Snake-in-the-eye.
Hans dóttir hét Ragnhildr, móðir Haralds ins hárfagra, er fyrstr réð öllum Noregi einn.	His daughter named Ragnhild, mother Harald the Hair-Fair, was first ruler-of all Norway one.	His daughter was named Ragnhild, mother of Harald Fair-Hair, who was the first ruler of all Norway as one.
En Ívarr réð fyrir Englandi allt til dauðadags ok varð sóttdauðr.	Then Ivar ruled for England altogether until death-day and was sickness-death.	Then Ivar ruled over England until his death day which was from sickness.
Ok þá er hann lá í banasótt, mælti hann, at hann skyldi þangat færa, er herskátt væi, ok þess kvaðst hann vænta, at þeir mundi eigi sigr fá, er þar kæmi at landinu.	And then was he laying in death-sickness, said he, that he should from-there be-brought, where invasion might-be, and this said he expected, that they would not success get, when they came to land.	And then when he was laying in death sickness, he said, that he should be brought from there, to where an invasion might be, and he said that he expected that they would not get success, when they came to land.
Ok er hann andast, var svá gert sem hann mælti fyrir, ok var þá í haug lagiðr.	And when he died, was so done as he spoke for, and was then a mound laid.	And when he died, so it was done as he had spoken about, and then a mound was laid.
Ok þat segja margir menn, þá er Haraldr konungr Sigurðarson kom til Englands, at hann kæmi þar at, er Ívarr var fyrir, ok fellr hann í þeiri för.	And that said many men, then when Harald king Sigurdarson came to England, that he came there to, where Ivar was present, and fell he about there before.	And many men said, that when King Harald Sigurdson came to England, that he came there to where Ivar was present, and he fell there abouts.

Old Norse	Literal	English
Ok er Vilhjálmr bastarðr kom í land, fór hann til ok braut haug Ívars ok sá Ívar ófúinn.	And when William Bastard came to land, travelled he to and broke mound Ivar's and saw Ivar un-decayed.	And when William the Bastard came to land, he travelled and broke Ivar's mound and saw that Ivar was undecayed.
Þá lét hann gera bál mikit ok lætr Ívar brenna á bálinu, ok eptir þat berst hann til landsins ok fær gagn.	Then had he made a-pyre great and had Ivar burned on the-pyre, and after that fought he for the-land and got won.	Then he had a great pyre made and had Ivar burned on the pyre, and after that he fought for the land and conquered it.
En frá Birni járnsíðu er komit margt manna.	And from Bjorn Ironside are come many people.	And many people have come from Bjorn Ironside.
Frá honum er komin mikil ætt: Þórðr, er bjó at Höfða á Höfðaströnd, mikill höfðingi.	From him are come great descendents: Thord, who lived at Hofud in Hofudastrond, a-great chieftain.	From him have come great descendents: Thord, who lived at Hofud in Hofudastrond, a great chieftan.
En þá er synir Ragnars váru allir líflátnir, dreifðist lið þeira á ýmsa vega, er þeim hafði fylgt, ok þótti þeim öllum, er verit höfðu með sonum Ragnars, einkis vert um aðra höfðingja.	And then when sons Ragnar's were all life-less, dispersed forces theirs about various ways, which they had followed, and seemed to-them all, that been had with sons Ragnar's, no worth in other chieftains.	And then when Ragnar's sons were all lifeless, their forces dispersed in various ways that they had followed, and it seemed to them all, those who had been with Ragnar's sons, found no worth in any other chieftans.
Þeir váru tveir menn, er fóru víða um lönd at leita, ef þeir fyndi nokkurn höfðingja þann, er þeim þætti sér eigi svívirðing í at þjóna, ok fóru þeir eigi báðir saman.	There were two men, who travelled widely about lands to search, if they found some chieftain then, who they seemed themselves not swine-worth of to serve, and travelled they not both together.	There were two men, who travelled widely about the lands to search, if they found some chieftan who was not swine-worthy to serve, and they did not travel together.
19	19	19
Sá atburðr hefir verit út í löndum, at einn konungr átti tvá sonu, ok tók hann sótt ok andaðist, en synir hans vilja drekka erfi eptir hann.	So happened had been out in the-lands, that one king had two sons, and took he sickness and died, and sons his willed drink-to inheritance after him.	So it happened in a distant land, that a king had two sons, and he took sickness and died, and his sons wanted to hold a funeral feast in his honour.

Old Norse	Literal	English
Þeir bjóða til þessar veislu svá, at allir menn skyldu koma þangat, þeir er á þrimr vetrum inum næstum spyrja þetta.	They invited to this feast so, that all men should come there, they were for three winters the next hearing-of this.	They invited people to this feast, so that everyone should attend, three winters from when they heard the news.
Nú spyrst þetta víða um lönd.	Now was-heard that widely about the-lands.	Now this was heard widely about the lands.
Ok á þessum þrimr vetrum búast þeir við þessi veislu.	And as this third winter prepared they with this feast.	And for this third winter, they prepared this feast.
Ok er þat sumar kemr, er erfi skyldi drekka, ok sú stund, er ákveðin var, þá verðr svá mikit fjölmenni, at engi vissi dæmi til, hvé mikit var, ok váru margar stórar hallir skipaðar ok mörg tjöld úti.	And as that summer came, when inheritance should drink, and so awhile, it agreed was, then became so much followers, that none knew deem about, how many were, and were many large halls fitted-out and many tents about.	And as that summer came, when the funeral feast was, the time it was agreed, then there came so many followers, that no one knew how many were there, and there were many large halls fitted out, and tents outside.
Ok er leið mjök it fyrsta kveld, kemr maðr einn til hallar þessarar.	And when passed most the first evening, came man one to hall this.	And when the first evening had mostly passed, one man came to these halls.
Þessi maðr er mikill, svá at þar var engi jafnmikill, ok þat sá á búnaði hans, at hann hafði hjá tignum mönnum verit.	This man was great, so that there were none equal-great, and that saw that dress his, that he had by honourable man been.	This man was so large, that there were none as large as him, and they saw from his dress that he had been an honourable man.
Ok er hann kemr í höllina, gengr hann fyrir þá bræðrna ok kveðr þá ok spyrr, hvar þeir vísi honum til sætis.	And as he came to the-hall, went he before they brothers and greeted them and asked, where they intended him to sit.	And as he came to the hall, he went before the brothers and greeted them and asked, where they intended him to sit.
Þeim leist vel á hann ok báðu hann sitja á inn æðra bekk.	They liked well of him and asked him to-sit about the higher bench.	They liked him well and asked him to sit on the higher bench.
Hann þurfti tveggja manna rúm.	He needed two men's room.	He needed the room of two men.

Old Norse	Literal	English
Ok þegar hann hafði niðr setst, var honum borin drykkja sem öðrum mönnum, ok ekki horn var svá mikit, at eigi drykki hann af í einum drykk, ok þat þóttust allir sjá, at honum þótti engis um vert um alla aðra.	And as-soon-as he had down sat, was he brought drink as other men, and no horn was so large, that not drank he of in one draught, and it seemed to-all-who saw, that he thought none about worth around all others.	And as soon as he sat down, he was brought a drink like the other men, and no horn was so large, that he could not drink it in one draught, and it seemed to all who saw, that he thought there was no worth in any of the others.
Svá verðr enn, at annarr maðr kemr til þessarar veislu.	So became yet, that another man came to this feast.	And then another man came to the feast.
Sá var heldr meiri en inn fyrri.	So was rather greater than the before.	He was even larger than the man before.
Þessir menn hafa síða höttu.	These men had long hoods.	These men had long hoods.
Ok er þessi maðr kemr fyrir hásætit inna ungu konunga, kveðr hann þá listuliga ok biðr þá vísa sér til sætis.	And when this man came before the-high-seat the young kings, greeted he then elegantly and invited they direct him to seat.	And when this man came before the hight seat of the young kings, he greeted them elegantly and they invited and directed him where to sit.
Þeir mæltu, at þessi maðr skyldi innar sitja á inn æðra bekk.	They spoke, that this man should closer sit about the higher bench.	They said, that this man should sit closer around the higher bench.
Nú gengr hann til sætis síns, ok eru þeir svá miklir í rúmi báðir saman, at fimm menn hafa upp risit fyrir þeim.	Now went he to seat his, and were they so much of room both together, about five men had up risen for them.	Now he went to his seat, and they took up so much room together, that five men had to get up for them.
En sá, er fyrr kom, er þó minni drykkjumaðr.	But so, was the-before coming, was thought lesser drinking-man.	But the one who arrived first was less of a drinker.
En inn síðari drakk svá skjótt, at hann hellti náliga í sik af hverju horni, ok eigi finna menn þó, at hann verði drukkinn, ok heldr lætr hann óþokkuliga við sínum sessunautum ok snýr baki við þeim.	Then the later drank so quickly, that he poured nearly by himself of every horn, and not found men though, that he became drunk, and rather had he unfairly-behaved with his sitting-next-to and turned-his back against them.	Then the second drank so quickly, that he poured for himself nearly every horn, and yet men had not found him to be drunk, and he behaved unfairly with those sitting next to him and turned his back on them.

Old Norse	Literal	English
Sá, er fyrri kom, bað, at þeir skyldi eiga gaman saman, "ok mun ek fyrri".	He, who before came, invited, that they should have a-game together, "And will I go-before".	The man who came before, bid that they should have a game together, "And I will go before".
Hann stakk við honum hendi ok kvað vísu:	He thrust to him hand and spoke a-verse:	He thrust his hand toward him and spoke a verse:
"Seg frá þegnsköpum þínum, þik ráðumst ek spyrja: hvar sáttu hrafn á hríslu	"Say from honour yours, You let-us-settle I ask: Where seen-you raven on perch	"Say to us of your honour, Let's settle this, I ask: Have you seen the raven on its perch,
hrolla dreyra fullan? Optar þáttu at öðrum,	Shiver blood full Often that-you about others,	Shivering, sated with blood, More often than you have around others,
í öndvegi fundinn, en dreyrug hræ drægir í dal fyr valfugla".	On the-foremost found, Than bloody corpses drawn In valley for corpse-birds".	On the foremost found, Than bloody corpses drawn, In the vally for corpse birds".
Nú þykkir þeim, er utar sat, til leitat við sik í slíku tilkvæði ok kvað vísu í móti:	Now seemed to-them, that outside sat, towards sought against him with such speaking and spoke a-verse to against:	Now it seemed to them, that the man who sat on the outside, the one who had addressed him, had challenged him, and he spoke a verse in response:
"Þegi heimdregi heitinn, hvat er þik vesallátan, hefir aldrigi unnit, er ek mega þrotna; feitaðir sverðs né sólar sækitík at leiki, gafta hálu hesti, hvat rækir þú, drykkju".	"Silence home-dragged name, What is-it you shabby, Have-you never won, What I may-have amassed Fattened swords not the-sun Seeker to play, Gave giantess's horse, What drove you, drinking".	Silence home-dragged name, What is it you shabby Have never won, What I may have amassed, Fattened swords not the sun, Seeker to play, Gave giantess's horse, What drove you, drinking".
Nú svarar hinn, er fyrri kom:	Now answered he, who before came:	Now the man who came before answered:
"Hafs létum vér hesta hlýr stinn á brim renna, meðan á bjartar brynjur blóði dreif um síður; ylgr gein, arnar, mönnum,	"Sea laid we horses Bow strong through surf ran, While that bright armour, Blood scattered about sides She-wolf's yawn, eagle, men,	"We laid sea horses, Strong bow ran through the surf, While that bright armour, Blood scattered about the sides, She wolf's yawn, eagle, men,

Old Norse	Literal	English
eyddist gráðr, of svíra,	Devastated hunger, of gullets,	Devastated hunger, of gullets,
harðmeldr gátum heiðan	Hard-melding got-we clearing	Hard-meldiing, we got clearing,
hveðnu, blóði roðna".	Fishes, bloodied reddened".	Fishes, bloodied reddened".
Ok nú kvað sá, er síðar kom:	And now said so, who after came:	And now the man who came after said:
"Alls engi sák yðarn,	"All none sake yours,	"All none sake yours,
þars upp lokinn fundum	There up ended meeting	There up ended meeting,
Heita vang fyr hvítum	Heiti's field before white	Heiti's field before white,
hesti máva rastar;	Horses seagulls currents	Horses seagulls currents,
ok við lasi lúðrar	And with weakness cringed	And with weakness cringed,
fyr landi vér undum	Before land we turned	Before land we turned,
hallar ríka mollu	Hall rich stifling	Hall rich stifling,
hrafns fyr rauðum stafni".	Ravens before red ship's-stem".	Ravens before red ship's stem".
Ok enn kvað sá, er fyrr kom:	And then spoke so, who before came:	And then the man who came before spoke:
"Samira okkr at öldrum	"Honour ours that age	"Honour ours that age,
í öndvegi þræta,	In foremost wrangle,	In foremost wrangle,
hvat okkarr hefir unnit	What ours have won	What ours have won
hvaðarr framar öðrum;	Where from others	Where from others,
þú stótt, þars bar bára	You stood, there bore waves	You stood, there bore waves,
brandahjört at sundi,	Sword-hart through the-sound,	Sword hart through the sound,
en ek sat, þars rá reiddi	Then I sat, there sail-yard rode	Then I sat, there sail yard rode,
rauðan stafn til hafnar".	Red stern to harbour".	Red stern to harbour".
Nú svarar sá, er síðar kom:	Now answered so, who after came:	Now the one who came after answered:
"Fylgdum Birni báðir	"Followed Bjorn both	"Followed Bjorn both,
at brandagný hverjum,	To blades-clash every,	To blades clash every,
váru reyndir rekkar,	When skilled warriors,	When skilled warriors,
en Ragnari stundum;	In Ragnar's time;	In Ragnar's time;
vark, þars bragnar börðust,	When, there heroes battled,	When, there heroes battled,
á Bolgaralandi	In Bulgar-land	In Bulgar-land,
því bark sár á síðu,	As bark wound in side,	As bark wound in side,
sit innar meir, granni".	Sit beside me, neighbour".	Sit beside me, neighbour".

Old Norse	Literal	English
Enda kenndust þeir þá við of síðir ok váru þar síðan at veislu.	It-concluded knew-they them then with of since and were they thereafter at the-feast.	And so it ended that they knew each other, and they stayed at the feast.
20	20	20
Ögmundr er maðr nefndr, er kallaðr var ögmundr inn danski.	Ogmund was a-man named, that called was Ogmund the Dane.	There was a man named Ogmund, that was called Ogmund the Dane.
Hann fór eitthvert sinn með fimm skipum ok lá við Sámsey í Munarvági.	He travelled once then with five ships and laid to Samso in Munar-Bay.	He once travelled with five ships an headed to Samso, in Munar Bay.
Þá er þat sagt, at matsveinar fóru á land at gera mat til, en aðrir menn fóru í skóg at skemmta sér, ok þar fundu þeir einn trémann fornan, ok var fertugr at hæð ok mosavaxinn, ok sá þó öll deili á honum, ok ræddu nú um með sér, hverr blótat mundi hafa þetta it mikla goð.	Then was it said, that the-ship's-cook went to land to get food to, but other men went into forest to amuse themselves, and there found they a wooden-man old, and was forty in height and moss-overgrown, and saw though all parts of him, and discussed now about among themselves, who sacrificed-to would have this the great god.	Then it was said, that the ship's cook went to land to get food, but other men went into the forest to amuse themselves, and there they found an old wooden man, and he was forty ells (18 metres) high, and overgrown with moss, and though they saw all his features, and they discussed among themselves, who would have sacrificed to this great god.
Ok þá kveðr trémaðrinn:	And then spoke wooden-man:	And then the wooden man spoke:
"Þat var fyr löngu, er í leið megir Hæklings fóru hlunnalungum fram um salta slóð birtinga, þá varðk þessa þorps ráðandi. Ok því settumk svarðmerðlingar suðr hjá salti, synir Loðbrókar; þá vark blótinn til bana mönnum í Sámseyju	"It was before long, Was in this-way may Sons-of-Haekling travelled Roller-warships From about the-salt Trail revealing, Then became this Village ruler. And therefore set Shining-sworded South beside salt, Sons Lothbrok's Then was sacrificed To death men In Samso	"It was long before, Rode this way, Sons of Hakeling travelled In roller warships, From about the salt, Trail revealing, Then became this, Village ruler. And therefore set, Shining sworded, South beside salt, Sons Lothbrok's, Then was sacrificed, To death men, In Samso,

Old Norse	Literal	English
sunnanverðri.	Southern-lands.	Southern lands.
Þar báðu standa,	There bid-they stay,	There they bid I stay,
meðan strönd þolir	While shore endures	While the shore endures,
mann hjá þyrni	Men beside thorns	Men beside thorns,
ok mosa vaxinn;	And moss overgrown	And moss overgrown,
nú skýtr á mik	Now cast to me,	Now cast to me,
skýja gráti,	Cloud tears,	Cloud tears,
hlýr hvárki mér	Covering neither to-me	Covering neither me,
hold né klæði".	Body nor clothes".	Body nor clothes".
Ok þetta þótti mönnum undarligt ok sögðu síðan frá öðrum mönnum.	And this thought men wonder-like and told since from other men.	And this the men thought a wonder, and since they told other men.

The Tale of Ragnar's Sons

Old Norse	Literal	English
1	1	1
Eptir dauða Hrings konungs tók Ragnarr, sonr hans, konungdóm yfir Svía veldi ok Dana.	After the-death-of Hring the-king took Ragnar, son his, kingship over the-Swedes ruling also the-Danes.	After the death of King Hring, his son Ragnar took kingship over the Swedes, also ruling the Danes.
Þá gengu margir konungar á ríkin ok lögðu undir.	Then went many kings to the-kingdom and subjected under.	Then many kings went to the kingdom and subjected it to their rule.
En því at hann var ungr maðr ok þeim sýndist hann lítt fallinn til ráðagerðar eða landstjórnar, þá var einn jarl í Vestra-Gautlandi, er Herrauðr hét.	But because that he was a-young man and they thought he little fallen to ruling or governing, then there-was an earl in West-Götaland, who-was Herraud named.	Because he was a young man and they thought he little equipped to ruling and governing, then there was an earl in West Götaland who was named Herraud.
Hann var jarl Ragnars konungs.	He was an-earl Ragnar's the-king.	He was an earl of King Ragnar.
Manna var hann vitrastr ok hermaðr mikill.	Of-men was he the-wisest and warrior great.	He was the wisest of men and a great warrior.
Hann átti eina dóttur, er Þóra borgarhjörtr var kölluð.	He had one daughter, who Thora Fortress-Hart was called.	He had a daughter who was called Thora Fotress-Hart.
Hún var allra kvenna fríðust, þeira er konungr hafði spurt til.	She was of-all women the-most-beautiful, they who the-king had heard of.	The was the most beautiful If all women that the king had ever heard of.
Jarlinn, faðir hennar, hafði gefit henni einn yrmling í morgingjöf.	The-earl, father hers, had given her a little-snake as morning-gift.	Her father the earl had given her a little snake as a morning gift.
Hún fæddi hann fyrst í eski sínu.	She raised him first in box hers.	She raised him first in a box of hers.
En þessi ormr varð svá mikill um síðir, at hann lá í kring um skemmuna ok beit í sporð sér.	But this snake was so large about since, that it lay in a-ring about the-sleeping-room and bit it tail his.	But this snake became so large since, that it lay in a ring around the sleeping room and bit its tail.

Old Norse	Literal	English
Hann gerðist þá svá ólmr, at menn þorðu eigi at koma nær skemmunni nema þeir, er honum gáfu mat eða þjónuðu jarls dóttur, en hann át uxa um dag.	He became then so savage, that many dared not to come near the-sleeping-room unless they, that him gave food or served the-earl's daughter, and he ate an-ox about-a day.	He became so savage, that many did not dare to come near the sleeping room, unless they gave it food or served the earl's daughter, and he ate an ox every day.
Fólkit óttaðist mjök, ok vissu, at hann mundi mikinn skaða gera, svá mikill ok ólmr sem hann var þá orðinn.	People were-afraid much, and knew, that he could much damage do, so much and savage as he was then become.	People were very afraid, and knew that he could do much damahe, so great and savage as he had then become.
Jarl strengdi þá þess heit at bragarfulli, at hann skyldi þeim einum manni gifta dóttur sína, Þóru, er dræpi orminn eða þyrði at ganga til tals við hana fyrir orminum.	The-earl boldly then this called a declaration, that he should them a man give daughter his, Thora, who killed the-serpent or dared to go to talk with her before the-snake.	The earl then boldly made this declaration, that he would give his daughter Thora to the man who killed the serpent or dared to go and talk with her before the snake.
Ok er Ragnarr konungr spyrr þessi tíðendi, þá ferr hann í Vestra-Gautland.	And when Ragnar the-king heard this news, then travelled he to West-Götaland.	And when King Ragnar heard this news, then he travelled to West Götaland.
Ok er hann átti skammt til býjar jarlsins, þá fór hann í rögguð klæði, brækr ok kápu, ok ermar á ok höttr.	And when he had short way-to estate the-earl's, then went he to rough clothes, breeches and cape, and sleeves and also hood.	And when he had gone a short way to the earl's estate, he changed into rough clothes, breeches, and a cape, and sleeves, and also a hood.
Þau klæði váru þæfð með sand ok tjöru ok tók í hönd sér eitt mikit spjót, en var gyrðr sverði, ok gekk svá einn frá sínum mönnum ok til býjar jarlsins ok skemmu Þóru.	These clothes were matted with sand and tar and took in hand his one great spear, which was girded sword, and went so alone from his men and to the-estate the-earl's and cabin Thora's.	These clothes were matted with sand and tar, and he took a great spear in his hand, which was girded with a sword, an he went alone from his men to the earl's estate and Thora's cabin.
Ok þegar ormrinn sá, at þar var kominn ókunnr maðr, þá reistist hann upp ok blés eitri móti honum.	And as-soon-as the-serpent saw, that there was coming an-unknown man, then rose he up and blew venom towards him.	And as soon as the serpent saw that there was an unknown man coming, then he rose up and blew venom towards him.

Old Norse	Literal	English
En hann skaut móti skildinum ok gekk at honum djarfliga ok lagði hann með spjóti í hjartat.	But he shot against the-shield and went at him boldly and laid him with spear to the-heart.	But he put his shield against this, and went at him boldly, and drove a spear into its heart.
Ok síðan brá hann sínu sverði ok hjó af orminum höfuðit, ok fór þat svá sem segir í sögu Ragnars konungs, at hann fekk síðan Þóru borgarhjört.	And then drew he his sword and hewed off the-serpent's head, and went that so as said in the-saga-of Ragnar the-king, that he married then Thora Fortress-Hart.	And then he drew his sword and hewed off the serpent's head, and it went as was said in the Saga of Ragnar the King, that he married Thora Fortress-Hart.
Ok síðan lagðist hann í hernað ok frelsti allt sitt ríki.	And since lay he to raiding and freed all his kingdom.	And since he headed off raiding and freed all his kingdom.
Hann átti með Þóru tvá syni.	He had with Thora two sons.	He had two sons with Thora.
Hét annarr Eiríkr, en annarr Agnarr.	Named one Erik, and another Agnar.	One was named Erik, and another Agnar.
Ok er þeir váru nokkurra vetra gamlir, þá tekr Þóra sótt ok andaðist.	And when they were a-few winters old, then took Thora sickness and died.	And when they were a few winters old, then Thora took sickness and died.
Síðan fekk Ragnarr Áslaugar, er sumir kalla Randalín, dóttur Sigurðar Fáfnisbana ok Brynhildar Buðladóttur.	Afterwards married Ragnar Auslag, who some called Randalin, daughter-of Sigurd Slayer-of-Fafnir and Brynhild Daughter-of-Budla.	Afterwards Ragnar married Auslag, who some called Randalin, daughter of Sigurd the Slayer of Fafnir and Brynhild, daughter of Budla.
Þau áttu fjóra syni.	Then had four sons.	Then they had four sons.
Ívarr beinlausi var ellstr, þá Björn járnsíða, þá Hvítserkr, þá Sigurðr.	Ivar the-Boneless was the-oldest, then Bjorn Ironside, then Hvitserk, then Sigurd.	Ivar the Boneless was the oldest, then Bjorn Ironside, then Hvitserk, then Sigurd.
Þat var mark í auga honum, at svá var sem ormr lægi um sjáldrit, ok því var hann kallaðr Sigurðr ormr í auga.	There was mark in eye his, that so was as a-snake laid about the-pupil, and therefore was he called Sigurd Snake-in-the-eye.	There was a mark in his eye, that was as a snake laid about the pupil, and he was therefore called Sigurd Snake-in-the-eye.

Old Norse	Literal	English
Nú er synir Ragnars váru vaxnir, þá herjuðu þeir víða um lönd.	Now when sons Ragnar's were grown, then raided they widely about the-lands.	Now when Ragnar's sons were grown, they then raided widely about the lands.
Þeir bræðr Eiríkr ok Agnarr fóru í öðrum stað, en í þriðja stað fóru þeir Ívarr ok þeir inir yngri bræðr hans með honum, ok gerði hann ráð fyrir þeim, því at hann var forvitri.	Their brothers Erik and Agnar travelled to other places, and a third place went they Ivar and they the younger brothers his with him, and made he plans for them, because that he was fore-knowing.	Their brothers Erik and Agnar travelled to other places, and Ivar went to a third place with his younger brothers, and he made plans for them, because he was fore-knowing.
Þeir lögðu undir sik Selund ok Reiðgotaland, Eygotaland ok Eyland ok öll smálönd í hafinu.	They subjected to themselves Zealand and Reidgotaland, Eygotaland and Islands also all small-lands in the-sea.	They subjected under their rule Zealand and Jutland, Gotland and the Islands, and also all small lands in the sea.
Settist þá Ívarr með inum yngrum bræðrum sínum af Hleiðru á Selundi, ok var þat þó móti vilja Ragnars konungs.	Set then Ivar with the younger brothers his of Lejre on Zealand, and was that though against the-will-of Ragnar the-king.	Ivar and his younger brothers set themselves up on Lerje in Zealand, even though that was against the will of King Ragnar.
Fóru synir hans með hernaði allir, því at þeir vildu eigi ófrægri vera en Ragnarr konungr, faðir þeira.	Travelled sons his with raiding everywhere, because that they willed no less-famous be than Ragnar the-king, father theirs.	His sons travelled everywhere with their raiding, because they wanted to be no less famous than King Ragnar.
Þat líkaði Ragnari konungi illa, er synir hans heldu móti honum ok tóku skattlönd hans móti hans vilja.	That liked Ragnar the-king badly, that sons his held against him and took tribute-paying-land his against his will.	That King Ragnar liked badly, that his sons resisted him and took his tribute paying lands against his will.
Hann setti þann konung yfir UppSvíaveldi, er Eysteinn beli hét, ok bað hann halda því ríki sér til handa, en verja fyrir sonum sínum, ef þeir kallaði til.	He set then a-king over Upper-Sweden, who Eystein Beli was-named, and ordered he hold with kingdom his to hand, but protect for sons his, if they claimed to.	He set a king over Upper Sweden who was named Eystein Beli, and order him to hold his kingdom, but protect against his sons if they claimed it.

Old Norse	Literal	English
Þat var eitt sumar, er Ragnarr konungr var farinn með her í Austrveg, at Eiríkr ok Agnarr, synir hans, kómu til Svíþjóðar ok heldu skipum sínum upp í Löginn.	It was one summer, when Ragnar the-king was travelling with war-band to Eastern-lands, that Erik and Agnar, sons his, came to Sweden and held ships theirs up in lying.	It was one summer, when King Ragnar was travelling with a war band to the Eastern Lands, that his sons Erik and Agnar came to Sweden and headed their ships in mooring.
Gerðu þeir þá boð Eysteini konungi til Uppsala, at hann kæmi til þeira.	Went they then to-ask Eystein the-king of Uppsala, that he come to them.	They then went to ask King Eystein of Uppsala, that he come to them.
Ok er þeir fundust, sagði Eiríkr, at hann vildi, at Eysteinn konungr heldi Svíaríki undir þá bræðr, ok kveðst þá fá vilja Borghildar, dóttur hans, ok segir, at þá megu þeir vel halda því ríki fyrir Ragnari konungi.	And when they met, said Erik, that he wished, that Eystein the-king hold Sweden under they the-brothers, and said then marry wished Borghild, daughter his, and said, that then may they well hold therefore the-kingdom for Ragnar the-king.	And when they met, Erik said that he wanted King Eystein to hold Sweden under the brothers, and that he wished to marry his daughter Borghild, and said that then they may well hold the kingdom for King Ragnar.
Eysteinn kveðst þetta vilja tjá innanlands höfðingjum, ok skildust þeir svá.	Eystein said that wished present-to inner-lands chieftains, and parted they so.	Eystein said that he wished to present this to the chieftans of the inner lands, and so they parted.
Ok er Eysteinn konungr bar þetta mál upp, þá urðu allir landsmenn á þat sáttir at verja landit fyrir sonum Ragnars, ok dregst nú saman óvígr herr, ok ferr Eysteinn konungr móti Ragnars sonum.	And when Eystein the-king bore this matter up, then became all landsmen in that agreed to protect land from sons Ragnar's, and drawn now together un-slayable-men band, and went Eystein the-king against Ragnar's sons.	And when King Eystein raised this matter, then all the landsmen agreed to protect the land from Ragnar's sons, and now was gathered together an unslayable war band, and King Eystein went against Ragnar's sons.
Ok er þeir finnast, verðr þar mikil orrosta, ok verða nú synir Loðbrókar ofrliði bornir, ok fellr svá lið þeira bræðra, at fátt eitt stóð upp.	And as they encountered, became then a-great battle, and were now sons Lothbrok's outnumbered borne, and fell so company theirs the-brothers, that few alone stood up.	And as they met, there was a great battle, and now Lothbrok's sons were outnumbered, and the brothers' company fell, so that few remained standing.
Þá fell ok Agnarr, en Eiríkr varð handtekinn.	Then fell and Agnar, but Erik was hand-taken.	Then Agnar fell, but Erik was captured.

Old Norse	Literal	English
Eysteinn konungr bauð Eiríki grið ok svá mikit fé af Uppsala veldi fyrir Agnar, bróður sinn, sem sjálfr vildi hann, ok þar með dóttur sína, þá er áðr hafði hann beðit.	Eystein the-king offered Erik mercy and so much wealth of Uppsala chosen for Agnar, brother his, as himself wished he, and there with daughter his, then as before he had proposed-to.	King Eystein offered Erik mercy and as much wealth of Uppsala as compensation for his brother Agnar as he wished, along with his daughter as he had proposed before.
Eiríkr vildi engar fébætr ok eigi konungs dóttur, ok eigi kveðst hann vilja lifa eptir þann ósigr, er hann hafði fengit, en þat kveðst hann þiggja vilja, at hann kjósi sér sjálfr dauðdaga.	Erik willed no compensation and no king's daughter, and not said he wished life after this defeat, as he had got, but so said he accept wished, that he choose he his-own death-day.	Erik did not want any compensation, and not the king's daughter, and did not wish to live after this defeat that he had got, but said that he would accept to choose his own death day.
Ok af því at Eysteinn konungr mátti enga sætt fá af Eiríki, þá játtar hann honum þat.	And from because as Eystein the-king may not settlement get of Erik, then agreed he to-him this.	And because King Eystein could not agree a settlement with Erik, he agreed to this.
Eiríkr bað, at þeir tæki undir hann spjótsoddum ok hefi hann svá upp yfir allan valinn.	Erik asked, that they take up-to he spear-points and have him so up over all fallen.	Erik asked that they take up spears, and place him over them.
Þá kvað Eiríkr:	Then said Erik:	Then Erik said:
"Vilkat boð fyr bróður *né baugum mey kaupa, Eystein kveða orðinn Agnars bana, heyra; grætr eigi mik móðir, munk efstr of val deyja,* *ok geirtré í gögnum gerr, látið mik standa".*	"Which bid before brother Nor ring maid buy, Eystein it-is-said became Agnar's bane, hear Weep not my mother, Remember uppermost of foe dead, And spear-tree to use willing, have me standing".	"Which offer before my brother, Nor buy a maid with rings, Eystein, it is said, became Agnar's bane, hear, Weep not, my mother, Remember above the slain, Let the ravenous spear tree, willing, have me standing".
Ok áðr hann væri hafinn upp á spjótin, þá sá hann einn mann ríða mikit.	And before he was raised up upon spears, then saw he one man riding much.	And before he was raised up on the spears, then he saw a great man riding fast.
Þá kvað hann:	Then said he:	Then he said:
"Þau berið orð it efra,	"There bear words these ever,	"There bear these final words,

Old Norse	Literal	English
eru austrfarar liðnar,	Are eastern-journeys passed,	That the eastern journeys are passed,
at mær hafi mína	That maiden have mine	That the maiden will have mine,
mjó, Áslaugu, bauga;	Slender, Auslag, rings	Slender Auslag, rings,
þá mun mest af móði,	Then shall most of mother,	Them shall most of mother,
ef mik spyrja dauðan,	Of me learn-of death,	Learn of my death,
mín stjúpmóðir mildum	My step-mother mild	My stepmother mild,
mögum sínum til segja".	Sons hers to tell".	Sons hers to tell".
Var nú svá gert, at Eiríki var lypt upp á spjótsoddunum, ok dó hann svá uppi yfir valnum.	Was now so done, that Erik was lifted up upon spear-points, and died he so up over as-chosen.	Now it was done, thar Erik was lifted up on the spear points, and he died up on them as chosen.
Ok er þessi tíðendi spyrjast út á Selund til Áslaugar, þá ferr hún þegar á fund sona sinna ok segir þeim þessi tíðendi.	And as this news was-heard out of Zealand to Auslag, then travelled she straight-away to find sons hers and said to-them this news.	And as this news was hear from Zealand to Auslag, then she travelled straight away to find her sons and said to them this news.
Þeir Björn ok Hvítserkr léku tafl, en Sigurðr stóð at framan.	There Bjorn and Hvitserk played table-game, and Sigurd stood by in-front-of.	There Bjorn and Hvitserk played table games, and Sigurd stood by in front.
Þá kvað Áslaug:	Then said Auslag:	Then Auslag said:
"Eigi mundi yðar,	"Not would you	"You would not,
ef ér dæið fyrri,	Without-vengeance being brothers	Without vengeance brothers be,
eitt misseri eptir	One season after,	One season after,
óhefnt vera, bræðra;	If were dead before	If you were dead before,
lítt ráðumk því leyna,	Little wearing therefore concealing,	Little wearing therefore concealing,
ef líf hafa knætti	If live have could	If live could have,
Eiríkr sitt ok Agnarr	Erik theirs and Agnar,	Theirs, Erik and Agnar,
óbornir mér niðjar".	Unborn of-me descendants".	Descendants unborn of me".
Þá svaraði Sigurðr ormr í auga:	Then answered Sigurd Snake-in-the-eye:	Then Sigurd Snake-in-the-eye answered:
"Þat skal þriggja vikna,	"It shall-be three weeks,	"It shall be three weeks,
ef þik tregar, móðir,	If you troubled, mother,	If you are troubled, mother,
leið eigu vér langa,	Journey our-own we long,	Our journey must be long,
leiðangr búinn verða;	Journeying prepared be;	For our forces to be ready,

Old Norse	Literal	English
skal Uppsölum eigi þótt ófafé bjóði, ef oss duga eggjar Eysteinn beli ráða".	Shall Uppsala not Though wealth offer, If we aided edges Eystein Beli's rule".	Uppsala shall not, Though wealth offered, If blade edges aid us, Eystein Beli's rule".
Þá kvað Björn járnsíða:	Then said Bjorn Ironside:	Then Bjorn Ironside said:
"Duga mun hugr ok hjarta í hauksnöru brjósti, þótt minnr um þat mæli, manni innan rifja; eigi er oss í augum ormr né fránir snákar, bræðr glöddu mik mínir, mank stjúpsonu þína".	"Help must mind and heart The hawk-snare breast, Though less about it speaks, Men inside review Not are ours in eyes Serpents nor flashing snakes, Brothers glad to-me mine, Remember stepsons yours".	"Heart and mind must help, The hawk snare breast, But little spoken about it, Men review inside, Not are in our eyes, Serpents or flashing snakes, My brothers merry to me, I remember your stepsons".
Þá svaraði Hvítserkr:	Then answered Hvitserk:	Then Hvitserk answered:
"Hyggjum at, áðr heitim, at hefnt megi verða; látum ýmsa illu, Agnars bana, fagna; hrindum húf á hrannir, höggum ís fyr barði, sjám á hitt, hvé snekkjur snemmst vér fáim búnar".	"Let-us-think about, before promising, That revenge may be, Let-us various evil, Agnar's bane, rejoice Early hull to waves, Blows ice before bow, Let-us-see to meet, how-to sailboats Soonest we get prepared".	"Let us plan before we promise, That revenge may be, Must bear various evils, Agnar's banesman, be glad, Shoot the hull to the waves, Shatter ice before the bow, Let us see how soon to sailboats, The soonest we can get prepared".
Þá kvað Ívarr beinlausi:	Then spoke Ivar Boneless:	Then Ivar the Boneless spoke:
"Hafið ofrhuga ærinn ok áræði bæði, þess mundi þá þurfa, at þrá mikit fylgdi; bera mun mik fyr bragna beinlausan fram verða, þó gatk hönd til hefnda, at hváriga nýtak".	"Have courage boundless And daring both, This would then need, To desire much follow Bore-up should-be me above heroes Boneless from being, Though get hand to revenge, That whichever new-take".	"Having courage boundless, And daring both, This would then need, To desire much to follow, Bore up should I be above heroes, From being boneless, I'll have a hand in revenge, Whichever I may take".

Old Norse	Literal	English
Eptir þat drógu Ragnars synir saman óvígan her.	After that drew Ragnar's sons together an-overwhelming war-band.	After that Ragnar's sons gathered together an overwhelming war band.
Ok er þeir váru búnir, þá fóru þeir með skipaher til Svíþjóðar, en Áslaug drottning ferr með fimmtán hundruðum riddara landveg, ok var þat fólk allvel búit.	When that they were prepared, then travelled they with naval-force to Sweden, but Auslag the-queen travelled with fifteen hundred riders land-ways, and were those people all-well prepared.	When they were prepared, then they travelled away with a naval force to Sweden, but Auslag the queen travelled with fifteen hundred riders across the land, and those people were all well prepared.
Sjálf bar hún herklæði ok var formaðr þess hers ok kallaðist Randalín, ok mætast þau í Svíþjóð ok ræna ok brenna, hvar sem þau fara yfir.	Herself wore she war-clothes and was commander this army and called Randalin, and met they in Sweden and raided and burned, where as they travelled across.	She war herself war clothes and as commander of this army was called Randalin, and they met in Sweden and raided and burned wherever they travelled.
Þetta spyrr Eysteinn konungr ok safnar her í móti þeim, hverjum þeim manni, er vígr var í hans ríki.	This heard Eystein the-king and gathered a-war-band to meet them, each-of those men, who were were in his kingdom.	King Eystein heard this and gathered a war band to meet them, of all the men who were in his kingdom.
Ok er þeir mætast, verðr þar mikil orrosta, ok fá Loðbrókar synir sigr, en Eysteinn konungr fell, ok spyrst þetta ok verðr mjök frægt.	And when they met, became there a-great battle, and got Lothbrok's sons success, but Eystein the-king fell, and learned was-this and became much fame.	And when they met, there became a great battle, and Lothbrok's sons got success, but King Eystein fell, and as this was learned they gained much fame.
Ragnarr konungr, þar sem hann var í hernaði, spyrr þetta ok líkar stórilla við sonu sína, at þeir létu eigi hefndina bíða hans.	Ragnar the-king, there as he was of raiding, heard this and was-displeased greatly with sons his, that they allowed not revenge to-wait-for his.	King Ragnar heard this news as he was raiding, and was greatly displeased with his sons, that they did not allow for his revenge.
Ok er hann kom heim í ríki sitt, þá segir hann Áslaugu, at hann skal gera eigi minna frægðarverk en synir hans höfðu þá gert.	And when he came home to kingdom his, then told he Auslag, that he would do no less famous-work than sons his had then done.	And then he came home to his kingdom, then he told Auslag, that he would do no less famous work than his sons had done.

Old Norse	Literal	English
"Hefi ek nú flest allt þat ríki aptr unnit undir mik, er mínir forellrismenn hafa átt, utan England eigi, ok því hefi ek nú látit gera knörru tvá í Líðum á Vestfold", því at hans ríki stóð allt til Dofrafjalls ok Líðandisness.	"Have I now almost all the kingdom back won under me, as my ancestors have had, except-for England alone, and therefore have I now had made knorrs two in Lidar in Vestfold", because that his kingdom stood altogether to Dovrefjell and Lindesnes.	"Now I have won almost all the kingdom back under me, as my ancestors have, except for England alone, and therefore I have now had two knorrs made in Lidar in Vestfold", because his kingdom stood together to Dovrefjell and Lindesnes.
Áslaug svaraði: "Mörg langskip máttu þér hafa gera látit með verði þessa knarra.	Auslag answered: "Might longships may you have made had with worth-of these knorrs.	Auslag answered: "You might have made longships for the same worth as these knorrs.
Vitu þér ok, at stórskipum er ekki gott at halda at Englandi sakir straums ok útgrynnis, ok er þetta ekki vitrliga ráðit".	Know you also, that large-ships are not good at heading to England for-the-sake-of currents and shallows, and are they not wise-like advised".	You also know that large ships are not good at heading to England on account of the currents and shallows, and they are not wisely planned".
En allt at einu ferr Ragnarr konungr með þessum knörrum vestr til Englands með fimm hundruð manna ok brýtr bæði skipin við England, en sjálfr hann ok allr herr hans kom heill á land.	But all the same travelled Ragnar the-king with these knorrs west to England with five hundred men and wrecked both ships in England, but himself he and all war-band his came safely to land.	But all the same King Ragnar travelled with these knorrs west to England with five hundred men, and wrecked both ships in England, but he and all his war band came to land safely.
Tekr hann nú at herja, hvar sem hann ferr.	Took he now to harrying, wherever which he travelled.	He now took to raiding wherever he travelled.
3	3	3
Í þann tíma réð sá konungr fyrir Norðhumbrulandi, er Ella hét.	In that time ruled so a-king for Northumberland, who Ælla was-named.	At that time there ruled a king in Northumberland who was named Aella.

Old Norse	Literal	English
Ok er hann spyrr, at herr er kominn í ríki hans, þá safnar hann miklu liði ok ferr móti honum með óvígan her, ok verðr þar orrosta mikil ok hörð.	And when he learned, that a-war-band had come to kingdom his, then summoned he a-great force and travelled to-meet him with an-unconquerable war-band, and became there battle great and hard.	And when he learned that a war band had come to his kingdom, he summoned a great force and travelled to meet him with an unconquerable war band, and there became a great battle.
Ragnarr konungr var yst í silkihjúp þeim, er Áslaug gaf honum at skilnaði.	Ragnar the-king was outermost in a-silk-tunic theirs, which Auslag gave him as they-had-parted.	King Ragnar wore on the outermost of his clothes a silk tunic which Auslag had given him when they had parted.
En því at landherrinn var mikill, svá at ekki mátti við haldast, þá fell náliga allt fólk hans, en hann gekk sjálfr vel fjórum sinnum í gegnum fylking Ellu konungs, en ekki járn festi á silkiskyrtu hans.	But because that land-warriors were great, so that not may with hold, then fell nearly all men his, but he got himself well four-times then in through the-ranks Ælla the-king's, and no iron fastened to silk-shirt his.	Because the land warriors were great, many could not withstand, and nearly all of his men fell, but he got himself four times well through the ranks of King Aella, and no iron fastened to his silk shirt.
Varð hann um síðir handtekinn ok settr í einn ormgarð, ok vildu ormarnir ekki koma nær honum.	Became he about eventually hand-taken and set in a snake-pit, and would snakes not come near him.	He eventually became captured and set in a snake pit, and snakes would not come near him.
Ella konungr sá, at hann bitu eigi járn um daginn, er þeir börðust, ok nú vildu eigi ormarnir granda honum.	Ælla the-king saw, that him was-bitten-by no iron about the-day, when they battled, and now willed not snakes to-injure him.	King Aella saw that he had not been bitten by any iron that day when they battled, and now the snakes did not want to injure him.
Þá lét hann fletta af honum klæði þat, er hann hafði yst haft um daginn, ok þegar hengu ormarnir á honum alla vega, ok lét hann þar líf sitt með miklum hraustleik.	Then had him stripped of his clothes that, which he had outermost had about the-day, and then hung serpents about him all ways, and laid he there life his with much bravery.	Then he had him stripped of his clothes, which he had been wearing outermost during the day, and then the serpents hung upon him in every direction, and there he laid down his life with much bravery.
Ok er synir Ragnars konungs spyrja þessi tíðendi, þá fara þeir vestr til Englands ok berjast við Ellu konung.	And when sons-of Ragnar the-king heard this news, then travelled they west to England and fought with Ælla the-king.	And when King Ragnar's sons heard this news, they then travelled west to England and fought with King Aella.

Old Norse	Literal	English
Ok af því at Ívarr vildi eigi berjast ok ekki hans fólk, en landherrinn var drjúgr, þá fengu þeir ósigr ok flýðu til skipa ok fóru við svá búit heim til Danmarkar.	And of there that Ivar willed not to-fight and not his people, but land-warriors were substantial, then got they defeated and fled to the-ships and travelled with so prepared home to Denmark.	And thereof, Ivar did not wish to fight, nor his people, but the defenders were substantial, and they were defeated and fled to their ships and prepared to travel home to Denmark.
En Ívarr var eptir í Englandi ok fór á fund Ellu konungs ok beiddist af honum bóta fyrir föður sinn.	But Ivar was afterwards in England and went to meet Ælla the-king and asked of him compensation for father his.	But afterwards Ivar was in England and went to meet King Aella and asked him for compensation for his father.
Ok því at Ella konungr sá, at Ívarr vildi eigi berjast með bræðrum sínum í móti honum, þá þótti honum trúligt at gera sætt við hann.	And because that Ælla the-king saw, that Ivar would not fight with brothers his to meet him, then thought he faithful to make a-settlement with him.	And because King Aella saw that Ivar would not fight with his brothers against him, then he thought it faithful to make a settlement with him.
Ívarr bað konung gefa honum svá mikit af landi í föðurgjöld sem hann breiddi yfir ina mestu öldungshuð, því at hann segir sér eigi vel munu fritt at fara heim fyrir bræðrum sínum.	Ivar asked the-king to-give him so much of land in father-payment as he broad over the most old-bull's-hide, because as he said himself not well would-be peace if travelled home before brothers his.	Ivar asked the king to give him such land in payment for his father, as broad as an old bull's hide, because he said that there would not well be peace if he travelled home before his brothers.
Ellu þótti þetta eigi ótrúligt, ok bundu þeir með þessu sætt sína.	Ælla thought this not treacherous, and bound they with this settlement theirs.	Aella thought that this was not treacherous, and they bound with their settlement.
Tekr Ívarr nú húðina hráblauta ok lætr þenja sem mest.	Took Ivar now hide raw-wet and had stretched as most.	Ivar now took a raw hide, and stretched it as much as could be.
Ok síðan lætr hann rista húðina í inn mjóvasta streng ok klýfr síðan sér hvárt, hárham ok holdrosu.	And then had he carved the-skin about the narrowest string and split then he each, the-hairy-side and the-fleshy-side.	And then he had the skin carved as the narrowest string, and he then split the hairy side and the fleshy side.

Old Norse	Literal	English
Síðan lætr hann draga um einn sléttan völl ok marka þar um utan grundvöll.	Afterwards had he drawn about one flat field and marked there about out foundations.	Afterwards he had drawn about one flat field and marked out the foundations.
Hann reisir þar á sterka borgarveggi, ok er sú borg nú kölluð Jórvík.	He raised there a strong city-wall, and was the city now called York.	He raised a strong city wall, and the city is now called York.
Hann vingaðist við allt landsfólk ok mest við höfðingja, ok svá kom, at allir höfðingjar hétu honum trúnaði ok bræðrum hans.	He befriended with all landsfolk and mostly with chieftains, and so came, that all chieftains called him trustworthy and brothers his.	He befriended with all the land folk and most with the chieftans, and so it came that all the chieftans called him and his brothers trustworthy.
Síðan sendir hann boð til bræðra sinna ok segir, at þá er meiri ván, at þeir megi hefna föður síns, ef þeir koma með her til Englands.	Afterwards sent he invite to brothers his and said, that then was more hope, that they may avenge father theirs, if they came with a-war-band to England.	Afterwards he sent an invite to his brothers and said that there was more hope that they may avenge their father, if they came with a war band to England.
Ok er þeir spyrja þat, bjóða þeir her út ok halda til Englands.	And as they learned that, invited they a-war-band out and headed to England.	As they learned that, they invited a war band out and headed for England.
Ok er Ívarr verðr þess varr, ferr hann þegar á fund Ellu konungs ok segir, at hann vill eigi leyna hann slíkum tíðendum, en segir, at hann má eigi berjast móti bræðrum sínum, en þó vill hann fara á fund þeira ok leita um sættir.	And as Ivar became of-this aware, went he straightaway to find Ælla the-king and said, that he willed not conceal from-him such news, then said, that he may not fight against brothers his, but though willed he travel to meet them and seek about reconciliation.	And as Ivar became aware of this, he went straightaway to find King Aella and said that he did not want to conceal such news from him, then said that he may not fight against his brothers, but though he wished to travel to meet them and seek some reconciliation.
Konungr þiggr þetta.	The-King accepted this.	The king accepted this.
Kemr Ívarr á fund bræðra sinna ok eggjar þá at hefna föður síns ok ferr síðan aptr til Ellu konungs ok segir, at þeir eru svá ólmir ok óðir, at þeir vilja fyrir hvetvetna fram berjast.	Came Ivar to meet brothers his and encouraged then to avenge father theirs and travelled afterwards back to Ælla the-king and said, that they were so wild and crazy, that they willed foremost whatever towards fighting.	Ivar came to meet his brothers and encouraged them to avenge their father, and travelled afterwards back to King Aella and said that they were so wild and crazy, that they willed most to fight.

Old Norse	Literal	English
Konungi sýnist þetta inn mesti trúleiki, er Ívarr gerði.	The-king thought that this the-most true-like, what Ivar had-done.	The king thought that this was most likely true, what Ivar had done.
Ferr hann nú móti þeim bræðrum með sinn her.	Went he now to-meet they the-brothers with his war-band.	He now went to meet the brothers with his war band.
Ok er þeir koma saman, þá snerust margir höfðingjar frá konunginum ok til Ívars.	And as they came together, then turned many chieftains from the-king and to Ivar.	And as they came together, many of the chieftans turned from the king and towards Ivar.
Varð konungr þá borinn ofrliði, svá at mikill þorri liðs hans fell, en sjálfr varð hann handtekinn.	Became the-king then born outnumbered, so that many majority men his fell, and himself became he hand-taken.	The king then became outnumbered, and so the majority of his men fell, and he himself became captured.
Ívarr ok þeir bræðr minntust nú, hversu faðir þeira var píndr.	Ivar and they brothers remembered now, how-so father theirs was tortured.	Ivar and the brothers remembered how their father was tortured.
Létu þeir nú rista örn á baki Ellu ok skera síðan rifin öll frá hrygginum með sverði, svá at þar váru lungun út dregin.	Had they now raised eagle about back Ælla's and scored afterwards ribs all from the-spine with swords, so that there were lungs out drawn.	They now had an eagle raised on Aella's back, and afterwards scored all his ribs from the spine with swords, so that the lungs were drawn out.
Svá segir Sighvatr skáld í Knútsdrápu:	So said Sighvat skald in a-Knuts-drapu:	So said Sighvat the skald in a Knuts-Drapu:
"Ok Ellu bak *at lét hinns sat* *Ívarr ara* *Jórvík skorit".*	"And Ælla's back That had his seat Ivar eagle York scored".	"And Aella's back That had his seat Ivar eagle York scored".
Eptir þessa orrostu gerðist Ívarr konungr yfir þeim hluta Englands, sem hans frændr höfðu fyrri átt.	After this battle made-he Ivar king over those parts-of England, as his kinsmen had before had.	After this battle Ivar made himself king over those parts of England as his kinsmen had before.

Old Norse	Literal	English
Hann átti þá tvá bræðr frilluborna, en annarr hét Yngvarr, en annarr Hústó.	He had then two brothers bastard-born, and one called Yngvarr, and another Husto.	He then had two brothers bastard born, and one was called Yngvarr, and another Husto.
Þeir pínuðu Játmund konung inn helga eptir boði Ívars, ok lagði hann síðan undir sik hans ríki.	They tortured Edmund king the holy after orders Ivar's, and had he afterwards from-under him his kingdom.	They tortured King Edmund the holy after Ivar's orders, and afterwards he took his kingdom from under him.
Loðbrókar synir fóru um mörg lönd með hernaði: England ok Valland ok Frakkland ok út um Lúmbardí.	Lothbrok's sons travelled about many lands with raiding: England and Wales and France and out as-far-as Lombardy.	Lothbrok's sons travelled about many lands raiding: England and Wales and France, and out as far as Lombardy.
En svá er sagt, at þar hafi þeir framast komit, er þeir unnu þá borg, er Lúna heitir.	And so is said, that there had they furthest come, that they won then the-city, was Luna named.	And so it is said, that the furthest they had come that they had conquered was a city named Luna.
Ok um eina stund ætluðu þeir at fara til Rómaborgar ok vinna hana, ok hefir þeira hernaðr frægstr verit um öll Norðrlönd af danskri tungu.	And about a while intended they to travel to Rome-City and win her, and had their harrying famous become about all North-Lands of Danish tongue.	And for a while they intended to travel to the City of Rome and conquer her, and their harrying had become famous across all the North Lands of Danish tongue.
Ok er þeir koma aptr í Danmörk í ríki sitt, þá skipta þeir löndum með sér.	And when they came back to Denmark the kingdom theirs, then divided they lands with themselves.	And when they came back to their kingdom of Denmark, they divided the lands among themselves.
Tók Björn járnsíða Uppsala ríki ok alla Svíþjóð ok þat, er þar til heyrir, en Sigurðr ormr í auga hafði Selund ok Skáni ok Halland ok alla Víkina ok Agðir tll Líðandisness ok mikinn þorra af Upplöndum, en Hvítserkr hafði Reiðgotaland ok Vindland.	Took Bjorn Iron-side Uppsala kingdom and all Sweden and that, which there to depended-on, and Sigurd Snake-in-the-eye had Zealand and Skane and, Halland but all Viken and Agder until Lindesnes and greater part of Uppland, and Hvitserk had Jutland and Wendland.	Bjorn Ironside took Uppsala and all the kingdom of Sweden and their dependencies, and Sigurd Snake-in-the-eye had Zealand and Skane and Halland and all Viken and Adger as far as Lindesnes and the greater part of Uppland, and Hvitserk had Jutland and Wendland.
Sigurðr ormr í auga átti Blæju, dóttur Ellu konungs.	Sigurd Snake-in-the-eye married Blaeja, daughter Ælla the-king's.	Sigurd Snake-in-the-eye married Blaeja, Aella's daughter.

Old Norse	Literal	English
Þeira sonr var Knútr, er kallaðr var Hörða-Knútr, er ríki tók eptir föður sinn í Selund, Skáni ok Hallandi, en Víkin hvarf þá undan honum.	Their son was Knut, who called was Horda-Knut, who the-kingdom took after father his in Zealand, Skane and Halland, but Viken broke-away then from-under him.	Their son was Knut, who was called Horda-Knut, who took over the rule of Zealand, Skane, and Halland after his father, but Viken broke away from him then.
Hann átti þann son, er Gormr hét.	He had then son, was Gorm named.	He had one sone who was named Gorm.
Hann var heitinn eptir fóstra hans, syni Knúts fundna.	He was named after foster-father his, son-of Knut Funda.	He was named after his foster father, the son of Knut Funda.
Hann helt allt land af sonum Ragnars, meðan þeir váru í hernaði.	He held all the-land of sons Ragnar's, as-long-as they were about raiding.	He held all the land of Ragnar's sons, as long as they were about raiding.
Gormr Knútsson var allra manna mestr ok sterkastr ok inn mesti atgervimaðr um alla hluti, en ekki var hann svá vitr sem verit höfðu inir fyrri frændr hans.	Gorm Knutsson was to-all men the-greatest and strongest and the most accomplished about all things, but not was he so wise as being had those before kinsmen his.	Gorm Knutsson was the largest and strongest of all men, and the most accomplished man in all things, but he was not as wise as his kinsmen before him.
4	4	4
Gormr tók konungdóm eptir föður sinn.	Gorm took kingship after father his.	Gorm took kingship after his father.
Hann fekk Þyri, er kölluð var Danmarkarbót, dóttur KlakkHaralds, er konungr var í Jótlandi.	He married Thyra, who called was Denmark's-benefit, daughter-of Klakk-Harald, who king was in Jutland.	He married Thyra, who was called Denmark's benefit, daughter of Klakk-Harald, who was king in Jutland.
En er Haraldr var andaðr, þá tók Gormr þat ríki allt undir sik.	And when Harald was dead, then took Gorm that kingdom altogether under himself.	And when Harald was dead, then Gorm took that kingdom altogether under himself.

Old Norse	Literal	English
Gormr konungr fór með her yfir allt Jótland ok eyddi öllum neskonungum allt suðr til Slés, ok svá vann hann mikit af Vindlandi, ok margar orrostur átti hann við Saxa, ok gerðist hann inn ríkasti konungr.	Gorm the-king travelled with a-war-band over all Jutland and devastated all sea-kings all south to Schlei-river, and so won he much of Wendland, and many battles had he with the-Saxons, and became he the mightiest king.	King Gorm travelled with a war band all over Jutland and devastated all the sea kings south to the Schlei river, and so he won much of Wendland, and he had many battles with the Saxons, and became the mightiest king.
Hann átti tvá syni.	He had two sons.	He had two sons.
Hét inn ellri Knútr, en Haraldr inn yngri.	Called the elder Knut, and Harald the younger.	The eldest was called Knut, and the younger was called Harald.
Knútr var allra þeira manna fegrstr, er menn hafa sét.	Knut was to-all they the-people fairest, that people had seen.	Knut was the fairest to all people, that people had seen.
Konungr unni honum um fram hvern mann ok þar með öll alþýða.	The-king loved him about from whom the-people and there among all popular.	The king lover him more than all the people, and he was popular with all.
Hann var kallaðr Danaást.	He was called Danes'-beloved.	He was called the Danes' beloved.
Haraldr líktist í móðurætt sína, ok unni móðir hans honum eigi minna en Knúti.	Harald likeness to mother's-kin his, and loved mother his him no less than Knut.	Harald had a likeness to his mother's kin, and his mother loved him no less than Knut.
Ívarr inn beinlausi var lengi konungr í Englandi.	Ivar the Boneless was long king in England.	Ivar the Boneless was king for a long time in England.
Hann átti ekki barn, því at hann var svá skapaðr, at honum fylgdi engi girnd né ást, en eigi skorti hann spekt eða grimmd, ok varð hann ellidauðr á Englandi ok var þar heygðr.	He had no children, because that he was so crafted, that he followed no lust or love, about no shortage his cunning or cruelty, and was he old-age-died in England and was there buried.	He had no children, because he was crafted in such a way, that he had no lust or love in him, but there was no shortage in his cunning or cruelty, and he was old in age when he died in England, and he was buried there.
Þá váru allir Loðbrókar synir dauðir.	Then were all Lothbrok's sons dead.	Then all of Lothbrok's sons were dead.
Eptir Ívar tók konungdóm í Englandi Aðalmundr.	After Ivar took kingdom in England Æthelmund.	After Ivar, Aethelmund took the kingdom of England.

Old Norse	Literal	English
Hann var bróðursonr Játmundar ins helga, ok kristnaði hann víða England.	He was brother's-son Edmund the holy, and Christianity he spread-in England.	He was brother's son of Edmund the Holy, and he spread Christianity in England.
Hann tók skatta af Norðhumrulandi, því at þat var heiðit.	He took tax of Northumbria, because that it was heathen.	He taxed Northumbria, because it was heathen.
Eptir hann tók konungdóm sonr hans, er Aðalbrigt hét.	After him took kingdom son his, was Æthelberht named.	After him, his son named Aethelberht took the kingdom.
Hann var góðr konungr ok varð gamall.	He was good king and became old.	He was a good king and became old.
Ofarliga á hans dögum kom Danaherr til Englands, ok váru formenn hersins Knútr ok Haraldr, synir Gorms konungs.	Not-far from his days came Danish-Army to England, and was leaders army-theirs Knut and Harald, sons-of Gorm the-king.	Not far from the end of his days, the Danish army came to England, and the army's leader was Knut and Harald, sons of King Gorm.
Þeir lögðu undir sik mikit ríki í Norðhumrulandi, þat er Ívarr hafði átt.	They laid under them large kingdom in Northumbria, that which Ivar had had.	They had large kingdom under them in Northumbria, which Ivar had had.
Aðalbrigt konungr fór móti þeim, ok börðust þeir fyrir norðan Kliflönd, ok fell þar margt af Dönum.	Æthelberht king went against them, and battled they for north Cleveland, and fell there many of the-Danes.	King Aethelberht went against them, and they battled for north Cleveland, and many of the Danes fell there.
Ok nokkuru síðar gengu Danir upp við Skarðaborg ok börðust þar ok fengu sigr.	And sometime later went the-Danes up against Scarborough and battled there and got success.	And sometime later the Danes went up against Scarborough and battled there with success.
Síðan fóru þeir suðr til Jórvíkr, ok gekk þar undir þá allt fólk, ok uggðu þeir þá ekki at sér.	Since travelled they south to York, and got they submitted then all people, and feared they then not for themselves.	Since they travelled south to York, and the people submitted to them, and they feared nothing.
Ok einn dag, er heitt veðr var, fóru menn á sund.	And one day, when hot weather was, went men in sound.	And one day when the weather was hot, men went swimming in a sound.

Old Norse	Literal	English
Ok svá sem konungssynir váru á sundi millim skipanna, hlupu menn af landi ofan ok skutu á þá.	And so as king's-sons were in sound between ships, ran men off land down and shot at them.	And as the king's sons were swimming between ships, men ran from the land and shot at them.
Var þá Knútr lostinn öru til bana, ok tóku þeir líkit ok fluttu út á skip.	Was then Knut struck arrow to death, and took they body and moved out to ships.	Knut was then struck with an arrow and killed, and they took the body carried it out to the ships.
Ok er landsmenn spyrja þetta, safnast þeir saman, svá at síðan fá Danir engar uppgöngur sakir safnaðar landsmanna ok fara síðan heim aptr til Danmarkar.	And when landsmen learned this, gathered they together, so that then got the-Danes no up-going for-the-sake-of the-gathering-of landsmen and travelled since home back to Denmark.	And when the landsmen learned this, they gathered together, so that the Danes would have no place to land because of the landsmen assembled, and afterwards they travelled home to Denmark.
Gormr konungr var þá á Jótlandi.	Gorm king was then in Jutland.	Then Gorm was king in Jutland.
Ok er hann spurði þessi tíðendi, þá hné hann aptr ok sprakk af harmi annan dag eptir at jafnlengd.	And when he learned this news, then knees he back and burst with grief next day died at the-same-time.	And when he learned this news, he fell to his knees, and died of grief at the same time the next day.
Þá tók konungdóm eptir hann yfir Danaveldi Haraldr, sonr hans.	Then took kingdom after him over Danish-realm Harald, son his.	Then his son Harald took over the Danish realm after him.
Hann tók fyrstr trú ok skírn sinna ættmanna.	He received first-of faith and baptism of-his relatives.	He was the first to receive faith and the baptism of his relatives.
5	5	5
Sigurðr ormr í auga ok Björn járnsíða ok Hvítserkr höfðu herjat víða um Frakkland.	Sigurd Snake-in-the-eye and Bjorn Ironside and Hvitserk had raided widely in France.	Sigurd Snake-in-the-eye and Bjorn Ironside and Hvitserk had raided widely in France.
Þá sneri Björn heim til ríkis síns.	Then turned Bjorn home to kingdom his.	Then Bjorn turned home to his kingdom.

Old Norse	Literal	English
Eptir þat barðist örnúlfr keisari við þá bræðr, ok fell þá af Dönum ok Norðmönnum hundrað þúshundraða.	After that battled Arnulf emperor with then brothers, and fell then of Danes and Norwegians hundred thousand.	After that the emperor Arnulf fought with the brothers, and a hundred thousand Danes and Norwegians fell there.
Þar fell þá Sigurðr ormr í auga, ok Guðröðr hét annarr konungr, er þar fell.	There fell then Sigurd Snake-in-the-eye, and Gudrod called another king, who there fell.	Then Sigurd Snake-in-the-eye fell, and another king named Gudrod.
Hann var sonr Óláfs Hringssonar, Ingjaldssonar, Ingasonar, Hringssonar, er Hringaríki er við kennt.	He was son Olaf son-of-Hring, son-of-Ingjald, son-of-Ingi, son-of-Hring, who Ringerike is with known.	He was the son of Olaf, the son of Hring, sin of Ingjald, son of Ingi, son of Hring, whom Ringerike is named after.
Hann var sonr Dags ok Þóru drengjamóður.	He was son Dag's and Thora Mother-of-Warriors.	He was the son of Dag and Thora the Mother of Warriors.
Þau áttu níu syni, ok er af þeim komin Döglinga ætt.	They had nine sons, and were of they coming Döglings descendents.	They had nine sons, and from them are descended the clan of the Doglings.
Helgi hvassi hét bróðir Guðröðar.	Helgi the-Keen was-named brother Gudrod's.	Gudrod's brother was named Helgi the Keen.
Hann hafði brott ór orrostunni merki Sigurðar orms í auga ok sverð hans ok skjöld.	He had brought from the-battle mark-of Sigurd Snake-in-the-eye and sword his and shield.	He had brought the banner of Sigurd Snake-in-the-eye, and his sword and shield, out of the battle.
Hann fór heim til Danmarkar með sínu liði ok fann þar Áslaugu, móður Sigurðar, ok sagði henni tíðendin.	He travelled home to Denmark with his forces and found there Auslag, mother Sigurd's, and said to-her the-news.	He travelled home to Denmark with his forces and found Auslag, Sigurd's mother, and said to her the news.
Þá kvað Áslaug vísu:	Then said Auslag verse:	Then Auslag said a verse:
"Sitja veiðivitjar vals á borgar halsum,	"Sit seekers The-slain about city neck,	"Sit seekers, The slain, about the city's neck,
böl er, þats hefir of hafnat	Lair which, that has of abandoned	Lair which, that has of abandoned,
hrafn Sigurðar nafni; blása nýtinjótar	Raven Sigurd's namesake; Blaze users	Raven, Sigurd's namesake; Blaze users,

Old Norse	Literal	English
nás í spán at hánum, ofsnemma lét Óðinn álf valmeyjar deyja".	Corpse about shiver that he, Too-early let Odin's Elf Valkyrie die".	Corpse about shivers that he, Too early let Odin's Elf Valkyrie die".
En af því at Hörða-Knútr var ungr, þá var Helgi þar með Áslaugu lengi til landvarnar.	But of because that Horda-Knut was young, then was Helgi there with Auslag long to defence.	But because Horda-Knut was young, Helgi stayed there a long time to defend.
Sigurðr ok Blæja áttu dóttur.	Sigurd and Blaeja had daughter.	Sigurd and Blaeja had a daughter.
Hún var tvíbura við Hörða-Knút.	She was twin with Horda-Knut.	She was Horda-Knut's twin.
Áslaug gaf henni nafn sitt ok fæddi hana upp síðan ok fóstraði.	Auslag gave her name hers and bore her up since and fostered.	Auslag gave her her own name and brought her up and fostered her since then.
Hana fekk síðan Helgi hvassi.	She married later Helgi the-Keen.	She later married Helgi the Keen.
Þeira sonr var Sigurðr hjörtr.	Their son was Sigurd Hart.	Their son was Sigurd Hart.
Hann var allra þeira manna fríðastr ok mestr ok sterkastr, er menn höfðu sét.	He was altogether of men handsome and greatest and strongest, as men had seen.	He was altogether the most handsome of men, and the greatest and strongest, that men had seen.
Þeir váru jafngamlir Gormr Knútsson ok Sigurðr hjörtr.	They were equal-age Gorm Knutsson and Sigurd Hart.	Gorm Knutsson and Sigurd Hart were equal in age.
En er Sigurðr var tólf vetra, þá drap hann berserk þann í einvígi, er Hildibrandr hét, ok þá tólf saman.	And when Sigurd was twelve winters, then killed he berserker then in duel, was Hildibrand named, and then twelve together.	And when Sigurd was twelve winters old, he killed a berserker in a duel, who was named Hildibrand, and then his band of twelve people.
Eptir þat gifti KlakkHaraldr honum dóttur sína, er Ingibjörg hét.	After that gave Klakk-Harald him daughter his, was Ingibjorg named.	After that Klakk-Harald gave him his daughter, who was named Ingibjorg.
Þau áttu tvau börn, Guðþorm ok Ragnhildi.	They had two children, Gudthorm and Ragnhild.	They had two children, Gudthorm and Ragnhild.

Old Norse	Literal	English
Þá spurði Sigurðr, at Fróði konungr, föðurbróðir hans, var dauðr.	Then learned Sigurd, that Frodi king, father-brother his, was dead.	Then Sigurd learned, that King Frodi, his father's brother, was dead.
Fór hann þá norðr til Noregs ok gerðist konungr yfir Hringaríki, ættleifð sinni.	Travelled he then north to Norway and became king over Ringerike, inheritance his.	He then travelled to Norway and became king over Ringerike, his inheritance.
Frá honum er löng saga, því at hann vann margs kyns þrekvirki.	From him is long saga, because that he won many wondrous brave-deeds.	From him there is a long saga, because he won many wondrous brave deeds.
En þat er at segja frá lífláti hans, at hann reið út á eyðimerkr at veiða dýr, sem vandi hans var til, ok kom þar móti honum Haki Haðaberserkr með þrjá tigu manna alvápnaðra ok barðist við hann.	But there is to say from life-laying his, that he rode out to deserted-forest to hunt wild-animals, as custom his was until, also came there to-meet him Haki Hadeland-Berserk with three ten men all-weaponed and fought with him.	But there is this to say about him laying his life, that he rode out to a deserted forest to hunt wild animals, and was his custom, until there also came to meet him Haki Hadeland-Berserk with thirty men all armed and fought with him.
Þar fell Sigurðr ok hafði drepit áðr tólf menn, en Haki konungr hafði látit hönd sína hægri ok hafði þó þrjú sár önnur.	There fell Sigurd and had killed about twelve men, that Haki the-king had laid hand his right and had though three wounds also.	There Sigurd fell and he had killed about twelve men, that King Haki lost his right hand and had though three other wounds.
Eptir þat reið Haki konungr með sínum mönnum á Hringaríki til Steins, sem bú Sigurðar var, ok tók brott Ragnhildi, dóttur hans, ok son hans, Guðþorm, ok mikit gós annat ok flutti heim með sér á Haðaland.	After that rode Haki king with his men to Ringerike to Stein, which dwelling Sigurd's was, and took away Ragnhild, daughter his, and son his, Gudthorm, and much property besides and brought home with him to Hadeland.	After that King Haki rode with his men to Ringerike to Stein, which was Sigurd's home, and took away his daughter Ragnhild, and his son Gudthorm, and much property besides, and brought them home with him to Hadeland.
Ok litlu síðar lét hann efna til veislu mikillar ok ætlaði at gera brullaup sitt, en þat dvaldist, því at sár hans höfðust illa.	And little later had he carried-out to feast great and intended to have wedding his, but that dwelled, because that wounds his had bad.	And a little later he had he had carried out a great feast, and intended to have his wedding, but that was delayed because his wounds were bad.

Old Norse	Literal	English
Ragnhildr var þá fimmtán vetra gömul, en Guðþormr fjórtán vetra.	Ragnhild was then fifteen winters old, but Godthorm fourteen winters.	Ragnhild was then fifteen winters old, but Godthorm was fourteen winters.
Leið svá haustit ok vetrinn fram um jól, at Haki lá í sárum.	Passed so autumn and winter from about Yule, that Haki lay so wounded.	So autumn and winter passed until Yule, as Haky lay wounded.
Þá var Hálfdan konungr svarti á Heiðmörk at búum sínum.	Then was Halfdan king the-Black at Heidmark about estates his.	King Halfdan the Black was at Heidimark at his estates.
Hann sendi Hárek gand ok með honum hundrað manna, ok fóru þeir yfir um ís á Mjörs á Haðaland á einni nótt ok kómu í dagan á bæ Haka konungs ok tóku allar dyrr á þeim skála, er hirðmenn sváfu í.	He sent Harek Wand and with him hundred men, and travelled they over about ice to Mjosa to Hadeland in one night and came at day to farmstead Haki the-king's and took all the-doors of the cabin, where the-guardsmen slept in.	He sent Harek Wand, and a hundred men with him, and they travelled over the ice on Lake Mjosa to Hadeland in one night, and came during the day to King Haki's farmstead, and blocked all the doors out of the house where his guard was sleeping.
Ok síðan gengu þeir til svefnskemmu Haka konungs ok tóku þar Ragnhildi ok Guðþorm, bróður hennar, ok allt þat fé, er þar var, ok hafa brott með sér.	And afterwards went they to sleeping-quarters Haki the-king's and took there Ragnhild and Gudthorm, brother hers, and all that wealth, which there was, and had away with them.	And afterward they went to King Haki's sleeping quarters and took Ragnhild and her brother Gudthorm and all the possesions that were there, and carried them off.
Þeir brenndu skálann ok þar inni í alla hirðina ok fara síðan brott.	They burned the-hut and there in about all guardsmen and went then away.	They burned the hall and all the guardsmen in it, and then went away.
En Haki konungr stóð upp ok klæddi sik ok gekk eptir þeim um hríð.	Then Haki the-king stood up and clothed himself and went after them about awhile.	Then King Haki stood up and clothed himself and went went after them for a while.
Ok er hann kom at vatnsísinum, þá sneri hann niðr hjöltunum á sverðinu ok lagðist á blóðrefilinn ok fekk þar bana ok er þar heygðr á vatnsbakkanum.	And when he came to water-ice, then turned he down hilt of sword and lay to sword-point and got there death and was there buried about water's-edge.	When he came to the ice, he turned the hilt of his sword downwards and fell on the point, and got his death, and was buried by the water's edge.

Old Norse	Literal	English
Hálfdan konungr sá, at þeir óku yfir ísinn með vagn tjaldaðan, ok þóttist vita, at þeira erendi mundi orðit hafa slíkt sem hann vildi.	Halfdan the-king saw, that they drove across ice with wagon covered, and thought certainly, that their errand could turned-out have such as he wished.	King Halfdan saw them driving over the ice with a covered wagon, and thought certainly, that their business could have turned out as he wished.
Lét hann þá senda boð um alla byggð ok bauð til öllu stórmenni á Heiðmörk ok gerði þann dag mikla veislu.	Had he then sent invitation about all settlement and invited to all great-men about Heidmark and made then day much feast.	He then had an invitation sent all about the settlement and invited the great men in Heidimark to the celebrations, and held a great feast that day.
Gerði hann þá brullaup til Ragnhildar, ok váru þau saman síðan marga daga.	Made he then wedding-feast for Ragnhild, and were they together afterwards many days.	He then made a wedding feast for Ragnhild, and they were together afterwards for many days.
Þeira sonr var Haraldr konungr inn hárfagri, er fyrstr varð einvaldskonungr yfir öllum Noregi.	Their son was Harald king the Hair-Fair, who first became sole-ruling-king over all Norway.	Their son was Harald Fair-Hair, who became the first sole ruling king over all Norway.

The Lay of Kraka

Old Norse	Literal	English
1	**1**	**1**
Hjoggum vér með hjörvi.	Struck we with swords.	We struck with our swords.
Hitt vas æ fyr löngu,	It was ever before long,	It was ever before long,
es á Gautlandi gingum	When in Götaland gone	When we went to Götaland,
at grafvitnis morði.	For ground-wolf slaughter.	For the ground wolf's slaughter.
Þá fingum vér Þóru,	Then won we Thora,	Then we won Thora,
þaðan hétu mik fyrðar,	From-there named me warriors,	From there the warriors named me,
es lyngölun lagðak,	As serpent laid,	As the serpent laid,
Loðbrók at því vígi;	Shaggy-breeches that because-of slaying;	Shaggy-breeches because of the slaying;
stakk á storðar lykkju	Thrust that wood coil	Thrust the wood coil,
stáli bjartra mála.	Steel bright matter.	Steel bright matter.
2	**2**	**2**
Hjoggum vér með hjörvi.	Struck we with swords.	We struck with our swords.
Heldr vask ungr, es skífðum	Rather was young, as we-sliced	Still was I young, when we-carved,
austr í Eyrasundi	Eastern to Eyrasundi	West east to Oresund,
undarn frekum vargi.	The eager wolf.	The eager wolf.
Ok fótgulum fogli	And gold legged birds,	And gold legged birds,
fingum vér, þars sungu	Grasped we, there singing	We grasped, singing there,
við háseymða hjalma	With high-seeing helmets	With high seeing helmets,
hörð járn, mikils verðar;	Hard iron, great worth;	Hard iron, great worth;
allr varð ægir sollinn,	All became ocean swollen,	All the ocean became swollen,
óð hrafn í valblóði.	Waded raven in slain-blood.	In slain blood waded the raven.
3	**3**	**3**
Hjoggum vér með hjörvi.	Struck we with swords.	We struck with our swords.
Hátt bárum þá geira,	High bearing there spears,	Spears held high there,
es tvítøgir tölðumk,	Were twenty we-reckoned,	Twenty we were reckoned,
ok tjör ruðum víða.	And pools reddened widely.	And pools reddened widely,
Unnum átta jarla	Won-we eight earls	We won eight earls,
austr fyr Dínu mynni;	East for Danube mouth;	Eastwards on the mouth of the Danube,

Old Norse	Literal	English
gera fingum þá gnóga	Did grasp there abundance	We did grasp abundance there,
gisting at því vígi;	Guested at then slaying;	Guested then at the slaying;
sveiti fell í sollinn	Sweat slaying about ocean	Sweat slaying about the ocean,
sæ, týndi lið ævi.	Sea, lost companions lives.	Sea, companions lost lives.

4	4	4
Hjoggum vér með hjörvi.	Struck we with swords.	We struck with our swords.
Heðins kvánar varð auðit,	Hedin's wife came fated,	Hedin's wife was fated to come,
þás Helsingja heimtum	Then Helsings hastened	Then Helsings hastened,
til heimsala Óðins.	To home Odin's.	To the home of Odin,
Lögðum upp í Ívu,	Laid up on Iva,	Laid up on the Iva,
oddr náði þá bíta,	Spears caught then cut,	Spears caught then cut,
öll vas unda gjalfri	All was under given	All was under given,
á sú roðin heitu;	River seen red brewed;	The river was seen red brewed,
grenjaði brandr við brynjur,	Howled brand with shield,	Blade howled against shield,
bensildr klufu skjöldu.	Bane-herrings cleft shields.	Bane herrings cleft shields.

5	5	5
Hjoggum vér með hjörvi.	Struck we with swords.	We struck with our swords.
Hygg engan þá frýðu,	Think none then withstood-us,	Thinking that no one then withstood us,
áðr á Heflis hestum	Until on Heflir's horses	Until, on Heflir's horses,
Herrøðr í styr felli.	Herrod in steering fell.	Herrod in steering fell.
Klýfrat ægis öndrum	Cleaved Aegir's others	Cleaved Aegir's others,
annarr jarl in frægri	Another earl the more-famous	Another earl more famous,
lunda völl til lægis	Puffins field to laying	Puffins field laying to,
á langskipum síðan;	About longships since;	About longships since;
sá bar siklingr víða	So bore king widely	So the king bore widely,
snart framm í styr hjarta.	Soon forward of brave heart.	Soon forwards of brave heart.

6	6	6
Hjoggum vér með hjörvi.	Struck we with swords.	We struck with our swords.
Herr kastaði skjöldum,	Warband cast shields,	The warband cast their shields,
þás rægagarr rendi	Then carrion-beast ran	Then the carrion beast ran,
ræstr at gumna brjóstum.	Swept up-to men's breasts.	Swept up to mens breasts.
Beit í Skarpa-skerjum	Grazing in Skarpa-Skerries	Grazing in Skarpa Skerries,

Old Norse	Literal	English
skœrubíldr at hjaldri; roðinn vas randar máni,	Shear-lancet about battle; Reddened was shield moon,	Shear lancet about battle; Reddened was the shield moon,
áðr Rafn konungr felli; dreif ór hölda hausum heitr á brynjur sveiti.	Before Rafn king fell; Scattering arrow flesh head Hot about armour sweat.	Before King Rafn fell; Scattering arrow flesh head, Hot about armour sweat.
7	7	7
Hjoggum vér með hjörvi. Hátt grenjuðu rottar, áðr á Ullarakri Eysteinn konungr felli. Gingum golli fáðir grundar vals af böndum, (rækyndill smó rauðar rítr) at hjalma móti; svíra virtr ór sárum sveif of hjarna kleifar.	Struck we with swords. High roared rats, Before that Ullr-acres Eystein king fell. Going gold went-they Ground choices for sword, (corpse-candle slipped red Written) to helms meeting; Neck ale from wounds Steerer of brain cliffs.	We struck with our swords. High roared rats, Before the field of Ullr, King Eystein fell, Going with gold they went, Ground choices for swords, (corpse candle slipped red, Written) to helms meeting; Neck ale from wounds, From brain cliffs it came.
8	8	8
Hjoggum vér með hjörvi. Hafa gátu þá rafnar fyr Inndyris-eyju œrna bráð at slíta. Fingum fálu hestum fullan verð at sinni, (ilt vas eins at gæta) með uppruna sólar; strenghömlur sák stíga, stökk malmr á skör hjalmi.	Struck we with swords. At-sea got then ravens Before Inndyr's-Island Plenty meat about tore. Fingers Fala's horses, Full worth that theirs, (hard was as to guard) With origin sun; Bow-string sake trod, Jumped metal to fragile helmet.	We struck with our swords. At sea the ravens got, Before Indyr's Island, Plenty of meat about torn. Fingers Fala's horses, Full meals that theirs, (It was hard to guard) With the origin of the sun; Bow string's sake trod, Metal jumped to fragile helmet.
9	9	9
Hjoggum vér með hjörvi. Háðum rendr í dreyra, þás benstara bræddum fyr Borgundarholmi. Hreggský slitusk hringa, hratt almr af sér malmi; Völnir fell at vígi,	Struck we with swords. Mock edged with blood, Then mortal-wound molten Before Bornholm. Clouds broken rings, Fast elm of one's metal; Volnir fell in slaying,	We struck with our swords. Mock edged with blood, Then mortal wound molten, Before Bornholm. Clouds broke rings, Fast elm of one's metal; Volnir fell in the slaying,

Old Norse	Literal	English
vasat einn konungr meiri;	Was one king better;	One king was better;
val rak vítt of strandir,	Foe driven charms of beaches,	Foe driven charms of beaches,
vargr fagnaði tafni.	Wolf got sacrifices.	The wolf received sacrifices.

10

Hjoggum vér með hjörvi.	Struck we with swords.	We struck with our swords.
Hildr vas sýnt í vexti,	Battle was shown to grow,	Battle was shown great grown,
áðr Freyr konungr felli	Before Freyr King fell	Before King Freyr fell,
í Flæmingja veldi.	In Flemings' empire.	In the Fleming's country.
Náði blár at bíta	Caught black-and-blue by bite	Caught black and blue by bites,
blóði smeltr í gyltan	Blood enamelled a sow	Blood enamelled a sow,
Högna kufl at hjaldri	Hogni cloak of battle;	Hogni's cloak of battle;
harðr bengrefill ferðum;	Hard battle-hoe voyages;	Hard battle hoe voyages;
mær grét morginskœru	Maidens wept morning-shear	Maidens wept as morning sheared,
mörg, en tafn fekkst vörgum.	Many, of sacrifices got wolves.	The wolves got many sacrifices.

11

Hjoggum vér með hjörvi.	Struck we with swords.	We struck with our swords.
Hundruðum frák liggja	Hundreds speared lay	Hundreds lay speared,
á Eynæfis öndrum,	About Eynaefi's others,	About Eynaefi's others,
þars Englanes heitir.	There Englanes called.	There Englanes called.
Siglðum vér til snerru	Sailed we to slaughter	We sailed to slaughter,
sex dœgr, áðr lið felli;	Six days, before host fell;	Six days, before the host fell;
áttum odda messu	Directed point mass	Directed mass of points,
við uppruna sólar;	By origin-of sun;	By the origin of the sun;
varð fyr várum sverðum	Went before we swords	Went before swords,
Valþjófr í styr hníga.	Valthjof about steered kneeling.	Valthjof bent in battle.

12

Hjoggum vér með hjörvi.	Struck we with swords.	We struck with our swords.
Hrunði -dögg af sverðum	Collapsed -dew of swords	Collapsed dew of swords,
brún í Barðafirði	Brown of Bardafjord	Brown of Bargarfjord,
bleika ná- fyr hauka.	Dark got before hawks.	Got dark before hawks.
Umði almr, þars oddar,	Whined elm, there point,	Elm bows whined, there points,

Old Norse	Literal	English
allstrítt bitu skyrtur	All-contended bit battle-shirts	All contended biting battle shirts,
at slíðrloga sennu	At sheath-flame at-once	At sheath flame at once,
Svölnis hamri þœfðar;	Svolnir's hammer quarrel;	Svolnir's hammer quarrel;
rendi ormr til unda,	Edge serpent to under,	Edge serpent to under,
eitrhvass drifinn sveita.	Envenomed driven sweat.	Envenomed driven sweat.
13	13	13
Hjoggum vér með hjörvi.	Struck we with swords.	We struck with our swords.
Heldum Lakkar tjöldum	Headed Hlökk's tents	Headed to Hlokk's shelters,
hátt at Hildar leiki	High at Hild's game	Held high at Hild's game,
fyr Hjaðninga vági.	Before Hjadninga inlet.	Before Hjadninga bay.
Sjá knáttu þá seggir,	Saw ball then said,	Saw the ball then said,
es sundruðum skjöldu	As asunder shields	As asunder shields,
at hræsíldar hjaldri,	From corpse-fish battle;	From corpse fish battle;
hjalm slitnaðan gotna;	Helmet worn men;	Helmet worn men;
vasat sem bjarta brúði	Was which bright bride	Was which bright bride,
í bing hjá sér leggja.	In bed beside her lying.	In bed beside her lying.
14	14	14
Hjoggum vér með hjörvi.	Struck we with swords.	We struck with our swords.
Hörð kom ríð á skjöldu,	Hard came ride upon shields,	Hard came ride upon shields,
nár fell niðr til jarðar	Dead fell down to earth	The dead fell down to earth,
á Norðimbralandi.	In Northumbria.	In Northumbria.
Vasat of eina óttu	Was of one incite	Was of one incited,
öldum þörf at frýja	None needed to refuse	No one needed to refuse,
Hildar leiks, þars hvassir	Hild's game, there sharp	Hild's game, there sharp,
hjalmstofn bitu skjómar;	Helm-staves bit shields;	Helm staves bit shields;
vasat sem unga ekkju	Was which young widow	Which the young widow was,
í öndvegi kyssa.	In foremost-seat kissing.	In foremost seat kissing.
15	15	15
Hjoggum vér með hjörvi.	Struck we with swords.	We struck with our swords.
Herþjófi varð auðit	Herthjof became fated	Herthjof became fated,
í Suðreyjum sjálfum	In South-Islands ourselves	In Southern Islands ourselves,
sigrs á várum mönnum.	Victory about we men.	Victory about we men,
Varð í randar regni	Became to shields rain	Became shields to rain,
Rögnvaldr fyrir hníga,	Rongvald before kneeled,	Rognvald kneeled before,
sá kom harmr of hölða	Saw came harm of hold	So came harm of hold,

Old Norse	Literal	English
hæstr at sverða gusti; hvast kastaði hristir hjalms strenglágar palmi.	High at sword gusts; Hiss cast shaking, Helms string-laid palms.	High at sword gusts; Hiss cast shaking, Helms string laid palms.

16

Hjoggum vér með hjörvi. Hverr lá þverr of annan; glaðr varð geira hríðar gaukr at sverða leiki. Léta örn né ygli, sás Írlandi stýrði, (mót varð malms ok rítar) Marstan konungr fasta; varð í Veðrafirði valtafn gefit hrafni.	Struck we with swords. Each lay heaped about each-other; Glad became spear storm Cuckoo about sword play. Had eagle not awful, So-is Ireland steered, (meeting became ore and drawn) Marstan king fasted; Became in Waterford Slain-offering given raven.	We struck with our swords. Each lay heaped about each other; Glad became the spear storm, The sword clash's cuckoo, Had the eagle, not awful, So is Ireland steered, (meeting became ore and drawn), King Marstan fasted; Became in Waterford, Slain offering given raven.

17

Hjoggum vér með hjörvi. Hundmargan sák falla morginstund fyr mæki mann at odda sennu. Syni mínum hneit snimma slíðra þorn við hjarta; Egill lét Agnar ræntan óblauðan hal lífi; glumði geirr við Hamðis gránserk, bliku merki.	Struck we with swords. Hundred-many attended fell Morning-while for-the sword Men about spear-point at-once. Son mine struck early Sheath thorn in heart; Egill had Agnar stolen Un-cowardly man's life; Roared spears against Hamdir's Grey-shirt, shimmering banner.	We struck with our swords. Hundred many attended fallen, While morning, for the sword, Men about spear points at once. Struck early, my son. Sheath thorn in his heart; Egill had Agnar stolen, Un-cowardly man's life; Roared spears against Hamdir, Grey shirt, shimmering banner.

18

Hjoggum vér með hjörvi. Haldorða sák brytja ekki smátt fyr ulfa Endils niðja bröndum; vasat á Víkaskeiði, sem vín konur bæri;	Struck we with swords. Held-words sake cut-up Not small before wolves Endil's descendants swords; Was as Vikaskeid, As wine women bore;	We struck with our swords. Held words sake cut up, Not small before wolves, Endil's descendants swords; Was as Vikaskeid, As wine women bore;

Old Norse	Literal	English
hroðinn vas ægis asni ófár í dyn geira;	Stripped was Aegir's donkey High among storm spears;	Aegir's donkey was stripped, High among the storm of spears;
skorin vas Sköglar kápa at skjöldunga hjaldri.	Scored was Skogul's cape At Skjoldungs' battle;	Scored was Skogul's cape, At Skjoldungs' battle;
19	19	19
Hjoggum vér með hjörvi. Háðum sverðs at morgni	Struck we with swords. Depending swords at morning	We struck with our swords. Depending swords at morning,
leik fyr Lindiseyri við lofðunga þrenna. Fár átti því fagna	Sported before Lindiseyri With kings three. Few had because-of celebrated	Sported before Lindiseyri; With three kings. Few had cause to celebrate,
(fell margr í gin ulfi, haukr sleit hold með vargi, at heill þaðan kœmi; Íra blóð í ægi œrit fell of skœru.	Fell many to jaws wolf, Hawks tore-up bodies with wolves, That whole from-there came; Irish blood in sea Enough fell to quarrel.	Fell many to the wolf's jaws, Hawks tore up bodies with wolves, That whole from there came; Irish blood in the sea, Enough fell to quarrel.
20	20	20
Hjoggum vér með hjörvi. Hárfagran sák røkkva meyjar dreng of morgin	Struck we with swords. Fair-haired sake darken Maiden's fellow about morning	We struck with our swords. Fair haired case darkened, Maiden's fellow about morning,
ok málvini ekkju. Vasat sem varmar laugar vínkers Njörun bæri oss í Álasundi, áðr Örn konungr felli; böðmána sák bresta, brá því fira lífi.	And friend's widow. Was as warm washing Wine-beaker Njörun brought Us in Álasund, Before Orn king fell; Bathing-moon saw burst, Drew therefore people's lives.	And friend's widow. Was as warm washing, Wine beaker Njorun brought, Us in Alasund, Before King Orn fell; Bathing moon saw burst, Drew therefore people's lives.
21	21	21
Hjoggum vér með hjörvi. Há sverð bitu skjöldu, þás gollhroðinn glumði geirr við Hildar næfri. Sjá mun í Önguls-eyju of aldr mega síðan,	Struck we with swords. High sword bit shields, Then cry-thrown roared Spears in battle skilfully. Saw would at Anglesey About age may since,	We struck with our swords. High sword bit shields, Then cry thrown roared, Spears in battle skilfully. Saw would at Anglesey, About age may since,

Old Norse	Literal	English
hversu at lögðis leiki	How-so about had played	How so about had played,
lofðungar framm gingu;	Kings from going;	Kings from going;
roðinn vas út fyr eyri	Reddened was out before island	Reddened was out before island,
ár flugdreki sára.	Early flight-dragon wound.	Early flight-dragon wound.
22	22	22
Hjoggum vér með hjörvi.	Struck we with swords.	We struck with our swords.
Hví sé drengr at feigri,	Why so fellow to cower,	Why should a warrior cower,
at hann í odda éli	As he about spear-points hail	As the spear points hail,
öndurðr látinn verði?	Breathing deceased will-be	Breathing deceased will be,
Opt sýtir sá ævi,	Often laments so life,	Often laments so life,
es aldrigi nistir,	Which never pierced,	Which never pierced,
(ilt kveða argan eggja)	(It's hard to encourage the weak),	(It's hard to encourage the weak),
örn at sverða leiki;	Eagle to sword plays;	To eagles in the edge game,
hugblauðum kømr hvergi	Thought-cowardly comes nowhere	Cowardly thoughts come nowhere,
hjarta sitt at gagni.	Heart his that of-use.	His heart that of use.
23	23	23
Hjoggum vér með hjörvi.	Struck we with swords.	We struck with our swords.
Hitt telk jafnt, at gangi	It shaped evenly, that went	It is shaped evenly, that which went,
at samtogi sverða	That come-together swords	That come together swords,
sveinn í móti einum.	Lad among meeting one.	Lad among meeting one.
Hrøkkvit þegn fyr þegni,	Draw-back thane before thane,	Draw back thane before thane,
þat vas drengs aðal lengi,	That was warriors nature long,	That was long the warrior's nature,
æ skal ástvinr meyja	Ever shall loved-friend maid	Ever shall loved friend maid,
einarðr í dyn sverða.	Determined in storm swords.	Determined in storm of swords.
24	24	24
Hjoggum vér með hjörvi.	Struck we with swords.	We struck with our swords.
Hitt sýnisk mér raunar,	It seems to-me ordeal,	It seems to me ordeal,
at forlögum fylgjum,	To fortune follow,	To fortune follow,
fár gengr of sköp norna.	Few go around craft The-Norns.	Few escape The Norn's craft.
Eigi hugðak Ellu	Not thought Aella	Not imagined Aella,
at aldrlagi mínu,	That age-laying mine,	That age laying mine,

Old Norse	Literal	English
þás blóðvali bræddak	Then blood-falcons melt	Then blood falcons melt,
ok borð á lög keyrðak;	And board of law drive;	And board of law drive;
vítt fingum þá vargi	Wide got then wolves	Wide then got the wolves,
verð í Skotlands fjörðum.	Worth in Scotland's fields.	Widely in Scotland's bays.

25

Hjoggum vér með hjörvi.	Struck we with swords.	We struck with our swords.
Hitt lœgir mik, jafnan	It gladdens me, evenly	It gladdens me evenly,
at Baldrs föður bekki	That Baldr's father bench	That Baldr's father bench,
búna veitk at sumblum.	Prepared given to banquet.	Prepared for the banquet,
Drekkum bjór af bragði	We-drink beer of taste	We drink beer of taste,
ór bjúgviðum hausa;	Of bent-tree skulls;	Of bent tree skulls,
sýtira drengr við dauða	Lament fellow with death	Lament the fellow's death,
dýrs at Fjölnis húsum;	Dear at Fjolnir's house;	Dear at Fjolnir's house;
eigi kømk með æðru	Not comes with higher	Not comes with higher,
orð til Viðris hallar.	Words to Vidrir's hall.	Words to Vidrir's hall.

26

Hjoggum vér með hjörvi.	Struck we with swords.	We struck with our swords.
Hér vildi nú allir	Here willed now all,	Here willed now all,
burir Áslaugar bröndum	Sons Auslag's burning	Sons of Auslag burning,
bitrum hildi vekja,	Bitter battle awaken,	Bitter battle awoken,
ef vandliga vissi	If closely knew	It closely knew,
of viðfarar ossar,	Of wide-travelled ours,	Of our wide travelling,
hvé ófáir ormar	How many serpents	How many serpents,
eitrfullir mik slíta;	Poison-full me stab;	Poison full, stab me,
móðernis fekk mínum	Mother's got mine	Of their mother's lineage, they have got,
mögum, svát hjörtu dugðu.	Sons, so-that hearts enough.	My sons, so that hearts enough.

27

Hjoggum vér með hjörvi.	Struck we with swords.	We struck with our swords.
Harðla líðr at ævi,	Hard passes at life,	Hard passes my life,
grimt stendr grand af naðri,	Fiercely stands hurt of serpent,	Fiercely stands the hurt of the serpent,
góinn byggvir sal hjarta.	Goinn settles hall heart.	Goinn scathes me sorely,
Væntum hins, at Viðris	Wish at Vidrir's	Wish at Vidrir's
vöndr í Ellu standi;	Wound of Aelle a time;	Wound of Aelle a time;
sonum mínum man svella	Sons mine should swell	Sons mine should swell,
sinn föður ráðinn verða;	Their father ruled become;	Their father ruled become;

Old Norse	Literal	English
munuat snarpir sveinar	Should-to sharply lads	Should sharply lads,
sitt kyrt vesa láta.	Their calm be allowed.	Their calm be allowed.

28

Hjoggum vér með hjörvi.	Struck we with swords.	We struck with our swords.
Hefr fimm tøgum sinna	Have five tens theirs	Fifty of theirs,
folkorrostur framðar	Folk-battles performed	Folk battles performed,
fleinþings boði ok eina.	Lance-meeting bid, and one.	Lance meeting bid, and one.
Minst hugða ek manna,	At-least mind I many,	At the least mind I many,
at mér vesa skyldi	About me being should	About me should be,
(ungr namk odd at rjóða)	(young tunic spear-point that reddened)	(Young tunic spear-point that reddened),
annarr konungr fremri;	Another king foremost;	Another king foremost,
oss munu æsir bjóða,	Us would Aesir invite,	Us would Aesir invite,
esat sýtandi dauði.	Glowing sweet death.	Glowing sweet death.

29

Fýsumk hins at hætta,	Face this the danger,	Face this danger,
heim bjóða mér dísir,	Home bid me Disir,	Home invite me Disir,
sem frá Herjans höllu	Who from Herjan's hall	Who from Herjan's hall,
hefr Óðinn mér sendar.	Has Odin to-me sends.	Has Odin sent for me,
Glaðr skalk öl með ásum	Gladly shall ale with the-gods	Gladly shall have ale with the gods,
í öndvegi drekka,	To foremost drink,	To drink foremost,
lífs eru liðnar stundr,	Life is passing time,	Life is passing time,
læjandi skalk deyja.	Laughing shall I-die.	Laughing I shall die.

Word List (Old Norse to English)

Old Norse	English
´, `	
'	

A, a

Old Norse	English
aætlaði	intended
aðal	nature
aðalbrigt	Æthelberht (a name), Ethelberht (a name)
aðalmundr	Æthelmund (a name), Ethelmund (a name)
aðra	another, another (feminine, dative, singular), another (masculine, accusative, plural), else, other, other (feminine, dative, singular), other (masculine, accusative, plural), others, second (feminine, dative, singular), second (masculine, accusative, plural)
aðrir	another (masculine, nominative, plural), other, other (masculine, nominative, plural), others, second (masculine, nominative, plural)
af	for, from, of, off, on, out, out-of, over, that, they, to, with
aflim	gain
agðir	Agder (a name)
agnar	Agnar (a name)
agnarr	Agnar (a name)
agnars	Agnar (a name)
aldr	age
aldri	age, never
aldrigi	never
aldrlagi	age-laying, never for-good
alfari	
alla	all
allan	all, every
allar	all
allir	all, everywhere, to-all-who
allmarga	all-many
allmikit	all-much
allnær	all-near, near
allnýs	all-prying
allólíkligt	all-un-likely
allóvæn	all-ugly
allr	all
allra	all, altogether, every, everyone's, of-all, to-all
allrar	all
alls	all
allstrítt	all-contended
allt	all, altogether
allvaldr	all-wielding
allvel	all-well, well
almenning	all-men
almr	elm
alnar	measure, measured, measures
alþýða	popular
alvápnaðra	all-weaponed
andaðist	died, ended
andaðr	dead
andast	die, died

137

Old Norse	English	Old Norse	English
andviðri	the-storm	annarra	another, another (feminine, genitive, plural), another (masculine, genitive, plural), another (neuter, genitive, plural), each-other, else, other, other (feminine, genitive, plural), other (masculine, genitive, plural), other (neuter, genitive, plural), second (feminine, genitive, plural), second (masculine, genitive, plural), second (neuter, genitive, plural)
andvíga	opposition		
ann	love, loved		
annan	accompany, another, another (masculine, accusative, singular), each-other, next, other, other (masculine, accusative, singular), others, second, second (masculine, accusative, singular)		
annarr	2nd, second, another, another, another (masculine, nominative, singular), each, other, other (masculine, nominative, singular), otherwise, second, second (2nd), second (masculine, nominative, singular)		
		annarri	another, another (feminine, dative, singular), other (feminine, dative, singular), second (feminine, dative, singular)
		annars	also, another, another (masculine, genitive, singular), another (neuter, dative, singular), another's, any-other, each-other, else, other, other (masculine, genitive, singular), other (neuter, dative, singular), others, others', second (masculine, genitive, singular), second (neuter, dative, singular), the-other's, to-another
		annast	take-care-of, taken-care-of, took-care-of

Old Norse	English
annat	another, another (neuter, dative, singular), any-other, besides, else, next, other, other (neuter, dative, singular), other-things, second, second (neuter, dative, singular), second-time, something-else
annathvárt	either, either-way
annk	purpose
aptan	evening
aptanninn	the-evening
aptr	again, back, return
ara	eagle
argan	wealkings
arnar	eagle
asni	donkey
at	a, about, as, as-to, at, back-from, but, by, for, from, had, if, in, it, man, of, on, out, than, that, the, then, therefore, this, through, to, to-be, towards, up-to, was, were, what, when, which
atbeina	assist, assistance
atburð	events
atburðr	event, happened
atburðum	events
atgervimaðr	accomplished
athugaleysi	carelessness
atsetu	a-seat, to-seat
atsókn	attack
auðig	wealthy
auðit	fated
auðr	Aud (a name), fortune, rich, wealth
auðsætt	obvious

Old Norse	English
auðvitat	obvious
auga	eye, eyes, the-eye, the-eyes
augna	eyes
augu	eyes
augum	eyes
aurriðanet	a-trout-net
ausinn	poured, sprinkled
austr	East, Eastern
austrfarar	Eastern-Journeys
austrveg	Eastern-Lands
austrvegi	Eastern-Lands

Á, á

Old Norse	English
á	a, about, all, am, and, are, a-river, as, at, at-the, be, by, for, from, had, has, have, he, in, into, is, it, of, on, on-the, onto, out, out-of, over, river, so, that, the, then, the-river, through, to, towards, upon, was, with, yet
áðr	about, after, around, back, before, earlier, return, returned, until
ágæst	the-greatest
ágæt	famous
ágætar	great
ágæti	excellent, glory
ágætir	renowned
ágætis	greatness
ágætr	famous, fine, great
ákafari	eager
ákafir	eager
ákafliga	extremely, very
áki	Aki (a name)
ákveðin	agreed
ákveðit	decided

Old Norse	English
álasundi	Alasund (a place)
álf	elf
álits	thought
álmsveig	elm-twig
án	without
ár	early
áræði	daring
áslaug	Aslaug (a name)
áslaugar	Aslaug (a name)
áslaugu	Aslaug (a name)
ást	affection, love
ástir	love
ástvinr	loved-friend
ásum	Æsir (a place, Norse Mythology), the-gods
át	ate
átrúnað	belief
átt	descendents, direction, had, have, married, owned
átta	8, eight
áttak	fed
áttar	born
átti	8th, eighth, had, married
áttu	directions, had, have, have-you, owned
áttum	directed, directions, had
ávallt	always
áverkann	would

Æ, æ

Old Norse	English
æ	ever
æðra	higher
æðru	higher
ægi	sea
ægir	ocean, the-ocean
Ægis	Ægir's (a name)
ælig	wretched
æptu	called-out, shouted
ærinn	boundless
ærir	insane
ærit	plenty-of
Æsir	Æsir (a place, Norse Mythology)
ætla	intend, intended, suppose, supposed, to intend
ætlaði	intended, supposed, thought
ætlar	intend, intended, intentions, supposed
ætlat	intend, intended, purpose
ætluðu	intended, supposed
ætt	ancestry, descendents, direction, family, family-line, generations, lineage, the-lineage
ættar	family, lineage, noble
ættbogi	descendents
ætti	had, have
ættleifð	inheritance
ættmanna	relatives
ævi	life, lives, our-lives

B, b

Old Norse	English
bað	asked, bid, bid, invited, ordered, proposed-to
báða	both, both (masculine, accusative)
báðir	both, both (masculine, nominative)
báðu	asked, bid, bid-they
báðuð	invite

The Sagas of Ragnar Lothbrok   *Word List (Old Norse to English)*

Old Norse	English	*Old Norse*	English
bæ	a-farm, dwelling, estate, farm, farmstead, town	barn	child, children
		barna	born, children
		barni	a-child, child
bæði	asked, as-well, bid, both, both (neuter, accusative), both (neuter, nominative), choose, choosing	báru	bearing, bore, brought, carried, waters
		bárum	bearing
		bastarðr	bastard
bæjar	farm	batni	better
bæjarins	the-estate	batt	bought
bæjum	farms	bauð	bid, invited, offered
bæn	begging, bidding	bauga	circle, rings
bær	farm, the-farm	baugi	rings
bæri	bore, brought	baugs	ring
bak	back	baugum	ring
baka	bake	beð	bed
bakaðist	warmed	beðit	bid, proposals, proposed-to
bakast	warmed		
baki	back	beggja	both, both (feminine, genitive), both (masculine, genitive), both (neuter, genitive)
bál	a-pyre, fire, the-fire		
baldrs	Baldr's (a name)		
bálinu	the-pyre		
bana	bane, death, kill, killer, to-death	beið	sought, waited
		beiddist	ask, asked, invited, to-ask
banasári	death-wound		
banasótt	death-sickness	beiddu	asked
bannat	banned	beiðir	asked
bar	bore, carried, carry, carrying, placed, surpassed, was-carried, wore	bein	bone, bones
		beinabót	benefit
		beini	bone
		beinlausan	Boneless (a name)
bára	waves	beinlausi	Boneless (a name)
barðafirði	Bardafjord (a place)	beinlauss	Bone-Less (a name)
bardaga	battle, the-battle, to-battle	beit	bit, grazing
		bekk	bench
bardagann	battle	bekki	bench
bardagi	battle, the-battle	beli	Beli (a name)
bardaginn	the-battle	beljar	bellowed
barðhjarls	land-snakes	ben	wound
barði	beat	bengrefill	battle-hoe
barðist	battled, fought	bensildr	bane-herrings
barist	bore	benstara	mortal-wound
bark	bark		

The Sagas of Ragnar Lothbrok   Word List (Old Norse to English)

Old Norse	English
ber	bare, be-bare, bore, carried
bera	bear, bore, bore-up, born, borne, bring, carried, carry, unload
bergja	taste
bergt	eaten
beri	bear, bore
berið	bear
berjast	battle, fight, fighting, fought, to-fight
berjumst	fight
berr	bears, bore
berserk	berserker
berst	bore, fought
bert	bare, uncovered
best	best, the-best
besta	best
bestu	best
bestum	best
betr	better
betra	better
betri	better
bið	ask, bid
bíða	bid, to-wait-for, wait
biðið	ask
biðim	wait
biðja	ask, bid, invite, offer, propose, propose-to, tell, to ask, to tell
biðr	asked, asked-for, bid, invite, invited
biðst	chose
biki	tar
binda	bind, tie
bing	bed
birni	bear
birtinga	revealing
bíta	bit, bite, cut
bíti	bite
bitrum	bitter

Old Norse	English
bitu	bit, bitten, was-bitten-by
bjarg	boulder, rock
bjargvel	well-enough
bjart	bright
bjarta	bright
bjartar	bright
bjartra	bright
bjó	dwelling, dwelt, lived, prepared, red, settled
bjóða	bid, invite, invited, offer, to invite, to offer
bjóði	offer
bjór	beer
björgum	rocks
björn	bear
bjúgviðum	bent-tree
blæða	bleed
blæja	Blaeja (a name)
blæju	Blaeja (a place)
blár	black-and-blue, blue
blása	blaze
blásit	blown
bleika	dark
bleikr	pale
blés	blew
bleyta	softened
blíðr	happy, pleased
blíðum	gentle
bliku	shimmering
blóð	blood
blóðbogi	blood-gush
blóði	blood, bloodied
blóðrefilinn	sword-point
blóðvali	blood-falcons
blót	sacrifices
blótat	sacrificed-to
blótim	sacrifice
blótin	sacrificed-to
blótinn	sacrificed

Old Norse	English	Old Norse	English
blótmaðr	a-sacrificing-man	borghlið	city-side
blótskap	sorcery	borgin	the-city
blótskapr	sorcery	borgina	borg, city, the-city
blótstaðr	sacrificial-places	borginni	the-city, the-city-walls
blótum	sacrifice		
boð	bid, invitation, invite, to-ask	borgir	cities, city
		borgundarholmi	Bornholm (a place)
böðheggr	offered-tree	borin	brought
boði	announced, asked, bringer, orders	borinn	born, brought, carried
böðmána	bathing-moon	börn	children
boga	bow	bornir	borne
bogamynd	bow-shape	bóta	compensation
bogastreng	bow-string	brá	drew, prepared, startled
bogi	bow		
böl	affliction, lair	bráð	meat
bolgaralandi	Bulgar-Land (a place)	bráðast	quickly
		bráðgerr	matured, quick
bör	bore	bráðir	prey
borð	board, table, tables	bráðr	haste
börðu	beat	bráðrakinn	hastening
börðust	battled, fought, thought	bræddak	melt
		bræddum	molten
borg	borg, city, the-city	bræðr	brothers, the-brothers
borga	city		
borgar	borg, city	bræðra	brothers, the-brothers
borgarhjört	Fortress-Hart (a name)	bræðrna	brothers
borgarhjörtr	Fortress-Hart (a name)	bræðrum	brothers, the-brothers
borgarhlið	city-gates	brækr	breeches
borgarinnar	the-city, the-townspeople	bragarfulli	declaration
		bragði	looking, taste
borgarmanna	townspeople	bragna	hero, heroes
borgarmenn	the-townspeople, townspeople	bragnar	heroes
		brandagný	blades-clash
borgarmönnum	townspeople	brandahjört	sword-hart
borgarveggi	city-wall, city-walls, the-city-walls	brandr	Brand (a name)
		brandrauðum	fiery-red
borgarveggina	the-city-walls	brást	startled, transformed
borgarveggir	city-walls	brátt	soon
borgarveggja	city-walls	brauð	bread
borgarvídd	city-wide	brauðit	the-bread
borghildar	Borghild (a name)		

Old Norse	English
braut	away, broke, brought, divided
brávelli	Bravellir (a place)
bregða	foreclose, unbelievable
bregðr	react, shocked, tricked
breiða	spread, widely
breiddi	broad
brenna	burn, burned, let
brenndu	burned
bresta	burst
breyta	bring, change
breytni	conduct
breytt	changed
brim	surf
brjósk	cartilage
brjósti	breast
brjóstum	breast, breasts
brjóta	break, broke, brought
brjótr	breaks
bróðir	brother, brother-of
bróður	brother
bróðursonr	brother's-son
brögð	trick, tricks
brögðum	strategy, tricks
brögnum	trickery
bröndum	burning, firewood, sword, swords
brotit	burned
brotnar	broken
brott	away, brought, out, to-away
brúði	bride
brúðlaup	a-wedding-feast, wedding, wedding-feast
brugðit	appeared, brought, brought-out, custom
brullaup	wedding, wedding-feast
brún	brown
brúna	brow, brown
brúnstein	brow-stones
brúnsteina	brow-stones
brúnsteinum	brow-stones
brygði	react
brynhildar	Brynhild (a name)
brynhildi	Brynhild (a name)
brynhildr	Brynhild (a name)
brynju	armour
brynjur	armour, shield
brytja	cut-up
brýtr	broke, divided, wrecked
bú	a-farm, dwelling, estate, farm, settlement
búa	dwell, dwelt, he, homes, laid, live, prepare, prepared, settle, to dwell, to live, to prepare
búast	prepare, prepared, settle, stay
búðir	booths
buðla	Budli (a name)
buðladóttur	Daughter-of-Budla (a name)
buðlungi	king
buðu	invited, offered
búin	done, prepared, readied, ready
búinn	prepared, prepared-with, ready
búit	be-prepared, dwelling, dwelt, lived, preparations, prepared, ready, settled, settlement, to-settle
búna	prepared
búnaði	clothing, dress
búnar	prepared
bundu	bound
búnir	prepared, preparing, ready, readying
burðarmenn	bearer-men

Old Norse	English
burir	sons
búum	estates
búumst	prepare
byði	invite
býðr	invite, invited, offer
byggð	settlement
bygghlaða	barley-barn
byggja	colonise, settle, settlement
byggvir	settles
býjar	estate, farm, the-estate
byr	fair-wind, wind
byrði	a-bundle, burden
byri	fair-wind, wind
byrja	brings-about
byrjuð	brought
byrla	pour
býst	prepared

C, c

D, d

Old Norse	English
dæið	dead
dælt	easy, genteel
dæmi	deem, examples
dag	day
daga	days
dagan	day
daginn	day, days, the-day
dagr	day
dagrýrir	day-diminishing
dags	dag's, day, day's, in-the-day
dal	valley
dana	The-Danes
danaást	Danes'-Beloved (a name)
danaherr	Danish-Army
danaveldi	Danish-Realm (a place)
danir	Danes, Danish, The-Danes
danmarkar	Denmark (a place)
danmarkarbót	Denmark's-Benefit (a name, poetic)
danmörk	Denmark (a place)
danmörku	Denmark (a place)
danski	Dane
danskri	Danish
dauða	dead, death, the-dead, the-death-of
dauðadags	death-day
dauðan	dead, death
dauðdaga	death-day
dauði	death
dauðir	dead, died
dauðr	dead, death
dauðs	dead, death
degi	day
deili	parts
deyja	dead, die, i-die, to-die
deyr	die, dies
dínu	Danube (a place)
dísir	Disir (a name)
djarfliga	boldly
djöfuls	Devil's (a name)
dó	died
dœgr	days
dofrafjalls	Dovrefjell (a place)
dögg	dew
döglinga	Of-The-Dead (a name)
dögum	days
dögurðar	day's-meal
dönum	Danes, The-Danes
dóttir	daughter, daughter of, daughter-of, the-daughter, the-daughter-of

Old Norse	English
dóttur	daughter, daughter-of
drægi	drew
drægir	drawn
dræpi	killed
draga	carry, drawn, drew
drakk	drank
drap	killed
drápu	drapa, killed
drápuð	killed
dregin	drawn
dregit	drawn
dregr	drew
dregst	drawn
dreif	scattered, scattering
dreifðist	dispersed
drekka	drank, drink, drinking, drink-to
drekkir	drink
drekkum	we-drink
dreng	fellow
drengiliga	bravely, fellow-like
drengir	warriors
drengja	fellow, fellows
drengjamóður	mother-of-warriors
drengr	fellow
drengs	warriors
drep	kill
drepa	kill, killed, kill-you, to kill
drepin	killed
drepit	killed, taken
dreyra	blood
dreyrug	bloody
drifinn	driven
drjúgr	substantial
drógu	drew
drottning	the-queen
drukkinn	drunk
drukkit	drank-to, drink, drunk
drykk	drank, draught, drink

Old Norse	English
drykki	drank
drykkja	drink
drykkju	drinking
drykkjumaðr	drinking-man
duga	aided, help
dugðu	enough
dugi	could, enough, good
dvaldist	dwelled
dveljast	dwell
dyggligast	most-virtuous
dýja	beast
dyn	storm
dýr	wild-animals
dýri	dear
dýrlig	dear
dýrligan	dear
dýrligu	dear
dyrr	the-doors
dýrra	dearer
dýrs	dear
dýrum	wild-animals

Ð, ð

E, e

Old Norse	English
eða	and, but, either, of, or
ef	as, if, maybe, of, whether
efna	carried-out, carry-out
efni	matter, prospect, prospects, the-matter
efra	ever, over
efstr	uppermost
eggja	encourage, encouragement
eggjan	encouragement

Old Norse	English
eggjar	edges, encouraged
eggjuðu	egged
egill	egil
eiða	oath
eiga	had, have, marriage, marry, own, owned, owning, owns, said-of, to own
eigi	alone, did-not, no, none, no-one, not, not, not-be, not-of, not-to, only, owned, was-not
eignast	own
eigu	our-own, own, owned
eigum	any, own
ein	1, one (feminine, nominative), a, alone, along, an, only, same
eina	1, one (feminine, accusative), a, as-one, only
einarðr	determined
einir	1, one, alone, only
einkar	especially, very
einkis	no, nothing
einn	1, one (masculine, accusative), 1, one (masculine, nominative), a, alone, an
einnar	1, one (feminine, genitive)
einnhvern	someone
einnhverr	any-of, one-of
einni	1, one (feminine, dative), alone
eins	1, one (masculine, genitive), 1, one (neuter, genitive), a, alone, as, likewise, one's
einu	1, one (neuter, dative), a, only, same
einum	1, one (masculine, dative), a, alone, any, to-one
einvaldskonungr	sole-ruling-king
einvígi	duel
eireki	Erik (a name)
eirekr	Eirek (a name)
eireks	Erik (a name)
eiríki	Erik (a name)
eiríkr	Erik (a name)
eitrfullir	poison-full
eitrhvass	envenomed
eitri	venom
eitt	1, one (neuter, accusative), 1, one (neuter, nominative), a, alone, along, an, once, only, single
eitthvert	once, some, something, some-time
ek	i, i-am
ekki	no, none, not, nothing, not-to
ekkils	Ekkil (a name)
ekkju	widow
eld	a-fire, fire
eldi	fire
eldinn	a-fire, the-fire
eldr	fire, flame
ella	Ælla (a name), or, other, otherwise
ellidauðr	old-age-died
elligar	or
ellri	elder
ellstr	oldest, the-oldest
ellu	Ælla (a name)
elr	gave-birth-to, nourishes, raised
em	am

Old Norse	English
en	about, and, as, before, but, but-for, except, in, of, than, that, the, then, though, when, where, which, while
enda	and yet, an-end, complete, conclude, end, ended, ending, in-the-end, it-concluded
endemi	unheard-of
endemlig	strange
endils	Endil's (a name)
enga	any, no, none, not, only
engan	no, none
engar	no, none
engi	no, no one, none, none-of, no-one, not, nothing
engir	none
engis	none
england	England (a place)
englandi	England (a place)
englands	England (a place)
englanes	Englanes (a place)
engrar	no-more, not
engu	none, not, nothing
engum	no, none
enn	but, it, still, then, was, yet
enskir	English
eptir	after, afterwards, back, behind, died

Old Norse	English
er	a, am, am-i, and, are, as, at, be, being, but, for, had, has, have, he, i, if, in, is, is-it, it, it-is, it-was, let-be, of, of-which, out, spoke, than, that, that-was, the, then, this, to, to-be, until, was, were, what, when, where, which, while, who, whose, who-was, with
erendi	business, errand, errands
erendis	errand, errands
erendum	errand, errands
erfi	inheritance
erfingja	heirs
ermar	sleeves
ert	are, your
eru	are, are-we, is, they, they-were, was, we-are, were, were-they
eruð	are
erum	are, are-we, we-are
es	as, was, were, when, where, which, who
esat	glowing
eski	box
eskinu	the-box
eskit	the-box
eta	eat
etja	provoke
eyða	devastated
eyddi	devastated
eyddist	devastated
eyddu	devastated
eyðimerkr	deserted-forest
eygotaland	Eygotaland (a place)
eyland	island, islands
eynæfis	Eynaefi's (a name)

Old Norse	English	Old Norse	English
eyrasundi	Eyrasundi (a place)	færr	capable
eyri	island	fæst	few
eystein	Eystein (a name)	fætr	feet
eysteini	Eystein (a name)	fáfnisbana	Slayer-of-Fafnir (a name)
eysteinn	Eystein (a name)	fagna	celebrated, rejoice, welcome, welcomed
eysteins	Eystein (a name)		
eytt	devastated	fagnaðaröl	celebrations, toasts
		fagnaði	celebrated, got, received

É, é

		fagnat	welcomed
éli	hail	fagra	fair, fairness
ér	is, that, were	fagran	beautiful
		fagrt	beautiful, fair, fairly

F, f

		fái	get, give
		fáim	get
		fáir	few, marry
fá	be, few, get, get-for, gets, give, got, have, marry, obtain, pay, to get, to obtain	fall	fall, fallen, falling
		falla	fall, fell
		falli	fall, fell
		fallinn	fall, fallen
faðir	father, father-of, fathers, father-to	fálu	hid
		fám	few, get
fáðir	went-they	fann	found
fæ	get	far	go, travel
fæða	bear, brought, feed, foster, give-birth	fár	few, have, malice
		fara	faring, go, going, journey, sent, to go, to travel, to-go, to-travel, travel, traveling, travelled, travelling, went
fæddi	bore, raised		
fæðslu	food		
fæðu	little		
fær	accomplish, accomplished, affected, can, could, did, gets, go, goes, got		
		fararinnar	of-the-journey
		fari	fare, go, goes, going, passage, take, travel, travelling, went
færa	be-brought, bring, brought, less, take, to-do		
		farin	gone
færðr	brought	farinn	travelled, travelling
færðu	carried, went	farit	fare, fared, going, gone, travel, travelled, went
færi	bring, brought, going, journey, opportunity, went		
		farmóðr	travel-weary
færir	brought	farnir	travelled

Old Norse	English	Old Norse	English
fast	close, fast, tightly	ferð	go, journey, travel, travelled, travelling, trip, voyage
fasta	fasted		
fastgarðr	stronghold		
fátæka	poor	ferðar	go, journey, to-journey, travel, voyage
fátæki	poverty, wealthiness		
fátt	few, little		
fé	cattle, fee, liquidity, livestock, money, movable wealth, pay, wealth	ferðinni	to-travel, travelling
		ferðum	voyage, voyages
		ferlíki	monstrous
		ferr	away, goes, journeyed, journeys, travel, travelled, went
fébætr	compensation		
feðr	father, fathers		
fegnir	celebrated		
fegrð	beauty, fairness	ferst	left, travelled
fegrst	fair, fairest, finest	fertugr	40, forty
fegrstr	fairest	festast	fastened
féhirði	fee-servant	festi	fastened, joined, to-propose
feigri	cower		
feigum	doomed	festum	promised-for
feitaðir	fattened	fimm	5, five, give
fekk	gave, got, married	fimmtán	15, fifteen
fekkst	found-is, got	fingi	getting
fékostnaðr	fee-costly	fingum	fingers, got, grasp, grasped, won
fell	fell, mountain, slaying		
		finna	find, found, to find, to-find, to-meet
fella	fell, felled		
felldi	fell, shed	finnast	encountered, found, meet-up
felli	falling, fell, rising		
fellingum	joints	finnst	finding, found
fellr	falls, fell	fira	burning, people's
fellt	fell	firr	far, forwards, further
fengi	get, got	fiski	fish, fishing
fengin	get	fjallinu	a-mountain
fengit	caught, found, got, had	fjár	finances, wealth
		fjarri	away, far, far-away
fengu	caught, gathered, got, held	fjöld	full-many
		fjölda	many
fengust	got-they	fjölmenn	many-people, populous
fer	go, goes, going, travel, travelled, went		
		fjölmenni	followers, many
		fjölmennis	the-crowd

Old Norse	English
fjölmennr	followers, full-many, many-men, numerous, well attended
fjölmenns	crowd
fjölnis	Fjolnir's (a name)
fjölrætt	discussed
fjóra	4, four (masculine, accusative)
fjörbrotum	death-throes
fjórði	4th, fourth
fjörðum	fields
fjórtán	14, fourteen
fjórum	4, four (feminine, dative), 4, four (masculine, dative), 4, four (neuter, dative)
flæmingja	Flemings' (a name)
flátt	craftily, lies
flaug	flown
fleinþings	lance-meeting
fleira	many, more, other
fleiri	more
flest	almost, most
flestir	most, mostly
flestum	most
fletta	stripped
flettr	stripped
flótta	extravagant, flee
flóttann	fleeing, to-escape
flugdreki	flight-dragon
flugu	flew
flutti	brought
fluttu	floated, moved
flýðu	fled
flýgr	flew, flies
flýja	fled, flee, fleeing
flýr	fled
flytr	advanced
föður	father, father's
föðurbróðir	father-brother
föðurgjöld	father-payment
fogli	birds
fögr	beautiful, fair, of-fair
fögru	fair
foldar	folds, on-land
fólk	folk, men
folka	folk
fólkit	folk
folkorrostur	folk-battles
föngum	provisions
fór	came, comes, do, fared, forwards, journeyed, returned, travelled, travelling, went
för	before, going, journey, voyage
forellrismenn	ancestors
forlögum	fortune
formaðr	chief, commander
formenn	leaders
fornan	old
fornir	old
fóru	before, travel, travelled, travelling, went
fórum	travelled, travelling
förunaut	companionship
forvitni	curiosity, curious
forvitri	for-knowing
fóstra	foster, foster-child, foster-father
fóstraði	fostered
fóstru	foster
föt	clothing
fótgulum	feet-gold
fótum	feet
frá	apart-from, away, away-from, from, from-there, of, time
frægð	fame
frægðar	fame
frægðarmark	birth-mark

Old Norse	English
frægðarverk	famous-work
frægir	famous
frægr	famous
frægri	more-famous
frægstr	famous
frægt	fame
fræknleik	bravery
frækrligast	the-braver
fræknustu	bravest
frændr	kinsman, kinsmen
frák	speared
frakkland	france
fram	ahead, forth, forward, forwards, from, from-forward, from-going, going-forward, towards
framan	in-front-of
framar	above, from
framast	foremost, furthest
framðar	performed
framm	forward, from
framvís	fore-knowing
fránan	from
fránir	flashing
frásögn	from-saying, said
fregit	news
freistat	tried
frekum	eager
frelsti	freed
fremr	from
fremri	foremost
frerin	frozen
frétt	news
frétta	heard-news
fréttir	news
fréttum	news
freyr	Freyr (a name)
freys	Frey's (a name)
fríðastr	handsome, most-handsome
friði	peace

Old Norse	English
fríðir	handsome
friðr	beautiful, love, peace
fríðust	most-beautiful, the-most-beautiful
frilluborna	bastard-born
fritt	peace
fróði	Frodi (a name)
frost	frost, frosted
frýðu	withstood-us
frýja	refuse
fuglar	birds
fullan	full
fullgott	full-good
fullting	assistance, help
fullu	full
fund	find, meet, meeting, to-meet, visit
fundar	meet
fundinn	found
fundna	funda
fundu	found
fundum	meeting
fundust	found, met, were-found
furða	a-wonder, fury
furðu	surprisingly
fylgdi	follow, followed
fylgdum	followed
fylgi	follow, followed, follows
fylgir	followed, following, follows
fylgja	follow, to-follow
fylgjum	follow
fylgt	followed
fylking	the-ranks
fylkingar	flanks, ranks, the-ranks
fylkingu	the-ranks
fylkingum	ranks, the-king
fylkir	command
fylkja	rallied

Old Norse	English
fylkt	mustered
fylli	fill
fyndi	found
fyr	before, for, for-the
fyrðar	warriors
fyrir	ahead, ahead-of, along, and, at, at-hand, because, because-of, because-of-a, before, before-them, before-us, by, for, foremost, for-the, from, in-front-of, present, therefore, they, to
fyrirætlan	before-intentions, for-intentions, intentions
fyrirrúm	first
fyrr	before, for, the-before, until
fyrri	before, for, former, go-before
fyrrum	before
fyrst	first
fyrsta	first
fyrstr	first, first-of, foremost
fyrstu	first
fýsumk	face

G, g

Old Norse	English
gáðu	heeded, looked
gærkveld	last-night
gæta	guard, guarded
gæti	got, to-guard
gætti	guarded
gaf	gave, given, was-given, were-given
gafta	gave
gáfu	gave
gagn	benefit, of-use, won
gagni	of-use
gagns	benefit, need
gall	bellowed
galtar	boar
gamall	old
gaman	a-game, delight, enjoyed, enjoyment, joy, joyed, joys
gamli	old
gamlir	old
gand	wand
ganga	go, going, go-they, to go, to walk, to-come, to-go, walk, walking, went
gangi	go, going, went
gatk	get
gátu	got
gátum	got-we
gaukr	cuckoo
gaum	heed
gautland	Gautland (a place)
gautlandi	Götaland (a place)
gautlands	Götaland (a place)
geðsligr	engaging
geðsligra	pleasing
gefa	gave, gift, give, to give, to-give
gefast	give
gefi	gave, give
gefin	be-given, given, married, marry
gefinn	be-given, gave
gefir	give
gefit	give, given
gefnir	given
gefr	are-given, gave, give, given, gives, were-given
gegn	against
gegna	going
gegnir	served

Old Norse	English
gegnt	opposite, straight
gegnum	through
gein	yawn
geira	spear, spears
geirnagla	spear-nail
geirr	spears
geirtré	spear-tree
geitr	goats
gekk	go, goes, going, got, walked, went
gellr	bellow, bellowed
geng	walking
gengit	go, gone, went
gengr	go, goes, going, happens, it-goes, to-go, went
gengu	going, went
ger	do, had-done, made, make
gera	be, be-done, be-made, did, do, done, get, have, made, make, send, to do, to make, to-do
gerast	be, will-be
gerða	made
gerði	did, done, gave, had-done, made, was, went
gerðist	became, became-a, becoming, happened, made, made-he
gerðu	did, made, make, was, went
gerir	did, does, made, makes
gerist	became, was
gerla	completely
gerr	done, made, willing
gersamliga	altogether
gersimar	precious
gersimum	jewels
gerst	done, made, to-do

Old Norse	English
gert	be, do, done, made, was, was-done
gervallir	all
gervar	skilled
gervir	made
get	can, do, get, guess
geti	could, mentioned
geysingi	forcefulness
geyst	rushed
gift	married
gifta	gift, give
gifti	gave
gin	jaws
gingu	going
gingum	going, gone
girnd	lust
gisting	guested
gjalfri	gifts, given
gjalla	scream, snorting, sounded
gjarn	willing
glaðr	be-glad, glad, gladly
glæp	a-crime
glöddu	glad
glumði	roared
gnípafirði	Gnipafjord (a place)
gnóga	abundance
gnótt	abundance
gný	rage
gnyðja	grumble
gnýinn	the-din
gnýr	a-din, din, the-noise
goð	god, gods, good
góð	good
góðr	a-good, good
goðum	the-gods
gögnum	use
góinn	goinn
gollhroðinn	cry-thrown
golli	gold
gömul	an-old, old

Old Norse	English
gormr	Gorm (a name)
gorms	Gorm (a name)
góz	property
gotna	men
gott	a-good, benefit, benefited, good
gráðr	hunger
grætr	weep
grafa	engrave
grafvitnis	ground-wolf
gram	warriors
grána	grey
grand	hurt
granda	injure, to-injure
grandi	injury
granni	neighbour
gránserk	grey-shirt
gránu	grey
gráti	tears
grenjaði	howled
grenjuðu	roared
grét	crying, wept
grið	mercy
griðum	safe-conduct
gríma	Grima (a name)
grimmd	cruelty
grimmleik	savagery
grimmliga	fiercely
grimmligu	fearful
grimmr	Grim (a name)
grimt	fiercely
grímu	Grima (a name)
grísir	piglets, the-piglets
grjót	gravel, rock
grön	green, moustache
grundar	ground
grundvöll	foundations
guðröðar	Gudrod's (a name)
guðröðr	Gudrod (a name)
guðþorm	Gudthorm (a name)
guðþormr	Godthorm (a name)

Old Norse	English
guðvefjarpell	fine-cloth
gull	gold
gullhring	gold-ring
gulli	gold
gullinu	gold
gullit	gold, the-gold
gullsaumaðr	gold-embroidered
gumna	men, men's
gusti	gusts
gyltan	sow
gyrðr	girded

H, h

Old Norse	English
há	high
haðaberserkr	Hadeland-Berserk (a place, a nickname)
haðaland	Hadeland (a place)
háðum	depending, mock
hæð	height
hæfi	has
hæfir	fits, had
hægri	right
hægt	possible
hæklings	Sons-of-Haekling (a name)
hæstr	high
hætt	end, ended, risked
hætta	concluded, danger, dared, end, leave, risk, the-danger
hætti	stop, way, ways
haf	have, sea, the-sea
hafa	at-sea, had, has, have, have-been, having, sea, they, to have, to-have, to-sea
hafast	have

Old Norse	English
hafði	had, had-been, has, have, he, held, married, that-had
hafi	had, has, have, sea
hafið	have
hafim	have
hafinn	raised, started
hafinu	the-sea
hafir	have
hafna	forsake, harbour, wary
hafnar	harbour, wary
hafnat	abandoned
hafs	sea
haft	had, have
hag	benefit, circumstances
hagleik	sports, the-strength
hagliga	skilfully
haglkorn	hailstone
haka	Haka (a name)
haki	Haki (a name)
hal	man, man's
halda	have, held, hold, holding, keep, to hold
haldast	held, hold
haldim	keep
haldit	held, hold, stayed
haldorða	held-words
hálfan	half
hálfdan	Halfdan (a name)
halland	halland
hallandi	halland
hallar	hall
hallargólfinu	the-hall-floor
hallir	halls
háls	hills, neck
hálsi	neck
halsum	neck
hálu	giantess's
hamðis	Hamdir's (a name)

Old Norse	English
hamri	hammer
hana	he, her, hers, it, she, she-is, she-was, that, to-her
handa	hand
handastaðinn	hand-print
handtekinn	captured, hand-taken
hann	from-him, had, he, he, health, he-is, held, here, he-was, him, himself, his, it, she, to-him, was
hans	he, him, his, to-him
hánum	he, him, his
hár	hair, has
harald	harald
haraldr	harald
haralds	harald
háram	the-hairy-side
harða	hard, roughly
harðfengi	toughness
harðfengnir	brave, war-taken
harðfengr	hardy
harðfengt	tough
harðger	hardy, strongly-built
harðla	hard, very
harðliga	hard
harðmeldr	hard-melding
harðr	hard
hárek	harek
hárfagra	Hair-Fair (a name)
hárfagran	Fair-Haired (a name)
hárfagri	Hair-Fair (a name)
hárham	the-hairy-side
hárit	hair
harmi	grief
harmr	grief, harm
harpa	harp
hársíma	hair-strands
hart	rough, roughly

Old Norse	English
hásætit	high-seat, the-high-seat
háseymða	high-seeing
hata	hate
hatar	hates
hátt	high, loud, loudly, way
haug	mound
hauka	hawks
haukr	hawks
hauksnöru	hawk-snare
hausa	skulls
haustit	autumn
hausum	head
heðan	from-here, hence
heðins	Hedin's (a name)
hefði	had, have, would-have-been
hefðir	have
hefi	had, have
hefik	had, have-i
hefir	did, had, had-it, has, have, have-you, holds
hefja	begin, have
hefk	have
heflis	Heflir's (a name)
hefna	avenge, revenge
hefnd	revenge
hefnda	revenge
hefndina	revenge
hefnið	revenge
hefnt	had, revenge
hefr	had, has, have
hegning	punishment
hegningar	punished
heiðan	clearing
heiðar	heath's
heiðir	high
heiðit	heathen
heiðmörk	Heidmark (a place)
heilagri	hallowed
heilan	healing
heill	a-whole, hail, healthy, luck, safely, whole
heilsar	greeted
heilug	holy
heim	home, homes, households, to home, towards home
heima	at-home, home, homes
heiman	from-home, home
heimanfylgja	home-following
heimdregi	home-drawn
heimi	heimir
heimir	heimir
heimis	Heimir's (a name)
heimsala	world
heimsins	of-the-world
heimtum	fastened
heit	named, pledge
heita	be named, be-named, name, name, named, named, to be named, to name, to-be-named
heiti	am-named, name, named, named
heitim	promising
heitinn	be-named, named, named
heitir	is-named, named, named, named-are
heitit	named, naming, the-name
heitr	hot
heitt	hot
heitu	brewed
heldi	held, hold, kept
heldr	advanced, behind, behold, held, heldr's, hold, rather, took

Old Norse	English
heldu	busy, held
heldum	than
helga	Helga (a name), holy
helgi	Helgi (a name)
helju	hel
hellti	poured
helsingja	helsings
helt	held
hélt	held
hendi	arm, hand, his-hand, to-hand
hendr	caught, hand, hands
hengu	hung
hennar	for-her, her, hers, she, to-her
henni	he, her, hers, him, she, to-her
her	an-army, army, a-war-band, the-forces, war, warband, war-band
hér	forces, here, she
herbergis	room
herbúðir	war-booths, war-camp
herða	shoulders
herfangi	raiding
herferð	war-voyage
herför	raiding, warfare, war-going
herinum	the-forces
herja	army, harry, harrying, wage-war
herjans	Herjan's (a name)
herjat	harried, raided
herjuðu	raided, raiding
herklæði	war-clothes
herliðs	a-war-band
hermaðr	warrior, warrior-man
hermenn	war-men
hermönnum	forces
hernað	raiding
hernaði	raiding

Old Norse	English
hernaðr	harrying
herópi	war-cry
herr	army, a-war-band, band, warband, war-band
herra	lord
herrauðr	Herraud (a name)
herrinn	harrying
herrøðr	Herrod (a name)
herruðr	Herrud (a name)
hers	army, war
hersaga	news-of-war
hersins	army-theirs
herskátt	invasion
herskildi	raiding, separated, separately, war-shields
herskipa	a-warship
herskipum	ships
hersögu	war-declaration
herþjófi	herthjof
hesta	horses
hesti	horse, horses
hestum	horses
hét	man, named, promised, names, was, was-named, was-named
héti	named
hétu	named, named, pledged
heygðr	buried
heyja	conducted, fight
heyra	be-heard, hear, heard
heyrða	heard
heyrði	heard
heyrðu	hear, heard
heyri	hear, hears
heyrir	depended-on, heard
hildar	battle
hildi	battle
hildibrandr	Hildibrand (a name)

Old Norse	English
hildingar	princes
hilditönn	wartooth
hildr	battle
hilmi	helm, prince
hingat	here, there
hinn	he, him, in, of, other, the, the other, then, this-one
hinns	his
hins	the, this
hirðik	wearing
hirðina	guardsmen
hirðir	cared, hid
hirðmenn	the-guardsmen
hitnaði	heated
hitt	encounter, find, found, it, meet, meeting, other, they
hitta	meet, met, to-meet
hittast	found, meet, met
hittir	hits, met
hittist	met
hittust	found, met
hjá	beside, by, heard, near, nearby
hjaðninga	Hjadninga (a name)
hjala	to-talk
hjalar	talked
hjaldri	battle
hjalm	helmet
hjálm	helmet
hjalma	helmets, helms
hjálma	helms
hjalmi	helmet
hjalms	helms
hjalmstofn	helm-staves
hjarna	brain
hjarta	heart, the-heart
hjartat	the-heart
hjó	hewed, struck
hjoggum	struck
hjöltunum	hilt
hjörtr	hart, the-hart
hjörtu	hearts
hjörvi	sword, swords
hjúpu	covering
hjúskaparfar	marital-status
hlakkar	screaming
hlaupa	leap, ran, run, to leap, to run
hlaupi	running
hleiðru	Lejre (a place)
hleypr	ran
hlið	the-sides
hlíf	protection
hlífa	protected
hljóð	listen, silence, sound
hljóðs	be-heard
hlunnalungum	roller-warships
hlunni	the-rollers
hlunnroð	rollers-red
hlupu	ran, running
hlut	less, loot, lot, part, share
hluta	lot, lots, part, part's, parts-of
hluti	part-of, parts, things
hlutr	lot, part, part of, thing
hlýða	listen, obey
hlymdölum	Hlymdal (a place)
hlýr	bow, covering
hné	knee, knees, knelt, sank
hneftafli	a-gaming-table
hneit	struck
hníga	kneeled, kneeling, sink
hniginn	declined, declining
höfða	headland, hofda, hofdi, hofud
höfðaströnd	Hofdastrond (a place)
höfði	head, heads, to-have

Old Norse	English
höfðingi	chief, chieftain, leader, the-chief
höfðinginn	the-chieftain
höfðingja	chieftain, chieftains, chieftans
höfðingjalaust	leader-less
höfðingjar	chieftains
höfðingjum	chiefs, chieftains
höfðu	had, had-they, have, heads, owned
höfðum	heads
höfðust	had
höfn	harbour
höfuð	hand, head, heads
höfuðit	head
höfuðsteypu	head-tumbled
höfum	have
högg	striking
höggr	hewed, hews
höggum	blows
höggva	blow, break, fell, strike, striking, to blow, to strike
höggvins	struck-off
höggvit	struck
högna	Hogni (a name)
hold	bodies, body
hölda	flesh
hölða	hold
holdrosu	the-fleshy-side
höll	hall
höllina	the-hall
höllu	hall, halls, the-hall, tilted
höllunni	the-hall
hönd	arm, hand
höndina	hand
höndum	hand, handed, hands
honum	he, her, him, himself, his, in-him, she, to-him, to-him-of, with-him

Old Norse	English
hörð	hard
hörða-knút	Harthacnut (a name)
hörða-knútr	Harthacnut (a name)
horfðu	looked
horfit	turned
horn	horn
horni	horn
hornum	horns
hörpu	harp
hörpuna	harp, the-harp
hörpunnar	the-harp
hörpunni	harp, the-harp
horskum	the-wise
hörund	skin
hött	a-hood
höttr	hood
höttu	hoods
hráblauta	raw-wet
hraðast	fastest
hræ	corpses
hræra	move
hræsíldar	corpse-fish
hrafn	Hrafn (a name)
hrafni	Hrafn (a name)
hrafns	Hrafn (a name)
hrannir	waves
hratt	fast, quickly
hraustleik	bravery
hreggský	clouds
hress	well
hreysti	valour
hríð	awhile, time, while
hríðar	storm
hrindum	early
hring	a-ring, ring
hringa	rings
hringaríki	ringerike
hringinn	the-ring
hringleginn	ring-like
hringr	hring
hrings	hring

Old Norse	English
hringssonar	Son-of-Hring (a name)
hríslu	perch
hristir	shaking, shook
hroðinn	stripped
hrøkkvit	draw-back
hrolla	shiver
hrunði	collapsed
hrundit	heaped
hrundu	raised
hrygg	spine, the-spine
hrygginum	the-spine
hrytr	snoring
húðina	hide, the-skin
húf	hull
hug	mind, think, thought, thoughts
hugat	thought
hugblauðum	thought-cowardly
hugða	affections, mind
hugðak	thought
hugði	thought
hugðist	thought
hugðu	thought
hugðum	thought
hugr	mind, minds, thought
hún	her, here, is-she, it, she, she-is, she-was, that-she, to-her
hund	dog
hundinn	the-dog
hundmargan	100-many, hundred-many
hundmörgum	countless
hundrað	120, one hundred and twenty (a 'long hundred') (neuter, accusative, singular), 120, one hundred and twenty (a 'long hundred') (neuter, nominative, singular)
hundrinn	the-dog
hundruð	120, one hundred and twenty (a 'long hundred') (neuter, accusative, plural), 120, one hundred and twenty (a 'long hundred') (neuter, nominative, plural)
hundruðum	120, one hundred and twenty (a 'long hundred') (neuter, dative, plural)
hungri	hunger
hús	house, houses
húsa	for-lodgings, houses
húsfreyja	housewife, the-lady-of-the-house
húsgangs	house-going
húsinu	the-house
húsit	the-house
húss	houses, the-house
hústó	husto
húsum	house
hvaðan	from-where, where
hvaðarr	where
hvar	everywhere, where, wherever
hvár	each
hvarf	broke-away, disappeared
hváriga	whichever
hvárir	each
hvárirtveggju	either-side
hvárki	neither
hvarmatúni	eyelids-enclosure
hvárr	each, where, which, which (of two), which two?, who, who (of two)
hvart	whether
hvárt	each, either, however, if, is, whether
hvárttveggja	each-way, either

Old Norse	English
hvárumtveggjum	each-way, either-way
hvarvetna	everywhere
hvass	sharp
hvassa	harsh
hvassi	the-keen
hvassir	sharp
hvast	hiss
hvat	how, that, what, whatever
hváta	urge
hvati	the-swift
hvé	how, how-to
hveðnu	fishes
hvell	sharp
hver	each, each-of, every, how, what, who, whose
hverfa	disappear, turn, turn-back, turned
hvergi	each, either, neither, nowhere
hverir	who, why
hverja	each, what
hverjan	each
hverju	each, every, how
hverjum	any, each, each-of, every, whether, which, who
hvern	each, every, how, what, which, who, whom
hverr	each, every, every-man, to-each, watch, what, which, who, who?
hverrar	each, how-so, whose
hvers	each, how, what, which, whose
hversu	how, how so, how-so, what
hvert	any, each, what, where, wherever, which
hvetvetna	whatever
hví	what, why
hvíli	rest
hvítabæ	Hvitabaer (a place)
hvítabær	Hvitabaer (a place)
hvítar	white
hvítserk	Hvitserk (a name)
hvítserki	Hvitserk (a name)
hvítserkr	Hvitserk (a name)
hvítum	white
hygg	mind, think
hyggja	observed, think, thought, thoughts
hyggjum	let-us-think, think
hyggr	considered, looked, think, thinks, thought, wondered, worries

I, i

Old Norse	English
iðju	occupation
iðnar	trade
ill	ill
illa	a-bad, bad, badly, evil, ill, wicked, wickedly
illgjarn	ill-doing, ill-tempered
illilig	ill-like
illr	bad, difficult, ill, of-ill
illt	disorderly, harm, ill
illu	evil
ilt	difficulty, hard
in	in, the
ina	the, these
ingasonar	Son-of-Ingi (a name)
ingibjörg	Ingibjorg (a name)
ingjaldssonar	Son-of-Ingjald (a name)
inir	the, those

Old Norse	English
inn	a, he, in, inside, of, that, the, then, this
inna	the
innan	in, inside, to, within
innanlands	inner-lands
innar	beside, closer, inside, the
inndyris-eyju	Inndyr's-Island (a place)
inni	in, inside, of-the, the
inniligast	deepest
ins	the
inum	in, the
it	the, these, those, to
ivarr	Ivar (a name)

Í, í

Old Norse	English
í	a, about, all, among, as, at, by, his, i, if, in, into, is, it, lived-at, of, on, out, so, that, the, this, to, with
íhugar	thought
íra	irish
írlandi	Ireland (a place)
ís	ice
ísinn	ice
íþróttir	sports
íþróttum	accomplished
ívar	Ivar (a name)
ívari	Ivar (a name)
ívarr	Ivar (a name)
ívars	Ivar (a name)
ívu	Iva (a name)

J, j

Old Norse	English
jafnan	equal, equally, evenly, ever, usually
jafnast	equal
jafnfrægir	equal-famous
jafngamlir	equal-age
jafngerla	equally
jafnilla	equally
jafningi	equal
jafningjar	equal
jafnlengd	the-same-time
jafnmikill	equal-great
jafnt	equal, equally, evenly
jafnvæn	equally
jafnvæna	equal
jarðar	earth, earth's
jarl	an-earl, earl, jarl, the-earl
jarla	earls
jarli	earl, the-earl
jarlinn	earl, the-earl
jarls	earl, earl's, jarl, jarl's, the-earl's
jarlsins	earl's, the-earl's
járn	iron
járnsíða	Ironside (a name)
járnsíðu	Ironside (a name)
járnskó	Iron-Shoes (a name)
jarteinir	tokens
játmund	Edmund (a name)
játmundar	Edmund (a name)
játtar	agreed
jöfra	ruler
jöfurr	ruler
jóku	increased
jól	Yule
jörð	earth, land, the-earth
jórvík	York (a name)
jórvíkr	York (a name)
jótland	Jutland (a place)
jótlandi	Jutland (a place)

The Sagas of Ragnar Lothbrok   *Word List (Old Norse to English)*

Old Norse	English
K, k	
kæmi	came, come
kaga	stare
kalla	call, called, to call
kallaði	call, called, claimed, for
kallaðist	called
kallaðr	called
kallar	called
kann	can, can-it, it, know, known, knows
kanntu	obstacles
kápa	cape
kapp	eagerness
kappi	champion, warrior
kápu	cape
karl	a-man, man, old-man, the-man, the-old-man
karli	the-old-man
karls	man's, peasant's, the-man, the-old-man
karlsdóttur	a-peasant's-daughter
kasta	cast, to-cast
kastaði	cast
kastala	castle, castles
kastar	cast
kasti	cast
kastið	cast
kaupa	bought, buy, purchase
kaus	chose
keisari	emperor
kem	come
kemba	comb
kemir	came
kemr	became, came, came-to, come, comes, coming
kemst	came
kenna	be-known, know, known
kennast	knew
kenndi	felt, knew, taught
kenndust	knew-they
kenningarnafn	nickname
kennir	knew
kennt	known, taught
kerling	an-old-woman, the-old-woman
kerlingar	the-old-woman
kerlingu	old-woman, the-old-woman
keyrðak	drive
kippir	drew
kjeðst	said
kjósi	choose, chose
klædd	clothed
klæddi	clothed
klæddr	clothed
klæði	cloth, clothes, clothing
klæðum	clothed, clothes, clothing
klækjum	shame
klakkharaldr	Klakk-Harald (a name)
klakkharalds	Klakk-Harald (a name)
kleifar	cliffs
kliflönd	Cleveland (a place)
klufu	cleft
klýfr	split
klýfrat	cleaved
knætti	could
knarra	knorrs
knátti	should
knáttu	ball
kné	allegiance, knee, knees
knerrir	knorrs
knífi	knife
knífrinn	the-knife

Old Norse	English
knjám	knees
knörru	knorrs
knörrum	knorrs
knúti	Canute (a name)
knútr	Canute (a name)
knúts	Canute (a name)
knútsdrápu	A-Knuts-Drapa (a name)
knútsson	Son-of-Knut (a name)
kœmi	came
koll	shaved
kölluð	called
kölluðu	called
kolsvörtum	coal-black
kom	came, come, comes, coming, had-come, went
koma	came, come, comes, coming, to come
komast	came, come, comes, coming
komi	come, comes, coming
komim	come
komin	come, coming
kominn	become, becoming, came, come, come-in, coming, have-come
komir	come
komist	come
komit	came, come, comes, come-to, coming
kømk	comes
komnir	came, come, coming, returning
kømr	comes
komst	came
kómu	came
komum	come
kona	as-a-woman, a-woman, lady, the-woman, wife, woman
konan	the-woman, woman
konar	kind-of, kinds, kinds-of
konu	a-wife, a-woman, wife, woman, woman's
konum	woman, women
konung	a-king, king, the-king
konunga	kings
konunganna	the-king's
konungar	kings
konungastefnu	king's-assembly
konungdóm	kingdom, kingship
konungi	king, the-king, to-the-king
konunginn	king, the-king
konunginum	the-king
konungr	a-king, king, king's, the-king, the-king's
konungrinn	the-king
konungs	a-king's, king, king's, the-king, the-king's
konungssynir	king's-sons
konunni	the-woman
konur	woman, women
kostar	benefit, choice, use
köstuðu	cast, threw
kráka	Kraka (a name)
kráku	crow, saw
kraptr	strength
krefr	craves
kreisti	crushed
kring	a-ring
kristnaði	Christianity
kú	cow
kufl	cloak
kúna	a-cow, the-cow

Old Norse	English
kunna	could, know, know-how, knowing, to-know
kunni	could, knew, know
kúnni	the-cow
kunnigt	known
kurteisust	well-mannered
kvað	asked, be-called, called, cried-out, said, saying, spoke
kvaddi	called
kvaddr	called
kvaðst	said, spoke
kváðu	said, saying
kváðust	said, said-they
kvæði	asked, poem, said
kvánar	wife
kvángaðr	married
kvángast	marriage, was-married
kvánríki	woman-ruled
kveð	ask, greet
kveða	greeted, it-is-said, providing, quote, quoted, speak, to speak
kveðir	say
kveðit	declared, spoken, sung
kveðja	a-greeting, called, greet, greeted
kveðju	greeting, greetings
kveðr	called-for, greeted, greets, said, spoke
kveðst	said, saying
kveld	evening
kveldit	evening, the-evening
kvelds	evening
kvenna	woman, women
kvensamliga	feminine-same-like
kveykja	kindled
kveykt	lit
kveyktr	lit

Old Norse	English
kvígendi	bullocks
kvígendin	the-bullocks
kvikt	alive
kvöð	obligations
kykvendis	creature
kynni	circumstance, knew, know
kyns	wonder, wondrous
kýr	cow, the-cow
kýrin	cow, the-cow
kyrr	quiet, still
kyrrðum	peaceful
kyrrir	still
kyrt	calm
kyssa	kissing

L, l

Old Norse	English
lá	laid, lay, laying, lying
lægi	laid, lay
lægis	laying
læjandi	laughing
læst	locked
læt	lay, let
læti	bellowing
lætr	acted, allow, allowed, behave, behaviour, bellowed, had, keep, laid, lay, let, lets
lag	layer, spear-shaft
lagða	enriched
lagðak	laid
lagði	became, had, laid, lay, left, took-to
lagðist	laid, lay
lagðr	laid
lagiðr	laid
lágu	laid, lay, laying, low
lakkar	Hlökk's (a name, Norse Mythology)
land	land, the-land

Old Norse	English
landherr	lord-of-the-land
landherrinn	land-warriors
landi	land, lands, the-land
landinu	land, lands, the-land, to-the-land
landit	land, the-land
landráða	land-ruling's
lands	land, lands
landsfólk	lands-folk
landsins	land, lands, the-land
landskjálfti	an-earthquake
landsmanna	countrymen, landsmen
landsmenn	landsmen
landstjórnar	governing
landvarnar	defence
landveg	land-way, land-ways
langa	long
langr	long
langskip	longships
langskipum	longships
langt	long
lásboga	lock-bow
lasi	weakness
lát	bellowing, have, let
láta	allow, allowed, bellowed, burn, burned, do, done, had, have, laid, lay, lay-out, leave, let, letting, lose, put, to allow, to let
látið	left, let
látin	dead, let
látinn	deceased
látit	caused, had, laid, made
látum	let, let-us
laugar	washing
lauk	closed, concluded, end, ended, leek
lauks	leek
launa	loan, repay, reward
launar	repaid
launi	reward
laus	less, loose, lost
lausafé	liquidity, loose-fee, treasure, wealth
lax	salmon
leggja	allow, grant, laid, lay, laying, let, lying, make, place, to lay
leggjum	let-us-lay
leggr	have, laid, lay, let, seated
leið	a-journey, during, journey, laid, lay, pass, passed, path, the-way, this-way, way
leiðangr	journeying
leiðangri	expedition
leiðar	route, the-way, way
leiddi	led
leik	sport, sported
leika	games, playing-tricks
leiki	game, play, played, plays, play-trickery, toyed
leiks	game
leist	impression, liked
leita	look for, search, seek, sought, to look for, to search
leitat	seek, seeking, sought
léku	played
lengi	a long time, along, for a long time, long, long time, longer
lengr	long, longer
lét	allowed, had, laid, lay, let, lost, put
léta	let
létk	let
létta	laid, let, relieve, rest
léttari	lighter

Old Norse	English
léttr	light
létu	allowed, had, laid, left, let, yet
létum	laid, made
leyfðu	laid
leygjar	of-the-flame
leyna	conceal, concealing, hiding
leyniliga	secretly
leynivág	hidden-creek
leynt	secret
leysa	releasing, solve
leyst	let-down
leystr	loosened, released
leystu	dismissed, loosened
lið	a-company, a-crew, a-group, assistance, companions, company, crew, following, forces, help, host, men, team, the-company-of, the-crew, troops
líða	pass, passed
líðandisness	Lindesnes (a place)
liði	a-crew, band, company, company, force, forces, group, help, men, team
liðin	a-company, company, passed, teams
liðinu	team, the-forces, the-men
liðit	company, forces, group, passed, team, the-company, the-men
liðnar	passed, passing
líðr	passed, passes
liðs	company, force, forces, help, men, team
liðsmenn	company-men
líðum	Lidar (a place)
líf	life, live, lives
lifa	life, live, living
lífi	life, live, lives, living
lífinu	his-life
lifir	live, lives, outlives
lífit	my-life
líflát	death, life-loss, loss
lífláti	life-laying
líflátnir	life-less
lífs	life
liggi	lying
liggja	lay, lie, lies, lying, the-alternative, to lie
liggr	laid, lay, lies, made
líkaði	liked
líkar	alike, like, liked, was-displeased
líkari	likened
líkendi	likely
líkit	body
líkligt	likely
líkr	alike, like
líkt	like
líktist	likeness
lím	mortar
limum	limbs
lindiseyri	Lindiseyri (a place)
líndúk	linen
líst	beheld, behold, beholding, like
listuliga	elegantly
líta	company, look
litfögr	fair-coloured
lítill	a little, little, little-be, small
lítils	little
lítinn	a-little
lítist	look
litit	considered, considering, looking
lítit	a-little, little
litla	little

Old Norse	English
litlu	a-little, little
litr	colour
lítt	a-little, little, little-with
loðbrækr	shaggy-breeches
loðbrók	shaggy-breeches
loðbrókar	Lothbrok (a name)
loðkápa	shaggy-cape
lœgir	gladdens
lofðunga	kings
lofðungar	kings
lög	law
lögð	laid
lögðis	let
lögðu	laid, lay, subjected
lögðum	laid
löginn	lying
logit	a-lie
lokinn	ended
lokit	concluded, ended, left
lönd	land, lands, the-lands
löndum	land, lands, the-lands
löng	delay, long
löngu	long
löngum	long
lostinn	shocked
lotum	sometimes
lúðr	trumpets
lúðrar	cringed
luku	finished
lúmbardí	Lombardy (a place)
lúna	Luna (a place)
lund	manner
lunda	puffins
lundúnaborg	London-City (a place)
lungun	lungs
lustu	struck
lý	concluded
lykkju	coil, loop
lýkr	concluded, ended, ends, it-ends, was-concluded
lyngölun	serpent
lyngorm	heather-snake
lypt	lifted
lypting	the-deck
lýsir	declare, declared

M, m

Old Norse	English
má	may, may-be, tha-may
maðr	a man, a person, a-man, man, men, person
mæddan	tired
mæki	sword
mæla	business, matter, matters, say, speak, spoke, the-matter, to speak, to-speak
mæli	speak, speaks
mælir	speak, speaks, spoke, talking, words
mælt	said, say, spoke, spoken
mælti	might, said, speaking, spoke
mæltu	speaking, spoke, was-said
mær	girl, maiden, maidens
mærin	the-girl
mæta	meet
mætast	meet, met
mætri	distinguished
mætta	might
mætti	could, it-might, may, met, might
mættir	might
magni	strength

Old Norse	English
maka	equal
maki	matched
mál	a-meal, case, conversations, language, matter, matters, said, say, speech, subject, the-matter
mála	matter
máli	having-a-meal, matter, speak, speech, the-matter
malmi	metallic
malmr	metal
malms	ore
máls	matter, speak, speech
málstefnu	council
málug	talking
málum	case, matters
málvini	friend's
man	bond-woman, girl, man, remembered, should
máni	moon
mank	remember
mann	a-man, man, men, person, the-people
manna	man, man's, man's, many, men, men, men's, of-men, people's, people's, the people, the-men, the-people
mannahöfðum	men's-heads
manngi	no-man, none, no-one
manni	a-man, man, man's, men, person
mannraun	trial
manns	husband, man, man's
mannsbani	man-slayer
mannsbarn	child, man's-son
mannskæðu	man's-damage

Old Norse	English
mánuð	month
már	gull
marga	many
margan	many
margar	as-much-as, many
margir	many
margr	many
margs	many, many's
margt	many
mark	mark, proof
marka	mark, marked, marks
mars	steed
marstan	Marstan (a name)
mat	food
matbúit	food-prepared
matr	food
matsveinar	cooks, ship's-cook, the-cooks, the-ship's-cook
mátti	as-may, could, may, might, that-might
máttu	could, may, might
máva	seagulls
mávangs	seagull's
með	about, along, among, as-well, between, it, well, while, with
meðalfærir	between-faring
meðan	as-long-as, long-as, meantime, meanwhile, while, with
mega	able, able-to, be, be-able, may, may-have
megi	may
megim	may
megin	may, might, most, side, ways
megir	may
megu	may
meguð	may

Old Norse	English
megum	may
meiðir	injure
mein	disease, harm
meini	harm
meins	harm
meir	me, more
meira	a-more, bigger, greater, more
meiri	better, greater, more
meirum	greater
menn	man, many, men, men, the-men
mennskr	a-human, human
mér	for-me, i, me, mine, more, my, myself, myself-to, of-me, to, to-me
merkðan	marked
merki	banner, imprint, mark-of
merkja	sign
messu	mass
mest	most, mostly, the-most
mesta	most, the-most
mestar	most
mesti	best, most, the-most
mestir	best, greatest, most
mestr	greatest, the-greatest
mestu	most
meta	appreciate, appreciated, evaluate
mett	sated
mey	a-maiden, daughter, girl, maid, maiden
meybarn	baby-girl
meyja	maid
meyjar	girls, maiden, maiden's
meyjunni	the-girl, the-maiden
meyna	the-girl

Old Norse	English
miðr	between, less, less than, middle
mik	i, me, mine, my, to-me
mikil	a-great, great, large, much
mikill	a-great, great, large, many, mighty, much, tall, very
mikilla	great
mikillar	great
mikilli	biggest, much
mikils	much
mikinn	a-great, as-big, great, greater, many, much
mikit	great, greatly, large, many, much, very
mikla	great, greatest, much, so-great
miklar	great, much
miklir	great, large, much
miklu	a-great, great, greater, many, much
miklum	much
mildri	tender
mildum	mild
milli	among, between
millim	between
mín	for-me, me, mine, my
mína	mine, my
mínir	mine, my
minn	me, mine, my
minna	less, mine
minnast	remember
minni	less, lesser, mind, mine
minnr	less
minnst	least
minntust	remembered
minnum	lesser
minst	at-least
mínu	me, mine, my

Old Norse	English
mínum	mine, my
mislagðar	mislaid, misplaced
misseri	a-season, season
mitt	mid, mine, my
mjó	slender
mjök	many, most, much, very
mjörs	mjosa
mjóst	thin
mjóvasta	narrowest
móðernis	mother's
móði	Móði (a name), mother
móðir	mother, mother-of, to
móðr	mother, mother-of, tired
móður	mother, mother-of
móðurætt	mother's-kin
mögnuð	mighty
mögr	skinny, sons
mögum	sons, stomach, stomachs
mollu	stifling
mönnum	man, men, men
morði	murder, slaughter
mörg	many, might
morgin	morning, the-morning
morgingjöf	morning-gift
morgininn	morning
morginn	morning
morginskœru	morning-shear
morginstund	morning-while
morgni	morning
mörgu	many
mörgum	many
mörk	a-mark, mark, timber
mörkina	the-trees, trees
mosa	moss
mosavaxinn	moss-overgrown

Old Norse	English
mót	against, meet, meeting, reply, return, towards
móti	against, meet, meeting, met, return, to-meet, towards
mun	could, must, shall, should, should-be, spirit, will, would, would-be
munarvági	munar-bay
munat	remembered
mundelds	hand-fire
mundi	could, could-be, remembered, remembering, should, shouldit-be, will, would, would-be
mundu	should, will, would, would-be
munduð	must-have
muni	shall, should, would
munk	remember
munr	difference, longing
munt	must, shall, should, would
muntu	shall, should
munu	shall, should, to will, will, would, would-be
munuat	should-to
munum	shall, should
munut	should
mynd	image
mynni	mouth, the-inlet, the-mouth-of
myrgininn	morning
myrkviðar	dark-forests

N, n

Old Norse	English
ná	near, reaching
ná-	got
náði	caught, got, got-not

Old Norse	English
naðri	serpent
næfri	skilfully
nær	brought, by, close-to, near, nearer, nearly, near-the, when
næst	near, nearest, next, next-to, then
næsta	next, next-to
næstum	next
nætr	nights
nafn	a-name, name, named
nafnfesti	name-fastening
nafni	name, namesake, the-name
nagl	nail
nagli	nail
nakkvat	not-any, somewhat
nálgast	approached
náliga	down, nearly, near-lying
namk	tunic
námu	took
nánd	close, close-by, close-to
nár	corpse, dead
nás	corpse
nátta	nights
náttar	night
náttúra	the-nature
náttverð	supper
nauð	distressing
naut	bulls, the-bulls
né	nor, not, or, the
nefndr	named
nefnir	named
nema	except, take, taken, taking, took, unless
nemr	take, taken, took
nemst	taken
neskonungum	sea-kings
niðja	descendants
niðjar	descendants
niðr	descendant, down, kin, nether
nistir	pierced
níu	9, nine
njörun	Njörun (a name, Norse Mythology)
njósn	spying
njóta	enjoy, the-night, useful
nokkur	any, anyone, certain, some, somewhat
nokkura	some
nokkurn	certain, some, somehow, someone
nokkurr	any, anything, someone
nokkurra	a-few, some, something
nokkurrar	some
nokkurs	someone
nokkuru	sometime, somewhat
nokkurum	any
nokkut	anything, something, somewhat
norðan	North, Northwards
norðhumbrulandi	Northumberland (a place)
norðhumrulandi	Northumbria (a place)
norðimbralandi	Northumbria (a place)
norðmönnum	Norwegians (a place)
norðr	North
norðrálfu	Northern-Lands (a place)
norðrlönd	Northern-Lands (a place)
norðrlöndum	The-Northern-Lands (a place)
noreg	Norway (a place)
noregi	Norway (a place)

Old Norse	English
noregs	Norway (a place)
norna	the-norns
nótt	night, the-night
nóttina	night, the-night
nú	not, now
numit	learned, taken
nýir	new
nýjari	new
nýju	again, new
nýtak	new-take
nýtinjótar	users

O, o

Old Norse	English
odd	point, spear-point
odda	point, spear-point, spear-points
oddar	point
oddhagastr	carving
oddr	odd, spears
of	about, for, of, to, too
ofan	above, down, downed, from above, from over, of, off, on, over
ofarliga	not-far
ofnu	woven
ofrefli	greater-force, overwhelming, overwhelming-force
ofrhuga	courage
ofrkapp	overkill
ofrliði	outnumbered
ofsnemma	too-early
ok	also, and, as, but, of, when
okkarr	ours, us (dual), us (two)
okkarrá	our
okkars	ours
okkart	our, ours
okkr	our, ours, us, we
okkra	our, ours
olli	cause, how-much
opt	often
optar	often
orð	word, words
orða	words
orðinn	became, become, have-become
orðit	become, been, of-words, turned-out, word, words
orðsending	message, messages, word-sending
orðstír	fame
orm	Orm (a name), snake
orma	serpent
ormar	serpents
ormarnir	serpents, snakes
ormgarð	snake-pit
ormi	serpent
orminn	the-serpent
orminum	serpent, serpent's, the-serpent, the-serpent's, the-snake
ormr	a-serpent, a-snake, serpent, Serpent (a name), serpents, snake, snakes
ormr-í-auga	Snake-in-the-eye (a name)
ormrinn	serpent, the-serpent
orms	serpent, snake
ormsins	serpent's
orrosta	battle
orrostan	battle
orrostu	battle, battles
orrostunni	the-battle
orrostur	battles
oss	ours, us, we
ossar	ours
oxa	an-ox

Old Norse	English

Ó, ó

Old Norse	English
óblauðan	un-cowardly
óbornir	not-born, unborn
óbúit	not-done
óð	waded
óðamálug	un-talkative
óðari	mad
óðinn	Odin (a name, Norse Mythology)
óðins	Odin (a name, Norse Mythology)
óðir	crazy
ófafé	wealth
ófáir	many
ófár	high
ófarar	impossible
ófni	sea-serpents
ófrægri	less-famous
ófriðr	hostility, terror, without-peace
ófúinn	un-decayed
ógert	undone
ógndjarfr	unafraid
óhefnt	without-vengeance
óherskátt	un-invaded
óhljóð	loudly
óklædd	unclothed
óku	drove
ókunnr	an-unknown
ókvíðandi	bravely
ókynligt	not-strange
óláfs	Olaf (a name)
ólíkar	unlike
ólmasti	wildest
ólmir	wild
ólmr	savage
ómegð	infancy, without
ómett	hungry
óp	cries-out, shouting
ópi	battle-cry, shrieking
ór	arrow, from, from out of, from-out-of, of, out, out from, out of, out-from, out-of, over
óráðligt	un-right
órunum	tales
ósigr	defeat, defeated
ósýnna	unseeing
óþokkuliga	unfairly-behaved
ótrúligt	treacherous
ótta	fear
óttaðist	were-afraid
óttast	fear, feared
ótti	fear
óttu	incite
óvænlig	unlikely
óvænni	fair, less-fair
óvænt	unexpected
óvættum	monsters
óvant	not-lacking
óvarlig	un-careful
óvart	un-warned
óvígan	an-overwhelming, an-unconquerable, unconquerable
óvígr	non-fighting-men, not-fighting
óvinir	enemies
óvinum	un-friends
óvirðuligar	unworthy
óx	grew

Ö, ö

Old Norse	English
öðru	another, other, other-things, otherwise, to-the-other
öðrum	another, each, next, other, others, the-other
ögmundr	Ogmund (a name)

Old Norse	English
öl	ale
öld	age, mankind
öldrum	age
öldum	age
öldungshuð	old-bull's-hide
öldungshúð	old-bull
öll	all
öllu	all
öllum	all, all-among, whole
öndrum	others
öndurðr	breathing
öndvegi	foremost, foremost-seat, the-foremost
öndverðri	at-the-front
önguls-eyju	Anglesey (a name)
önnur	also, another, other, second
örin	arrow
örlög	fate
örn	eagle, the-eagle
örnúlfr	Arnulf (a name)
örr	open-handed
öru	arrow
örvar	arrow, arrows
örvarboð	arrow-messages, arrow-summons
öxi	axe
öxin	axe, the-axe

Ǫ, ǫ

Ø, ø

Ǭ, ǭ

Œ, œ

Old Norse	English
œrit	enough
œrna	plenty

P, p

palmi	palms
peir	they
píndr	tortured
pínuðu	tortured

Q, q

R, r

rá	sail-yard
ráð	advice, advise, advised, authority, counsel, decide, decision, matter, obliged, plan, plans, proposal, propose, ride, rule, the-business
ráða	advice, advise, advised, agreed, decide, decision, discussed, plan, planned, plans, prevail, rule, to advise, to decide, to give advice, to make a decision, to rule, to-rule
ráðagerðar	ruling
ráðahag	marriage-proposal
ráðandi	ruled
ráði	advice, advised, counsel, plan, talk

The Sagas of Ragnar Lothbrok *Word List (Old Norse to English)*

Old Norse	English	*Old Norse*	English
ráðinn	decided, determined, ruled	*randar*	shield, shields
ráðir	advise, command	*rangendum*	wrong-doing
ráðit	advice, advised, discussed, resolved, ruling	*rastar*	currents
		rauðan	red
		rauðar	red
ráðligra	more-advisable	*rauðr*	red, The-Red (a name)
ráðs	advice, advise, counsel, plan, plans, solution	*rauðum*	red
		raunar	ordeal
ráðum	advice, counsel	*réð*	advised, appointed, decided, dominated, engaged, hired, rode, ruled, ruler-of, ruling
ráðumk	counsel		
ráðumst	let-us-settle		
ræða	decided, discussed, discussing		
ræddi	advised, decided, discussed, discussed-with, talked	*réði*	leader, ruled
		réðst	appointed, decided, discussed, moved, rode, went
ræddu	advised, decided, discussed	*réðu*	discussed, rode, ruled
ræðir	discussed	*regni*	rain
ræðr	advice, discussed, ruled, rules, ruling	*reið*	riding, rode
		reiddi	aimed, driven, rode
ræðst	decided	*reiðgotaland*	Jutland (a place)
ræðu	speech	*reiði*	anger
rægagarr	carrion-beast	*reiðir*	angry
rækir	drove	*reiðr*	angry, decided
rækyndill	corpse-candle	*reisa*	raise, raised, rise
ræna	raided	*reisir*	raised
ræntan	stole	*reistist*	rose
ræsis	prove	*reka*	drive, drove, expel, expelled
ræstr	swept		
rafn	Rafn (a name)	*rekkar*	warriors
rafnar	Ravens (a name)	*rekkja*	covers
ragnar	Ragnar (a name)	*rekkju*	bed, in-bed, to-bed
ragnari	Ragnar (a name)	*reknar*	driven
ragnarr	Ragnar (a name)	*rekum*	drive, foraging
ragnars	Ragnar (a name)	*rendi*	edge, ran
ragnhildar	Ragnhild (a name)	*rendr*	edged
ragnhildi	Ragnhild (a name)	*renna*	ran, run, split
ragnhildr	Ragnhild (a name)	*réttir*	right
rak	driven, drove	*reyna*	attempt, test, tested
randalín	Randalin (a name)	*reyndi*	experienced, test

Old Norse	English
reyndir	skilled
reynt	experienced, tested, tried
ríð	ride
ríða	raise, ride, riding, rode, smear
riddara	riders
riddaralið	riding-men
rifin	rib, ribs
rifja	consider, review
ríka	rich
ríkasti	mightiest
ríki	authority, kingdom, kingdoms, the-kingdom, the-kingdom-of
ríkin	the-kingdom
ríkinu	kingdom, the-kingdom
ríkis	kingdom, kingdoms
ríkjum	rule
ríkr	a-rich, kingdom, of-the-kingdom, powerful
ríkt	ruled
rínar	Rhine's (a place)
risit	risen
ríss	rose
rista	carved, raised
rítar	drawn
rítr	written
rjóða	redden, reddened
rjóðr	clearing
rjúfa	broken
rödd	voice
roðin	red
roðinn	reddened
roðna	reddened
röf	amber
rögguð	rough
rögnvaldr	Rognvald (a name)
rögnvalds	Rognvald's (a name)
røkkva	darken
rómaborgar	Rome-City (a place)
rómaveldi	Roman-World (a place)
róms	Rome (a place)
rómu	battle
rönd	against, shield
rönum	peace
röskva	seasoned
rottar	rats
ruðum	reddened
rúm	room
rúmi	room
rýfst	fails
rýrt	reduced

S, s

Old Norse	English
sá	except, he, looked, saw, see, seen, so, that, that one, the, then, this, was, was-seen, when
sæ	sea
sæfært	seaworthy
sæi	saw, seen
sækitík	seeker
sækja	seek, seek-to, sought
sæl	happy
sælir	happy, lucky
sælu	happiness
sæmd	honour
sæmdar	honour
sætis	seat, sit
sætt	a-settlement, settled, settlement
sætta	settle
sættir	reconciled, reconciliation
safna	raise, raised
safnaðar	the-gathering-of

Old Norse	English
safnar	collected, gathered, summoned
safnast	gathered
saga	saga, story, the-story
sagði	said, told
sagt	said, told
sák	attended, sake, saw
saka	blame
sakaði	accused
sakar	conviction, harmed, sake
sakast	harm
sakir	conviction, for-the-sake-of, sake
saklausan	innocent
sal	hall
salta	the-salt
salti	salt
sama	same, the-same, together
saman	together
samdrátt	gathering
samför	togetherness
samir	same, so
samira	honour, same
sámsey	Samso (a place)
sámseyju	Samso (a place)
samt	same, the-same, together
samtogi	come-together
sand	sand
sanda	sands
sandinum	sands, the-sand
sandr	sand
sanni	prove
sannliga	truly
sár	wound, wounded, wounds
sára	wound, wounds
sárinu	the-wound, wound
sárr	wound, wounded
sárum	wounded, wounds

Old Norse	English
sás	so-is, this-who
sat	sat, seat
satt	true, truth
sáttir	agreed
sáttu	seen-you
sátu	sat, sitting
saumaðan	sewn-and-stitched
saxa	The-Saxons
sé	as, be, being, he, he-be, his, is, is-being, know, saw, say, see, see-me, seen, so, this, was, which
sefr	sleeping, slept
seg	say
seggir	said
segi	said, say
segið	say, saying, telling
segir	answered, said, say, says, spoke, tell, told
segja	answer, said, said-to, say, say-of, says, say-to, talk, tell, to say, told, to-say
segjum	say
seilist	reached
selund	Zealand (a place)
selundi	Zealand (a place)
sem	as, as-if, as-though, himself, how, if, it-was, me, since, so, such-as, than, that, the, then, they, was, when, where, wherever, which, while, who
senda	send, sent, to send
sendar	sends
sendi	send, sent
sendimenn	messengers, sending-men, the-messengers

Old Norse	English
sendir	sent
sennu	at-once
sent	sent
sér	as, as-he, for-him, he, her, hers, herself, him, himself, himself-to, his, is, one's, privately, saw, see, seeing, seen, so, that, the, their, theirs, them, themselves, these, they, this, to, to-him, to-see, to-you, with, yourself
serk	shirt
serknum	the-shirt
sessunautum	sitting-next-to
sest	sat
set	sit
sét	saw, seen
setit	sat
setja	set, set-out, sit, to set
setr	sat, seats, set
setst	sat
sett	set
setti	put, set
settist	sat, set
settr	set
settumk	set
sex	6, six
síbilja	Sibilja (a name)
síbilju	Sibilja (a name)
síða	improved, long
síðan	after, afterwards, later, since, then, thereafter
síðar	after, afterwards, later, since
síðari	later
síðasti	next
síðir	eventually, since

Old Norse	English
síðr	heathens, less, sides
síðu	side
síður	less, sides
sighvatr	Sighvat (a name)
siglðum	sailed
signuð	signed
sigr	success, successful
sígr	victory
sigrast	be-victorious, conquered, victory
sigrs	victory
sigrumst	gain-victory
sigurðar	Sigurd (a name)
sigurðarson	Son-of-Sigurd (a name)
sigurði	Sigurd (a name)
sigurðr	Sigurd (a name)
sik	he, her, herself, him, himself, them, themselves
siklingr	king
silfd	silver
silfr	silver
silfri	silver
silki	silk
silkihjúp	a-silk-tunic
silkiskyrtu	Silk-Shirt (a name)
sín	her, hers, him, himself, his, theirs, them, themselves, they
sína	her, hers, himself, his, their, theirs
sínar	hers, his, theirs
sinn	he, her, her own, hers, his, his own, occasion, one-day, that, the, their, their own, theirs, then, they, time
sinna	hers, his, of-his, their, theirs
sinnar	hers, his, their, theirs, this

Old Norse	English
sinni	his, mind, once, opinion, ours, their, theirs, them, this, with
sinnum	then
síns	hers, his, their, theirs, they
sínu	her, hers, his, their, theirs, themselves, they
sínum	her, hers, his, their, theirs, with-his
síst	at-least, little-as-possible, none
sit	sit
sitja	sat, set, sit, sitting, to sit, to-sit
sitr	sat, sit, sits, sitting
sitt	her, hers, his, long, one's, the, their, theirs, there, these, they, this
sjá	he-saw, it-seemed, looked, saw, say, see, seeing, seen, see-this, so, such, they-saw, this, to see, to-see
sjáldrit	the-pupil
sjálf	herself
sjálfan	himself, itself, self
sjálfir	themselves
sjálfr	himself, his-own, myself, self
sjálft	himself
sjálfum	ourselves, yourself
sjám	let-us-see, see, we-see
sjást	looked, see, seen
sjau	7, seven
skaða	damage, damages
skal	shall, shall-be, should, would
skála	cabin
skálann	hut, the-hut
skáld	poet

Old Norse	English
skalk	rogue's, shall
skalt	shall
skamma	short
skammt	a-short-distance, short, short-distance, shortly, shortly-distance, short-way
skáni	Skane (a place)
skap	mood
skapaðr	crafted
skapsmuni	temperament
skapt	shaft
skaptinu	the-spear-shaft
skaptit	shaft, the-shaft
skarðaborg	Scarborough (a place)
skarpa-skerjum	Skarpa-Skerries (a place)
skatta	tax
skattlönd	tribute-paying-land
skaust	launched
skaut	hem, lap, shot, stern
skefr	planed
skelfr	shook
skemman	cabin
skemmr	short
skemmta	amuse, entertain
skemmtan	amusement
skemmtanar	entertain
skemmu	cabin, storehouse
skemmuna	cabin, sleeping-room, the-cabin, the-sleeping-room
skemmunnar	the-cabin
skemmunni	the-cabin, the-sleeping-room
skera	scored
skeyti	arrows
skíðgarðinn	fence, the-fence
skíðgarðr	plank-fence
skífðum	we-sliced
skikkjuskaut	the-lap-of-cloak

Old Norse	English
skildi	shield, shields, understood
skildinum	shield, the-shield
skildir	shields
skildu	knew, left, separated, understood
skildust	parted, separated
skilja	a-part, know, part, separate, separated, to part, to separate, to understand, understand, understood
skiljast	parted, separate, separated
skiljum	understand
skilnaði	parted, separate, separated, separation, they-had-parted
skip	a-ship, ship, ships, then
skipa	command, divide, ship, ships, the-ship, the-ships
skipabúnað	ship-preparing
skipaðar	fitted-out
skipaði	directed
skipaðir	fully-loaded
skipaher	naval-force
skipanna	of-the-ships, ships
skipast	been-done, change, changed
skipat	directed, prepared
skipi	a-ship, equip, ship, ships, the-ship
skipin	ships
skips	ship, ships
skipta	change, divide, divided, exchange, exchanged, of-exchange
skiptum	exchange
skipuð	arranged, equipped, prepared
skipum	ship, ships, the-ship, the-ships
skipunum	boats, ship, ships, the-ship
skírn	baptism
skjöld	shield, shields
skjöldu	shields
skjöldum	shields
skjölduna	shields
skjöldunga	Skjoldungs' (a name)
skjómar	shields
skjóta	launch, launched
skjótast	quickest, quickly, soonest
skjótt	quickly, shortly, soon, swiftly
skjótum	early
skœru	quarrel
skœrubíldr	shear-lancet
skóf	scraped
skóg	forest, the-forest
skógar	forests, the-woods, woods
skóginn	forest, the-forest, the-woods, woods
skóginum	forest, the-forest
sköglar	Skogul's (a name)
skógr	a-forest, forest
sköp	craft
skör	fragile
skoraði	challenged
skorin	scored
skorit	scored
skorti	shortage, shortage-of
skotit	shot
skotlands	Scotland's (a place)
skraut	decoration
skuli	shall
skulu	shall, should, should-be, to shall
skuluð	should
skulum	shall, should

Old Norse	English
skunda	hurry
skutu	launched, shot
skýja	cloud
skylda	should
skyldi	as-should-be, should, should-be, should-it, wished, would
skyldu	should, would
skyli	shall, shelter, should, should-be
skýlihöggum	axe-cuts
skyrtur	battle-shirts
skýtr	cast, shot
slá	strike, struck
sleit	tore-up
slés	Schlei-River (a place)
sléttan	flat
slíðra	sheath
slíðrloga	sheath-flame
slíka	so, such
slíkan	such
slíkar	silver, such
slíkir	such
slíkrar	such
slíkri	such
slíkt	so, such
slíku	such
slíkum	such
slíta	stab, tear, tore
slitnaðan	worn
slitnir	broken
slitnu	broken
slitusk	broken
sló	struck
slóð	trail
smæri	smaller
smálönd	Smaland (a place)
smátt	small
smeltr	enamelled
smiða	smiths
smiði	smiths
smó	slipped
smýgra	piercing
snákar	snakes
snarbrýnir	sharpened
snarpir	sharply
snart	fast, soon
snekkjur	sailboards, sailboats
snemma	early, soon
snemmst	soonest
sneri	turned
snerru	slaughter
sneru	turned
snerust	turned
snimma	early
snótu	attractive
snúa	turned
snýr	turned, turned-his
sofa	sleep, sleeping
sofnar	slept
sögð	said, told, told-to
sögðu	said, told
sogit	sucked-at
sögn	said, said-of, say, story
sögu	saga, said, story, the-saga, the-saga-of
sök	blame, cause, fault, reason
sólar	sun, the-sun
sollinn	ocean, swollen
sömu	same
son	a-son, son, son-of
sona	son, sons
sonar	son
sonr	of, son, son-of
sonu	sons
sonum	son, sons
sótt	attended, sickness, sought
sóttan	sought

Old Norse	English
sóttar	symptoms, to-be-sick
sóttdauðr	sickness-death
sóttu	looked, sought
spán	shiver
spangareiði	Spangarheith (a place)
spangarheiði	Spangarheid (a place)
spara	save, spare, withold
spari	save, spare
speki	wisdom
spekingr	wise
spekt	cunning
spektar	peaceful
spjalli	friends
spjöll	to-tell
spjót	a-spear, spear, spears
spjóti	spear, spear-tip
spjótin	spears, the-spears
spjótinu	spear, spear-tip
spjótit	spear, spear-tip, the-spear-head, the-spear-point, the-spear-tip
spjótskapt	spear-shaft
spjótskaptinu	spear-shaft
spjótskepti	a-spear-shaft, spear-shaft
spjótsoddum	spear-points
spjótsoddunum	spear-points
spjótunum	spears
sporð	tail
sporðr	tail
sprakk	burst
spurdaga	news
spurði	asked, heard-of, learned
spurðr	asked
spurðu	asked
spurt	asked, heard
spyrja	ask, asked, heard, hearing-of, learn, learned, learn-of, to ask, to learn
spyrjast	spread, was-heard
spyrr	ask, asked, asks, heard, heard-of, learned
spyrst	heard, heard-of, learned, was-heard
stað	land, place, places, stand, stands, stay, stood
staðar	place, places, stand
staddir	present, standing
staðinn	there
staðist	steadfast, withstood
stæði	steady, stood
stærstum	greatest
stafkarl	beggar, poor-beggar
stafn	stern
stafni	ship's-stem
stakk	thrust
stáli	steel
standa	stand, standing, stay, stood, to stand, withstand
standast	stand-you, withstand
standi	hurts
stefna	agreement, direct
stefnir	summoned
stefnt	located
stefnu	summons
steins	Stein (a name)
stendr	standing, stands, stood
sterka	strong
sterkari	stronger
sterkasta	strongest
sterkastr	strongest
sterki	strong
stíga	trod
stigum	level

Old Norse	English
stinn	strong
stirðar	stiff
stjúpmóðir	step-mother
stjúpsona	stepsons
stjúpsonu	stepsons
stóð	stayed, stood, was, withstood
stoðar	supports
stöðva	stop
stofnuð	established
stökk	jumped, split, spurted
stöngum	poles
stór	great, large
stórar	large
storðar	wood
stórilla	greatly
stórlyndr	generous
stórmenni	great-men
stórskipum	large-ships
stótt	stood
strandir	beaches
straums	currents
streng	string
strengdi	boldly
strenghömlur	bow-string
strengir	bound
strenglágar	string-laid
strengr	string
strönd	shore
studdist	stood
stund	awhile, time, while
stundir	awhile
stundr	time
stundu	awhile, while
stundum	awhile, sometimes, time
stungit	pierced
styr	steered, steering
stýrði	steered
stýrir	steer, steers, turned
sú	seen, so, that, the, their, this, was, yours
suðr	South
suðreyjum	South-Islands (a place)
suðrríki	Southern-Lands (a place)
súlur	the-pillars
sumar	some, summer
sumblum	banquet
sumir	some
sumra	some, summer
sumt	some, some-of
sumu	some
sund	a-strait, strait
sundi	sound, the-sound
sundr	apart, asunder, distribute, down
sundruðum	asunder
sungu	singing
sunnan	from-the-south, South
sunnanverðri	Southern-Lands (a place)
svá	as, so, so-as, so-did, so-much, such, that
sváfu	slept
svara	answer, answered, to answer
svaraði	answered
svarar	answered
svardaga	oath
svarðmerðlingar	shining-sworded
svarit	sworn
svarti	The-Black (a name)
svát	so, so-that
svefn	sleep
svefnhúss	sleeping-house
svefni	sleep
svefns	sleep
svefnskemmu	sleeping-quarters
sveif	steerer

Old Norse	English
svein	boy
sveinar	lads
sveinbarn	a-baby-boy, baby-boy, boy
sveini	boy, in-the-boy
sveininn	boy, the-boy
sveininum	the-boy, the-boy's
sveinn	boy, lad, the-boy, young man
sveinninn	boy, the-boy
sveita	sweat
sveiti	sweat
svella	swell
svelta	slain
sverð	sword, swords
sverða	sword, swords
sverði	sword, swords
sverðinu	sword
sverðs	swords
sverðum	swords
sverja	swear
sverr	swore
svía	Sweden, The-Swedes
svíar	Swedes
svíaríki	Sweden
sviðr	rapid, wise
svíkja	betray
svíra	gullets, neck
svíþjóð	Sweden
svíþjóðar	Sweden
svíþjóðu	Sweden
svívirðing	a-disgrace, swine-worth
svölnis	Svolnir's (a name)
svörum	answer, answers
syfjaðan	sleepy
syfjaðr	sleepy
sýna	show
sýndist	seemed, thought, thought-fit
sýndu	showed
sýndum	appearance
syngja	song
syni	son, son-of, sons
synir	sons, sons-of
sýnisk	seems
sýnist	seem, seemed, seems, thought
synjar	refuse, refused
sýnt	seemed, showed, shown
sýnum	appeared, seen, thought
sýsla	pursue
sýslu	business, do-business, looking-after, work
sýtandi	sweet
sýtir	laments
sýtira	lament

T, t

Old Norse	English
tæki	take, took
tækist	takes, took
tafl	table-game
taflit	game-pieces
tafn	sacrifices
tafni	sacrifices
taka	be-taken, take, taken, to take, took, to-take
takast	take, took
tala	say, speak, talk, to-speak
talað	told
talar	talk
tals	talk
tár	tears
tauma	bridle, reins
tek	take
tekin	taken
tekinn	taken

The Sagas of Ragnar Lothbrok   *Word List (Old Norse to English)*

Old Norse	English
tekit	taken
tekr	pulled, take, takes, took
tekst	took
telgja	carve, told
telk	shaped
telr	counted, talked
teygði	stretch
tíðar	frequent, this-time, visit
tíðenda	news, of-news, the-news, tidings
tíðendi	news, tidings
tíðendin	news, the-news
tíðendum	news
tignum	honourable
tigu	10, ten
til	about, at, come-to, for, of, that, them, to, too, towards, until, way-to
tilkvæði	speaking
tilræði	advised
tilskipun	directions
tilsýndar	appearance
tiltekju	change
tíma	time, times
tíu	10, ten
tjá	expressed, present-to
tjaldaðan	covered
tjöld	tents
tjöldum	tents
tjör	pools
tjöru	tar
tll	until
töfl	a-game-piece, table-games
tøgum	10s, tens
tók	received, taken, took, touched
tókk	took
tókst	took
tóku	taken, took, took-to
tölðumk	we-told
tólf	12, twelve
tölu	count, speech
törruðu	arranged
torveldi	difficult, difficulties
tötrum	rags
trautt	scarcely
tré	beam, beams, tree, trees, wood
trefr	fringes
tregar	troubled
trémaðrinn	wooden-man
trémann	wooden-man
trénu	the-tree
treystist	trusted
treystust	trusted
tröllskap	troll-like
tröllskapnum	sorcery
trú	faith
trúa	believe, trust, trusted
trúðu	believed
trúi	believe, trust
trúir	believes, true, trust
trúleiki	true-like
trúligt	faithful
trúnaði	trustworthy
trúr	true
tungu	tongue
tvá	2, two (masculine, accusative)
tvær	2, two (feminine, accusative), 2, two (feminine, nominative)
tvau	2, two (neuter, accusative), 2, two (neuter, nominative)
tveggja	2, two (feminine, genitive), 2, two (masculine, genitive)

The Sagas of Ragnar Lothbrok   Word List (Old Norse to English)

Old Norse	English
tveimr	2, two (feminine, dative), 2, two (masculine, dative), 2, two (neuter, dative)
tveir	2, two (masculine, nominative)
tvíbura	twin
tvítøgir	20, twenty
týna	destroy, lose
týndi	lost
týndist	lost

Þ, þ

Old Norse	English
þá	than, that, the, them, then, there, they, this, those, to-them, when
þaðan	from-there, there
þæfð	matted
þær	there, therefore, they, those
þærs	of-that
þætti	seemed, seems
þættist	thought
þagði	silent
þagnaði	silenced
þangat	from-there, get, that, there, to there
þann	he, him, than, that, that-one, the, then, then-one, they, this, those
þanninn	that-way
þar	here, it, that, their, then, there, therefore, they, where
þarf	need, needed
þars	there
þás	then
þat	it, it-was, ship, so, that, that-is, that-it-is, that-which-is, the, then, there, they, this, those, to
þats	that
þáttu	that-you
þau	hers, his, that, the, them, then, there, therefore, these, they, they-were, those
þegar	already, as-soon, as-soon-as, at once, straightaway, straight-away, then, there, they, when
þegði	silence, silent
þegi	silence, silent
þegn	free-man, thane
þegni	thane
þegnsköpum	honour
þeim	of-them, that, the, their, theirs, them, then, these, they, those, to, to-them, were-they, with-them
þeir	the, their, theirs, them, then, there, these, they, they-were, this, those, you
þeira	are-they, of, of-them, the, their, theirs, them, there, they, this, those
þeirar	their, there
þeiri	their, there, they
þekk	known
þengill	prince
þenja	stretched
þenna	that, then, these, this, those

188

Old Norse	English
þér	then, they, to-you, to-your, you, your, yours, you-to
þess	of-this, that, these, this, this-is
þessa	his, these, this
þessar	these, this
þessarar	that-kind-of, this
þessi	these, this
þessir	these
þessu	his, these, this
þessum	these, this
þetta	at-this, it, of-this, that, the, they, this, thus, was-this
þiggja	accept, accepted, receive, to-receive
þiggr	accept, accepted
þik	you, your, yours
þín	you, your, yours
þína	your, yours
þing	assembly, the-assembly
þinginu	assembly
þingit	assembled, assembly, the-assembly
þings	assembly, the-assembly
þingsins	assembly, the-assembly
þingstefnu	the-assembly
þínir	yours
þinn	you, your, yours
þinna	your, yours
þínu	yours
þínum	your, yours
þit	you
þitt	you, your, yours
þjóna	serve
þjónuðu	served
þjónustukonur	servant-maids
þjónustumenn	servants-of
þjóta	whistling

Old Norse	English
þó	also, nevertheless, then, thoug, though, thought, yet
þœfðar	quarrel
þokar	shook, stretches
þökk	thanks
þolið	enduring
þolir	endures
þóra	Thora (a name)
þorði	dared
þórðr	Thord (a name)
þorðu	dared
þörf	need, needed, needs
þori	dare, greater-part
þorik	deny, greater-part
þorir	dared
þorn	thorn
þorn-bil	Brooch-Bil (a name)
þorp	villages
þorps	village
þorra	part
þorri	majority
þóru	Thora (a name)
þótt	although, though, thought
þótti	as-seemed, seem, seemed, think, thinks, thought, was-thought
þóttist	thought
þóttu	thought
þóttust	seemed, thought
þrá	desire
þræta	wrangle
þrekvirki	brave-deeds
þrenna	3, three
þrévetr	three-winters
þriðja	3rd, third
þriðji	3rd, third
þriðjung	3rd, third-of
þriðjungr	3rd, a-third-of

Old Norse	English
þriggja	3, three (feminine, genitive), 3, three (masculine, genitive), 3, three (neuter, genitive)
þrimr	3, three (feminine, dative), 3, three (masculine, dative), 3, three (neuter, dative)
þrír	3, three
þrisvar	three-times
þrjá	3, three
þrjár	3, three
þrjú	3, three
þrotna	amassed
þróttarsnjallr	bold-and-brave
þrútinn	swollen
þú	are-you, you, your
þung	heavy
þungr	heavy
þurfa	need, needed
þurfti	needed
þurftu	need, needed
þúshundraða	#N/A
þvær	washed
þvengr	Thong (a place)
þverr	decreases, heaped
því	according, accordingly, according-to, as, because, because-of, before, for, in, of, since, that, the, then, therefore, this, what, with
þvílíkr	how-like, such, therefore-like
þykki	seems, seems-to, think, thought
þykkir	consider, considered, seemed, seems, think, thought
þykkist	seemed, think, thought
þykkja	be-valued, seem, seeming, think, thought, to seem, valued
þykkjast	realised, seem-to, think, thought
þykkjumst	think, think-us
þyldi	suffered
þyrði	dared
þyri	Thyra (a name)
þyrma	mercy
þyrni	thorns

U, u

Old Norse	English
ugga	feared
uggðu	feared
uggi	fear
ulfa	wolves
ulfi	wolf
ullarakri	Ullr-Acres (a place)
um	about, about-a, among, around, as-far-as, at, contrary-to, for, from, in, inclined, of, over, regarding
umði	whined
und	and, under
unda	beneath, under
undan	ahead, away, away-from, from, from-under, further, out-from, under
undarligt	wonder-like
undarligum	strange
undarn	strange

Old Norse	English
undir	behind, below, depended, from-beneath, from-under, near, submitted, to, under, up-to
undleygs	wound-flame
undum	turned
ung	young
unga	young
ungi	young
ungr	a-young, young, younger
ungu	young
unna	grant, love
unnar	won
unni	love, loved
unnit	committed, deserved, earned, spared, win, winning, won, work
unnu	won
unnum	won-we
uns	until
upp	above, open, to-open, up, upped, up-to-the-mountains
uppgöngu	up-going
uppgöngur	up-going
upphafi	the-beginning
uppi	about, stand-up, up
upplöndum	Uppland (a place)
uppruna	origin, origin-of
uppsala	Uppsala (a place)
uppsölum	Uppsala (a place)
uppsvíaveldi	Upper-Sweden (a place)
urðu	became, came
utan	except-for, out, out-of, outside
utar	out, outside
uxa	an-ox
uxahúð	an-ox-hide

Ú, ú

Old Norse	English
út	back, back-from, from, out, out-from, out-of, outside
útan	from out, from out of, of, out, out from, out-of, outside-of, to-out, travel
útgrynnis	shallows
úti	about, out, outside

V, v

Old Norse	English
vá	difficulty, slew
váðum	clothes, vestments
væi	might-be
væn	fair, fairness
væna	fair, kind
vænligt	promising, promisingly
vænn	a-fair, beautiful, handsome, kind
vænni	fairer
vænst	expected, fair, fairest
vænta	expect, expected, hoped
væntir	expect
væntum	wish
væri	had, is, it-was, it-would-be, should-be, was, were, would, would-be
værim	being
vættr	gored
vági	inlet, wave
vagn	wagon
vák	fought
vaka	awake
vaki	awake, wake
vakna	awake, woken

The Sagas of Ragnar Lothbrok — Word List (Old Norse to English)

Old Norse	English
vaknar	awoke
val	foe
valblóði	slain-blood
valda	wield
valdi	chose
valfalli	slain-fall
valfugla	corpse-birds
valinn	fallen
valland	Wales (a place)
valmeyjar	Valkyrie (a name, Norse Mythology)
valnum	as-chosen
valr	falcon, slain
vals	choices, rolled, roller, the-slain
valslöngur	war-slings
valtafn	slain-offering
valþjófr	Valthjof (a name)
vammlausa	blemish-free
ván	expected, hope, in-vain, looked
vanda	accustomed, custom, problems
vandamálum	problems
vandi	custom
vandliga	closely
vang	field
vani	usually
vanir	friends
vann	performed, won
vannst	defeated
vanr	accustomed, custom, free, lacking, without
vant	difficulty, missing, wanting
vápn	weapon, weapons
vápnabúnað	weapons-prepared
vápnföt	weapon-clothes
vápnhæft	weapon-capable, weapon-handy
vápnum	weapons
var	as, it-was, stayed, then, there-was, was, were, when, where, who
vár	be, been, our, spring, sprung, were, what-was, will
várar	our, ours, spring
varð	became, came, there-was, was, went, were
varðhöld	a-watch, watch-holders
varði	expectation, expected
varðk	became
vargi	wolf, wolves
vargr	wolf
varir	aware, foreseen
vark	was, when
varla	barely, hardly, rarely
varmar	warm
várn	ours
varr	aware, wary, where
várs	ours
várt	our, ours, us
varu	were
váru	being, ours, that-was, wares, was, were, when
várum	ours, we
vas	was
vasat	was
vask	was
vatnföllum	waterfalls
vatni	river, water
vatnsbakkanum	water's-edge
vatnsísinum	water-ice
vaxa	grew, grow
vaxinn	growing, grown, overgrown
vaxnir	grown
veðr	weather, wind, winds

The Sagas of Ragnar Lothbrok   *Word List (Old Norse to English)*

Old Norse	English
veðrafirði	Waterford (a place)
vefja	wrap
veg	fell, way
vega	fight, ways
veggirnir	the-walls
veiða	hunt
veiðivitjar	seekers
veikan	weak
veisla	feast, the-feast
veislu	a-feast, feast, the-feast
veisluna	feast
veislunni	feast, the-feast
veist	know
veistu	know-you
veit	knew, know, knowing, known, knows
veita	grant, know, lead, provide, supplied, supply, to grant
veiti	will
veitk	given
veitti	grant, granted, provided-for, support, supported
veittu	gave, grant, had, supported
vekja	awake, awaken, awoke
vel	a, well
veldi	chosen, empire, ruling
veldr	brought-about, caused, wielded
vella	boil, boiled
velli	field, fields, plains
veltist	rolled
ver	be, were
vér	our, we, we-are

Old Norse	English
vera	be, been, being, be-it, come-to, had-been, it-be, it-was, shall-be, to be, to-be, was, were
verð	deserve, worth
verða	as, be, became, become, becoming, being, to become, to-be, was, were
verðar	meal
verði	be, became, become, meal, will-be, worth-of
verðið	become
verðkaupit	worth-price
verðr	became, become, becomes, bring, was, were, worth, worthy
verit	be, became, become, been, being, did, have-been, made, was
verja	guard, protect, protection
verk	work
verki	work
verkit	the-work, work
verkum	actions, works
veröldin	the-world
veröldu	the-world
verr	the-worst, worse
verra	worse, worst
verri	worse, worsen
verst	the-worst, worst
verstr	worse
vert	be, worth, worthy
vesa	be, being
vesallátan	shabby
vestfold	Vestfold (a place)
vestr	West
vestra-gautland	West-Gautland (a place)

Old Norse	English
vestra-gautlandi	West-Gautland (a place)
vetra	of-winters, winter, winters
vetrinn	winter
vetrum	winter, winters
vetta	blade
vex	grew, grows
vexti	grow, grown, well-built
við	about, against, as, at, by, from, in, known, of, off, on, that, therefore, thereore, to, we, with, within, wood
víða	many, spread-in, widely
víðfarar	wide-travelled
viðinn	the-trees, trees
viðreignar	dealt-with
viðris	Vidrir's (a name), weather's
viðskiptis	business
viðtöku	resistance
vífill	Vifil (a name)
vífilsborg	Vifilsborg (a place)
vífilsborgar	Vifilsborg (a place)
vígi	slaying, the-fort
vígr	spear-man, were
víkaskeiði	Vikaskeid (a place)
víkin	Viken (a place)
víkina	Viken (a place)
víkingar	vikings
vikna	weeks
vil	will, wish
vilda	will, willed, wish, wished
vildi	wanted, will, willed, willed-it, willing, wills, wish, wished, would
vildu	wanted, will, willed, willing, would
vilhjálmr	william
vili	will, willed, wished
vilið	will
vilir	will, will-you
vilja	he-willed, the-will-of, to want, to will, want, will, willed, willing, wish, wished, would
viljum	will, wish, wish-to
vilkat	which
vill	wanted-to, will, willed, willed-to, willow, wills, wish, wished, wished-to, wishes, would
vilt	like, will, wish
viltu	will-you
vin	a-friend, friend
vín	wine
vinátta	friendship
vindland	Wendland (a place)
vindlandi	Wendland (a place)
vinfengi	friendship
vingaðist	befriended
vingott	friends-good
vini	friends
vínkers	wine-beaker
vínlauk	wine-leek
vinna	deserve, do-work, win, work-on
vinni	work
vinnir	work
vinnr	friend, won
vinnst	worked
vinsæll	befriended, popular, popularity
vinst	won
virðing	honour
virðir	value, valued
virðuliga	worthily
virtr	ale
vísa	direct, verse

Old Norse	English
vísi	certainly, intended
vissa	knew
vissi	knew, know
vissu	knew
víst	certain, certainly, know, known, made, surely, wise
vistir	food, lodging, provisions, shelter, supplies
vísu	a-verse, certainly, know, verse
vit	into, knew, know, known, sense, to, we, wit, with
vita	certainly, he-knew, knew, know, knowing, to know, to-know
viti	knew, knowing
vitir	know
vitja	visit
vitr	wise
vitrastr	the-wisest, wisest
vitrliga	wise-like
vitrust	wise
vitrustu	wisest
vítt	charms, wide
vitu	know
vitum	knowing, we-know
völd	powerful
völl	field, ground, the-field
völlum	fields
völlunum	the-fields
völnir	Volnir (a name)
vöndr	wand
vörðr	guardian
vörðust	guarded
vörgum	wolves
vöxtr	grown

W, w

X, x

Y, y

Old Norse	English
yðar	you, yours
yðarn	you, yours
yðarra	your, yours
yðarrar	yours
yðarri	yours
yðr	to-you, you, you (plural), your, yours
yðru	yours
yðvarn	your, yours
yfir	about, across, over, up
yfirbætr	compensate
yfirbátr	above
yfirbót	redress
yfirlit	appearance
yfirlits	to-look-at
yfirlitum	looks
ygli	awful
ykkr	to-you, you
ylgr	she-wolf's
yngri	younger
yngrum	younger
yngstr	young
yngvarr	Yngvarr (a name)
ynni	won
yrði	became, could, should, should-be, would
yrmling	little-snake
yst	outer, outermost

Ý, ý

Old Norse	English
ýmsa	various
ýmsi	various
ýmsum	various
ýta	launch, launched, out-to, pressed, pushed, towards

Z, z

Word List (English to Old Norse)

English	Old Norse

0-9

A, a

English	Old Norse
a	á, at, at, eina, einn, eins, einu, einum, eitt, er, í
a-baby-boy	sveinbarn
abandoned	hafnat
about	á, áðr, at, en, í, með, of, til, um, uppi, úti, við, yfir
about-a	um
above	yfirbátr
abundance	gnóga, gnótt
a-bundle	byrði
accept	þiggja
accepted	þiggja, þiggr
accomplished	atgervimaðr, færr, íþróttum
according	því
accordingly	því
according-to	því
accused	sakaði
accustomed	vanr
a-child	barni
a-company	lið
a-cow	kúna
a-crew	lið, liði
a-crime	glæp
across	yfir
acted	lætr
actions	verkum
a-din	gnýr
a-disgrace	svívirðing
advanced	flytr
advice	ráð, ráða, ráðum
advised	ráðit, ræddi, réð, tilræði
a-feast	veislu
a-few	nokkurra
affected	færr
a-fire	eld, eldinn
a-forest	skógr
a-friend	vin
after	áðr, eptir, síðar
afterwards	eptir, síðan
against	gegn, mót, móti, rönd, við
a-game	gaman
a-game-piece	töfl
a-gaming-table	hneftafli
agder	agðir
age	aldr, aldri, öld, öldrum, öldum
age-laying	aldrlagi
agnar	agnar, agnarr, agnars
agnar's	agnars
a-good	gott
a-great	mikil, mikill, mikinn, miklu
agreed	ákveðin, játtar, ráða, sáttir
a-greeting	kveðja
a-group	lið
ahead	fram
ahead-of	fyrir
a-hood	hött
a-human	mennskr
aided	duga
a-journey	leið
aki	áki
a-king	konung, konungr
a-king's	konungs

The Sagas of Ragnar Lothbrok *Word List (English to Old Norse*

English	Old Norse	English	Old Norse
a-knuts-drapu	knútsdrápu	amuse	skemmta
Alasund	álasundi	amusement	skemmtan
ale	öl, virtr	an	einn
a-lie	logit	a-name	nafn
a-little	lítinn, lítit	an-army	her
alive	kvikt	ancestors	forellrismenn
all	á, alla, allan, allar, allir, allr, allra, allrar, alls, allt, allt, gervallir, í, öll, öllu, öllum	and	á, eða, en, er, ok
		an-earl	jarl
		an-earthquake	landskjálfti
		anger	reiði
		anglesey	önguls-eyju
all-contended	allstrítt	angry	reiðir, reiðr
allegiance	kné	announced	boði
all-many	allmarga	an-old	gömul
all-men	almenning	an-old-woman	kerling
all-much	allmikit	another	aðra, annarr, annarr, annarra, annarri, annat, önnur
all-near	allnær		
allow	lætr, láta		
allowed	lætr, láta, létu	an-overwhelming	óvígan
all-prying	allnýs	an-ox	oxa, uxa
all-ugly	allóvæn	an-ox-hide	uxahúð
all-un-likely	allólíkligt	answer	segja, svörum
all-weaponed	alvápnaðra	answered	segir, svara, svaraði, svarar
all-well	allvel		
all-wielding	allvaldr	an-unconquerable	óvígan
almost	flest	an-unknown	ókunnr
alone	eigi, ein, einn, eins, einum, eitt	any	eigum, hverjum, nokkur, nokkurr, nokkurum
already	þegar		
also	ok, önnur, þó	any-other	annars, annat
altogether	allra, allt, allt, gersamliga	anything	nokkurr, nokkut
		apart	sundr
always	ávallt	a-part	skilja
am	em, er	apart-from	frá
a-maiden	mey	a-peasant's-daughter	karlsdóttur
a-man	karl, maðr, mann		
amassed	þrotna	appearance	sýndum, tilsýndar, yfirlit
amber	röf		
a-meal	mál	appeared	brugðit, sýnum
among	í, með, milli	appreciated	meta
a-more	meira	approached	nálgast
a-mountain	fjallinu	a-pyre	bál

English	Old Norse	English	Old Norse
are	er, ert, eru, eruð, erum	as-one	eina
		a-spear	spjót
are-given	gefr	a-spear-shaft	spjótskepti
are-they	þeira	as-seemed	þótti
are-we	erum	assembly	þinginu, þingsins
a-rich	ríkr	assistance	atbeina
a-ring	hring, kring	as-soon	þegar
armour	brynju, brynjur	as-soon-as	þegar
army	her, herr, hers	as-though	sem
army-theirs	hersins	as-to	at
arnulf	örnúlfr	a-strait	sund
around	um	asunder	sundr, sundruðum
arranged	skipuð, törruðu	at	á, at, í, til, við
arrow	ór, örin, öru, örvar	ate	át
arrow-messages	örvarboð	a-third-of	þriðjungr
arrows	örvar, skeyti	at-home	heima
arrow-summons	örvarboð	at-least	minst, síst
as	á, at, ef, eins, en, er, es, í, ok, sem, svá, því, verða, við	at-once	sennu
		a-trout-net	aurriðanet
		at-sea	hafa
a-sacrificing-man	blótmaðr	attack	atsókn
as-chosen	valnum	attended	sák
a-seat	atsetu	at-the-front	öndverðri
a-serpent	ormr	attractive	snótu
a-settlement	sætt	auslag	áslaug, áslaugar, áslaugu
as-far-as	um		
as-he	sér	auslag's	áslaugar
a-ship	skip	autumn	haustit
a-short-distance	skammt	avenge	hefna
as-if	sem	a-verse	vísu
a-silk-tunic	silkihjúp	awake	vaka, vaki
ask	bið, biðið, kveð, spyrja	awaken	vekja
		a-war-band	her, herliðs, herr
asked	bað, báðu, beiddist, beiddu, beiðir, biðr, kvað, kvæði, spurði, spurðr, spurðu, spyrja, spyrr	aware	varir, varr
		a-warship	herskipa
		a-watch	varðhöld
		away	brott, frá, undan
asked-for	biðr	away-from	frá, undan
aslaug	áslaug, áslaugar, áslaugu	a-wedding-feast	brúðlaup
		awful	ygli
as-long-as	meðan		
a-snake	ormr		

English	Old Norse	English	Old Norse
awhile	*hríð, stund, stundir, stundum*	bark	*bark*
a-whole	*heill*	barley-barn	*bygghlaða*
awoke	*vaknar*	bastard	*bastarðr*
a-woman	*konu*	bastard-born	*frilluborna*
a-wonder	*furða*	bathing-moon	*böðmána*
axe	*öxi, öxin*	battle	*bardaga, bardagann, bardagi, berjast, hildar, hildi, hildr, hjaldri, orrosta, orrostan, orrostu, rómu*
axe-cuts	*skýlihöggum*		
a-young	*ungr*		

Æ, æ

Ægir's	*Ægis*	battle-cry	*ópi*
Ælla	*ella, ellu*	battled	*barðist, börðust*
Ælla's	*ellu*	battle-hoe	*bengrefill*
Æsir	*Æsir*	battles	*orrostu, orrostur*
Æthelberht	*aðalbrigt*	battle-shirts	*skyrtur*
Æthelmund	*aðalmundr*	be	*gera, gerast, mega, sé, ver, vera, verða, vert, vesa*
		beaches	*strandir*
		bear	*bera, beri, berið*

B, b

		bearer-men	*burðarmenn*
		bearing	*bárum*
		bears	*berr*
		beast	*dýja*
baby-girl	*meybarn*	beat	*barði, börðu*
back	*áðr, aptr, aptr, bak, baki, eptir, út*	beautiful	*fagran*
		beauty	*fegrð*
bad	*illa*	be-bare	*ber*
badly	*illa*	be-brought	*færa*
bake	*baka*	be-called	*heitinn*
baldr's	*baldrs*	became	*gerðist, gerist, kemr, orðinn, urðu, varð, varðk, verða, verði, verðr, yrði*
ball	*knáttu*		
band	*herr*		
bane	*bana*		
bane-herrings	*bensildr*	because	*fyrir, því*
banned	*bannat*	because-of	*fyrir, því*
banner	*merki*	become	*orðinn, orðit, verða, verði, verðið, verðr, verit*
banquet	*sumblum*		
baptism	*skírn*	becomes	*verðr*
bardafjord	*barðafirði*	bed	*beð, bing, rekkju*
bare	*bert*	be-done	*gera*

English	Old Norse	English	Old Norse
been	orðit, verit	best	best, besta, bestu, bestum
been-done	skipast	be-taken	taka
beer	bjór	betray	svíkja
before	áðr, för, fóru, fyr, fyrir, fyrr, fyrri, fyrrum, því	better	batni, betr, betra, betri, meiri
before-intentions	fyrirætlan	between	miðr, milli, millim
before-them	fyrir	between-faring	meðalfærir
before-us	fyrir	be-victorious	sigrast
befriended	vingaðist	bid	bað, bauð, bíða, biðr, bjóða, boð
beggar	stafkarl	bidding	bæn
begin	hefja	bid-they	báðu
be-given	gefin, gefinn	biggest	mikilli
be-heard	hljóðs	birds	fogli, fuglar
beheld	líst	birth-mark	frægðarmark
behind	eptir, undir	bit	beit, bitu
behold	heldr, líst	bite	bíta, bíti
being	er, værim, váru, vera, verða, verit, vesa	bitten	bitu
		bitter	bitrum
be-it	vera	bjorn	birni, björn
be-known	kenna	black-and-blue	blár
beli	beli	blade	vetta
belief	átrúnað	blades-clash	brandagný
believe	trúa, trúi	blaeja	blæja, blæju
believed	trúðu	blame	saka, sök
believes	trúir	blaze	blása
beli's	beli	bleed	blæða
bellow	gellr	blemish-free	vammlausa
bellowed	beljar, gall, lætr, láta	blew	blés
bellowing	læti, lát	blood	blóð, blóði, dreyra
be-made	gera	blood-falcons	blóðvali
be-named	heita	blood-gush	blóðbogi
bench	bekk, bekki	bloodied	blóði
beneath	unda	bloody	dreyrug
benefit	beinabót, kostar	blown	blásit
bent-tree	bjúgviðum	blows	höggum
be-prepared	búit	blue	blár
berserker	berserk	boar	galtar
beside	hjá, innar	bodies	hold
besides	annat	body	hold, líkit
		boiled	vella

The Sagas of Ragnar Lothbrok   Word List (English to Old Norse)

English	Old Norse	English	Old Norse
bold-and-brave	þróttarsnjallr	breathing	öndurðr
boldly	djarfliga, strengdi	breeches	brækr
bone	bein, beini	brewed	heitu
boneless	beinlausan, beinlausi	bride	brúði
		bridle	tauma
bone-less	beinlauss	bright	bjart, bjarta, bjartar, bjartra
bones	bein		
booths	búðir	bring	breyta
bore	bæri, bar, barist, báru, bera, beri, berr, berst, bör, fæddi	bringer	boði
		brings-about	byrja
		broad	breiddi
		broke	braut, brjóta, brýtr
bore-up	bera	broke-away	hvarf
borghild	borghildar	broken	brotnar, rjúfa, slitnir, slitnu, slitusk
born	áttar, borinn		
borne	bera, bornir	brooch-bil	þorn-bil
bornholm	borgundarholmi	brother	bróðir, bróður
both	báða, báðir, bæði, beggja	brothers	bræðr, bræðra, bræðrna, bræðrum
bought	batt	brother's-son	bróðursonr
boulder	bjarg	brought	bæri, borin, borinn, brjóta, brott, byrjuð, færa, færðr, færi, færir, flutti
bound	bundu, strengir		
boundless	ærinn		
bow	boga, bogi, hlýr		
bow-shape	bogamynd	brought-out	brugðit
bow-string	bogastreng, strenghömlur	brown	brún, brúna
		brow-stones	brúnstein, brúnsteina, brúnsteinum
box	eski		
boy	svein, sveini, sveinn	brynhild	brynhildar, brynhildi, brynhildr
brain	hjarna		
brand	brandr	budli	buðla
brave	harðfengnir	bulgar-land	bolgaralandi
brave-deeds	þrekvirki	bullocks	kvígendi
bravellir	brávelli	bulls	naut
bravely	drengiliga, ókvíðandi	buried	heygðr
bravery	fræknleik, hraustleik	burn	brenna
bravest	fræknustu	burned	brenna, brenndu, brotit, láta
bread	brauð		
break	brjóta, höggva	burning	bröndum
breaks	brjótr	burst	bresta, sprakk
breast	brjósti	business	sýslu, viðskiptis
breasts	brjóstum	but	eða, en, er, ok

English	Old Norse	English	Old Norse
buy	*kaupa*	castles	*kastala*
by	*á, at, hjá, í, við*	cattle	*fé*
		caught	*náði*
		celebrated	*fagna, fegnir*
		celebrations	*fagnaðaröl*

C, c

English	Old Norse	English	Old Norse
		certain	*nokkur, víst*
cabin	*skála, skemman, skemmu, skemmuna*	certainly	*vísi, víst, vísu, vita*
		challenged	*skoraði*
		champion	*kappi*
call	*kalla*	change	*breyta, skipast, tiltekju*
called	*heit, heita, heitinn, heitir, heitit, hét, hétu, kalla, kallaðist, kallaðr, kallar, kölluð, kölluðu, kvaddi, kvaddr, kveðja*	changed	*breytt, skipast*
		charms	*vítt*
		chieftain	*höfðingi, höfðingja*
		chieftains	*höfðingja, höfðingjar, höfðingjum*
called-for	*kveðr*	child	*barn, barni, mannsbarn*
calm	*kyrt*		
came	*kæmi, kemir, kemr, kemst, kœmi, kom, koma, komast, komit, komnir, komst, kómu, urðu, varð*	children	*barn, barna, börn*
		choices	*vals*
		choose	*bæði, kjósi*
		chose	*biðst, kaus, kjósi, valdi*
came-to	*kemr*	chosen	*veldi*
can	*kann*	christianity	*kristnaði*
capable	*færr*	circumstances	*hag*
cape	*kápa, kápu*	cities	*borgir*
captured	*handtekinn*	city	*borg, borga, borgar, borgina, borgir*
cared	*hirðir*		
carelessness	*athugaleysi*	city-gates	*borgarhlið*
carried	*borinn, færðu*	city-side	*borghlið*
carried-out	*efna*	city-wall	*borgarveggi*
carrion-beast	*rægagarr*	city-walls	*borgarveggi, borgarveggir, borgarveggja*
carry	*bera, draga*		
cartilage	*brjósk*		
carve	*telgja*	city-wide	*borgarvídd*
carved	*rista*	claimed	*kallaði*
carving	*oddhagastr*	clearing	*heiðan, rjóðr*
cast	*kasta, kastaði, kastar, kasti, kastið, skýtr*	cleaved	*klýfrat*
		cleft	*klufu*
		cleveland	*kliflönd*
castle	*kastala*	cliffs	*kleifar*

English	Old Norse	English	Old Norse
cloak	kufl	completely	gerla
close	fast	conceal	leyna
close-by	nánd	concealing	leyna
closely	vandliga	conclude	enda
closer	innar	concluded	lauk, lokit, lý, lýkr
close-to	nánd	conduct	breytni
cloth	klæði	conducted	heyja
clothed	klædd, klæddi, klæddr	conquered	sigrast
		consider	rifja
clothes	klæði, váðum	considered	hyggr
clothing	búnaði, föt, klæði, klæðum	conversations	mál
		cooks	matsveinar
cloud	skýja	corpse	nár, nás
clouds	hreggský	corpse-birds	valfugla
coal-black	kolsvörtum	corpse-candle	rækyndill
coil	lykkju	corpse-fish	hræsíldar
collapsed	hrunði	corpses	hræ
collected	safnar	could	dugi, fær, geti, knætti, kunna, mætti, mátti, máttu, mun, mundi, yrði
colour	litr		
comb	kemba		
come	kæmi, kem, kemr, koma, komast, komi, komim, komin, kominn, komir, komist, komit, komnir, komum		
		council	málstefnu
		counsel	ráðumk
		count	tölu
		countless	hundmörgum
comes	fór, kemr, komi, komit, kømk, kømr	countrymen	landsmanna
		courage	ofrhuga, ofrhuga
come-to	komit, til, vera	covered	tjaldaðan
come-together	samtogi	covering	hjúpu, hlýr
coming	kemr, kom, koma, komast, komin, kominn, komit	covers	rekkja
		cow	kú, kýr, kýrin
		cower	feigri
command	fylkir, ráðir, skipa	craft	sköp
commander	formaðr	crafted	skapaðr
committed	unnit	craftily	flátt
companions	lið	craves	krefr
companionship	förunaut	crazy	óðir
company	lið, liði, liðit	creature	kykvendis
company-men	liðsmenn	crew	lið
compensate	yfirbætr	cringed	lúðrar
compensation	bóta, fébætr	crowd	fjölmenns
complete	enda		

English	Old Norse
cruelty	grimmd
crushed	kreisti
crying	grét
cry-thrown	gollhroðinn
cuckoo	gaukr
cunning	spekt
curious	forvitni
currents	rastar, straums
custom	vanda, vandi, vanr
cut	bíta
cut-up	brytja

D, d

English	Old Norse
dag's	dags
damage	skaða
dane	danski
danes	danir, dönum
danes'-beloved	danaást
danger	hætta
danish	danskri
danish-army	danaherr
danish-realm	danaveldi
danube	dínu
dared	þorði, þorðu, þorir, þyrði
daring	áræði, áræði
dark	bleika
darken	røkkva
dark-forests	myrkviðar
daughter	dóttir, dóttur
daughter-of	dóttur
daughter-of-budla	buðladóttur
day	dag, dagan, dagr, degi
day-diminishing	dagrýrir
days	daga, dœgr, dögum
day's-meal	dögurðar
dead	andaðr, dæið, dauðir, dauðr, dauðs, deyja, nár
dealt-with	viðreignar
dear	dýri, dýrlig, dýrligan, dýrligu, dýrs
dearer	dýrra
death	bana, dauða, dauðan, dauði, dauðr, líflát
death-day	dauðadags, dauðdaga
death-sickness	banasótt
death-throes	fjörbrotum
death-wound	banasári
deceased	látinn
decide	ráða
decided	ákveðit, ræða, ræddu, ræðst
decision	ráða
declaration	bragarfulli
declare	lýsir
declared	kveðit
declined	hniginn
decoration	skraut
deem	dæmi
deepest	inniligast
defeat	ósigr
defeated	ósigr, vannst
defence	landvarnar
delay	löng
denmark	danaveldi, danmarkar, danmörk, danmörku
denmark's-benefit	danmarkarbót
deny	þorik
depended	undir
depended-on	heyrir
depending	háðum
descendant	niðr
descendants	niðja, niðjar
descendents	ætt, ættbogi
deserted-forest	eyðimerkr
deserve	vinna
deserved	unnit
desire	þrá

English	Old Norse	English	Old Norse
destroy	týna	down	náliga, niðr, ofan
determined	einarðr	do-work	vinna
devastated	eyða, eyddi, eyddist, eyddu, eytt	drank	drakk, drekka, drykki
		drank-to	drukkit
devil's	djöfuls	draught	drykk
dew	dögg	draw-back	hrøkkvit
did	fær, gera, gerir, hefir	drawn	drægir, draga, dregin, dregit, dregst, rítar
did-not	eigi		
die	deyja		
died	andaðist, andast, dó, eptir	dress	búnaði
		drew	brá, drægi, draga, dregr, drógu, kippir
dies	deyr		
difference	munr	drink	drekka, drekkir, drykkja
difficult	illr, torveldi		
difficulties	torveldi	drinking	drykkju
difficulty	ilt, vant	drinking-man	drykkjumaðr
din	gnýr	drink-to	drekka
direct	stefna, vísa	drive	keyrðak, reka, rekum
directed	áttum, skipaði		
directions	tilskipun	driven	drifinn, rak, reknar
disappear	hverfa	drove	óku, rækir, reka
discussed	fjölrætt, ráða, ráðit, ræddu, ræðir, réðst, réðu	drunk	drukkinn, drukkit
		duel	einvígi
		during	leið
discussing	ræða	dwell	dveljast
disir	dísir	dwelled	dvaldist
dismissed	leystu	dwelling	bú
dispersed	dreifðist	dwelt	bjó, búa
distinguished	mætri		
distressing	nauð		

E, e

English	Old Norse
distribute	sundr
divide	skipa
divided	skipta
do	ger, gera, láta
do-business	sýslu
dog	hund
döglings	döglinga
done	gera, gerr, gerst, gert, láta
donkey	asni
doomed	feigum
dovrefjell	dofrafjalls

English	Old Norse
each	annarr, hvár, hvárir, hvárr, hvárt, hver, hverja, hverjan, hverjum, hvern, hverr, hverrar, hvert, öðrum
each-of	hverjum
each-other	annan, annarra
each-way	hvárttveggja, hvárumtveggjum
eager	ákafari, ákafir, frekum

English	Old Norse	English	Old Norse
eagerness	kapp	encouragement	eggja, eggjan
eagle	ara, arnar, örn	ended	lokinn, lokit, lýkr
earl	jarl	endil's	endils
earls	jarla	endures	þolir
earl's	jarls	enduring	þolið
early	ár, hrindum, skjótum, snemma, snimma	enemies	óvinir
		engaging	geðsligr
		england	england, englandi, englands
earned	unnit		
earth	jarðar, jörð	englanes	englanes
east	austr	english	enskir, grafa
eastern	austr	engrave	grafa
eastern-journeys	austrfarar	enough	dugðu, dugi, œrit
eastern-lands	austrveg, austrvegi	enriched	lagða
eat	eta	entertain	skemmtanar
eaten	bergt	envenomed	eitrhvass
edge	rendi	equal	jafnast, jafningi, jafningjar, jafnt, jafnvæna, maka
edged	rendr		
edges	eggjar		
edmund	játmund, játmundar	equal-age	jafngamlir
egged	eggjuðu	equal-famous	jafnfrægir
egill	egill	equal-great	jafnmikill
eight	átta	equally	jafngerla, jafnilla, jafnt, jafnvæn
eirek	eirekr		
either	annathvárt, eða, hvárt, hvárttveggja	equip	skipi
		equipped	skipuð
either-side	hvárirtveggju	erik	eireki, eirekr, eireks, eiríki, eiríkr
either-way	annathvárt, hvárumtveggjum	erik's	eireks
		errand	erendi, erendis
ekkil	ekkils	errands	erendi, erendis, erendum
elder	ellri		
elegantly	listuliga	established	stofnuð
elf	álf	estate	býjar
elm	almr	estates	búum
elm-twig	álmsveig	evening	aptan, kveld, kveldit, kvelds
else	aðra, annarra		
emperor	keisari	evenly	jafnan, jafnt
empire	veldi	events	atburð, atburðum
enamelled	smeltr	eventually	síðir
encountered	finnast	ever	æ, efra
encourage	eggja	every	hverju, hverjum, hverr
encouraged	eggjar		

English	Old Norse	English	Old Norse
every-man	hverr	faithful	trúligt
everywhere	allir, hvar, hvarvetna	fall	fall, falla
evil	illa, illu	fallen	fall, fallinn, valinn
examples	dæmi	falling	felli
except	en, nema, sá	falls	fellr
except-for	utan	fame	frægð, frægðar, frægt, orðstír
exchange	skiptum	family	ættar
expect	væntir	family-line	ætt
expectation	varði	famous	ágæt, ágætr, frægir, frægr, frægstr
expected	vænst, vænta, ván		
expedition	leiðangri	famous-work	frægðarverk
expelled	reka	far-away	fjarri
experienced	reynt	fare	farit
expressed	tjá	fared	farit, fór
extremely	ákafliga	faring	fara
eye	auga	farm	bæjar, bær, býjar
eyelids-enclosure	hvarmatúni	farms	bæjum
eyes	auga, augna, augu, augum	farmstead	bæ
		fast	fast, hratt, snart
eygotaland	eygotaland	fasted	fasta
eynaefi's	eynæfis	fastened	festast, festi, heimtum
eyrasundi	eyrasundi		
eystein	eystein, eysteini, eysteinn, eysteins	fastest	hraðast
		fate	örlög
eystein's	eysteins	fated	auðit
		father	faðir, feðr, föður
		father-brother	föðurbróðir
		father-payment	föðurgjöld

F, f

English	Old Norse	English	Old Norse
face	fýsumk	fattened	feitaðir
fails	rýfst	fault	sök
fair	fagra, fagrt, fögru, óvænni, væn, væna, vænst	fear	ótta, óttast, ótti, uggi
		feared	ugga, uggðu
		fearful	grimmligu
fair-coloured	litfögr	feast	veisla, veislu, veisluna, veislunni
fairer	vænni		
fairest	fegrst, fegrstr, vænst	fed	áttak
fair-haired	hárfagran	fee-costly	fékostnaðr
fairly	fagrt	fee-servant	féhirði
fairness	fegrð, væn	feet	fætr, fótum
fair-wind	byr	feet-gold	fótgulum
faith	trú		

English	Old Norse	English	Old Norse
fell	falla, falli, fell, felldi, felli, fellr, fellt	flesh	hölda
		flew	flugu, flýgr
felled	fella	flies	flýgr
fellow	dreng, drengr	flight-dragon	flugdreki
fellows	drengja	flown	flaug
felt	kenndi	foe	val
feminine-same-like	kvensamliga	folk	folka
few	fá, fæst, fáir, fám, fár, fátt	folk-battles	folkorrostur
		follow	fylgdi, fylgja, fylgjum
field	vang, velli, völl	followed	fylgdi, fylgdum, fylgi, fylgir, fylgt
fields	fjörðum, velli, völlum	followers	fjölmenni
fiercely	grimmliga, grimt	follows	fylgir
fiery-red	brandrauðum	food	fæðslu, mat, matr, vistir
fifteen	fimmtán		
fifty	fimm	food-prepared	matbúit
fight	berjast, berjumst, heyja	for	á, af, at, fyr, fyrir, fyrr, fyrri, því, til
fighting	berjast	force	liði, liðs
fill	fylli	forcefulness	geysingi
find	finna, fund	forces	hér, hermönnum, lið, liði, liðit, liðs
fine-cloth	guðvefjarpell		
finest	fegrst	fore-knowing	framvís
fingers	fingum	foremost	framast, fremri, fyrir, öndvegi
finished	luku		
fire	bál, eldi, eldr	foremost-seat	öndvegi
first	fyrirrúm, fyrst, fyrsta, fyrstr, fyrstu	foreseen	varir
		forest	skóg, skóginum
first-of	fyrstr	for-good	alfari
fish	fiski	for-him	sér
fishes	hveðnu	for-intentions	fyrirætlan
fits	hæfir	for-knowing	forvitri
fitted-out	skipaðar	for-lodgings	húsa
five	fimm	for-me	mér
fjolnir's	fjölnis	forsake	hafna
flame	eldr	forth	fram
flanks	fylkingar	for-the	fyr
flashing	fránir	for-the-sake-of	sakir
flat	sléttan	fortress-hart	borgarhjört, borgarhjörtr
fled	flýðu, flýr		
flee	flótta, flýja	fortune	forlögum
fleeing	flóttann	forty	fertugr
flemings'	flæmingja	forward	fram, framm

English	Old Norse	English	Old Norse
forwards	firr, fram	frozen	frerin
foster	fæða, fóstra, fóstru	full	fullan, fullu
fostered	fóstraði	full-good	fullgott
foster-father	fóstra	full-many	fjöld
fought	barðist, berjast, berst, vák	fully-loaded	skipaðir
found	fann, fengit, finna, finnast, finnst, fundinn, fundu, fyndi, hitt, hittust	funda	fundna
		furthest	framast
		fury	furða

G, g

English	Old Norse
foundations	grundvöll
found-is	fekkst
four	fjóra
fourteen	fjórtán
fourth	fjórði
four-times	fjórum
fragile	skör
france	frakkland
freed	frelsti
frequent	tíðar
freyr	freyr
frey's	freys
friends	spjalli, vanir, vini
friend's	málvini
friends-good	vingott
friendship	vinátta, vinfengi
fringes	trefr
frodi	fróði
from	á, af, at, at, frá, fram, framar, framm, fránan, fremr, fyrir, ór, um, undan, við
from-here	heðan
from-him	hann
from-home	heiman
from-out-of	ór
from-saying	frásögn
from-there	frá, þaðan, þangat
from-the-south	sunnan
from-under	undan, undir
from-where	hvaðan
frosted	frost

English	Old Norse
gain	aflim
gain-victory	sigrumst
game	leiki, leiks
game-pieces	taflit
games	leika
gathered	fengu, safnar, safnast
gathering	samdrátt
gautland	gautland
gave	gaf, gafta, gáfu, gefa, gefi, gefr, gifti
gave-birth-to	elr
generous	stórlyndr
genteel	dælt
gentle	blíðum
get	fá, fæ, fái, fáim, fengin, gatk, gera, þangat
get-for	fá
gets	fær
getting	fingi
giantess's	hálu
girded	gyrðr
girl	mær
give	fá, gefa, gefast, gefir, gefit, gifta
given	gefin, gefit, gefnir, gefr, gjalfri, veitk
glad	glaðr, glöddu
gladdens	lægir
gladly	glaðr

English	Old Norse	English	Old Norse
glory	ágæti	great	ágætar, ágætr, mikil, mikill, mikilla, mikillar, mikinn, mikit, mikla, miklir, miklu, stór
glowing	esat		
gnipafjord	gnípafirði		
go	far, fara, ganga, gengr		
goats	geitr	greater	meiri, meirum, mikinn, miklu
go-before	fyrri	greater-force	ofrefli
god	goð	greater-part	þori, þorik
gods	goð	greatest	mestir, mestr, mikla, stærstum
godthorm	guðþormr		
goes	fær, fari, ferr, gengr	greatly	mikit, stórilla
going	færi, fara, för, gegna, gengr, gingu, gingum	great-men	stórmenni
		greatness	ágætis
		greeted	heilsar, kveðja, kveðr
going-forward	fram		
goinn	góinn	greeting	kveðju
gold	golli, gull, gulli, gullinu, gullit	greetings	kveðju
		grew	óx, vex
gold-embroidered	gullsaumaðr	grey	grána, gránu
gold-ring	gullhring	grey-shirt	gránserk
gone	farin, farit, gengit, gingum	grief	harmi, harmr
		grim	grimmr
good	góð, góðr, gott	grima	gríma, grímu
gored	vættr	ground	grundar, völl
gorm	gormr, gorms	ground-wolf	grafvitnis
got	fá, fær, fagnaði, fekk, fekkst, fengi, fengit, fengu, fingum, gátu, gekk, ná-	group	liðit
		grow	vaxa, vexti
		grown	vaxnir, vexti, vöxtr
		grows	vex
götaland	gautlandi, gautlands	grumble	gnyðja
gotland	gautlandi	guard	gæta
got-they	fengust	guarded	gætti, vörðust
got-we	gátum	guardian	vörðr
governing	landstjórnar	guardsmen	hirðina
grant	leggja, unna, veita	gudrod	guðröðr
granted	veitti	gudrod's	guðröðar
grasp	fingum	gudthorm	guðþorm
grasped	fingum	guess	get
gravel	grjót	guested	gisting
grazing	beit	gull	már
		gullets	svíra

English	Old Norse	English	Old Norse
gusts	gusti	handsome	fríðastr, fríðir, vænn
		hand-taken	handtekinn
		happened	atburðr
H, h		happens	gengr
		happiness	sælu
had	á, at, átt, átti, átti, áttu, áttum, eiga, er, fengit, hæfir, hafa, hafði, hafi, haft, hann, hefði, hefir, hefr, höfðu, höfðust, lætr, lagði, láta, látit, lét, létu, veittu	happy	sæl
		harald	harald, haraldr, haralds
		harbour	hafna, hafnar, höfn
		hard	harða, harðla, harðliga, harðr, hörð, ilt
had-been	hafði, vera	hardly	varla
had-come	kom	hard-melding	harðmeldr
had-done	ger, gerði	hardy	harðfengr, harðger
hadeland	haðaland	harek	hárek
hadeland-berserk	haðaberserkr	harm	harmr, illt, mein, meini, meins, sakast
had-it	hefir	harmed	sakar
had-they	höfðu	harp	harpa, hörpu, hörpuna, hörpunni
hail	éli, heill		
hailstone	haglkorn	harried	herjat
hair	hár, hárit	harry	herja
hair-fair	hárfagra, hárfagri	harrying	herja, hernaðr, herrinn
hair-strands	hársíma		
haiti's	heita	harsh	hvassa
haka	haka	hart	hjörtr
haki	haki	has	á, er, hæfi, hafa, hafði, hafi, hefir, hefr
half	hálfan		
halfdan	hálfdan	haste	bráðr
hall	hallar, hallar, höll, höllu, sal	hastening	bráðrakinn
		hate	hata
halland	halland, hallandi	hates	hatar
hallowed	heilagri	have	á, ætti, átt, eiga, fá, gera, hafa, hafast, hafi, hafið, hafim, hafir, halda, hefðir, hefi, hefir, hefja, hefk, hefr, höfðu, höfum, lát, láta
halls	hallir		
hamdir's	hamðis		
hammer	hamri		
hand	handa, hendi, hendr, hönd, höndina, höndum		
		have-i	hefik
hand-fire	mundelds	have-you	hefir
hand-print	handastaðinn	having-a-meal	máli
hands	hendr, höndum	hawks	hauka, haukr

English	Old Norse	English	Old Norse
hawk-snare	hauksnöru	helgi	helgi
he	búa, er, hafði, hana, hann, hans, hánum, hinn, honum, sá, sér, þann	helm	hilmi
		helmet	hjalm, hjálm, hjalmi
		helmets	hjalma
		helms	hjalma, hjálma, hjalms
head	hausum, höfði, höfuð, höfuðit	helm-staves	hjalmstofn
heads	höfðum	help	duga, fullting, lið
head-tumbled	höfuðsteypu	helsings	helsingja
healing	heilan	her	hana, hennar, henni, hún, sér, sín, sína, sitt
heaped	hrundit, þverr		
hear	heyra, heyri		
heard	heyra, heyrða, heyrði, heyrðu, heyrir, spurt, spyrja, spyrr, spyrst	here	hér, hún
		herjan's	herjans
		hero	bragna
heard-news	frétta	heroes	bragna, bragnar
heard-of	spyrr, spyrst	herraud	herrauðr
hearing-of	spyrja	herrod	herrøðr
heart	hjarta	herrud	herruðr
hearts	hjörtu	hers	hana, hennar, henni, sér, sína, sinna, sinnar, sínu, sitt
heated	hitnaði		
heathen	heiðit		
heather-snake	lyngorm	herself	sér, sjálf
heath's	heiðar	herthjof	herþjófi
heavy	þung, þungr	he-was	hann
he-be	sé	hewed	hjó, höggr
hedin's	heðins	hews	höggr
heed	gaum	hid	fálu, hirðir
heeded	gáðu	hidden-creek	leynivág
heflir's	heflis	hide	húðina
heidmark	heiðmörk	high	há, hæstr, hátt, heiðir, ófár
height	hæð	higher	æðra, æðru
heimir	heimi, heimir	high-seat	hásætit
heimir's	heimis	high-seeing	háseymða
heirs	erfingja	hildibrand	hildibrandr
he-is	hann	hild's	hildar
he-knew	vita	hilt	hjöltunum
hel	helju	him	hann, hans, henni, honum, sér, sik, sín
held	fengu, halda, haldit, heldr, heldu, helt, hélt		
		himself	honum, sem, sér, sik, sína, sjálfan, sjálfr, sjálft
held-words	haldorða		

English	Old Norse	English	Old Norse
himself-to	sér	house-going	húsgangs
his	hann, hans, hinns, honum, sér, sín, sína, sínar, sinn, sinna, sinnar, sinni, síns, sínu, sitt, þau, þessa	households	heim
		houses	hús
		how	hvat, hvé, hver, hvers, hversu, sem
		howled	grenjaði
his-hand	hendi	how-like	þvílíkr
his-life	lífinu	how-much	olli
his-own	sjálfr	how-so	hverrar, hversu
hiss	hvast	how-to	hvé
hjadninga	hjaðninga	hring	hringr, hrings
hlokk's	lakkar	hull	húf
hlymdal	hlymdölum	human	mennskr
hofud	höfða	hundred	hundrað, hundruð, hundruðum
hofudastrond	höfðaströnd	hundred-many	hundmargan
hogni	högna	hundreds	hundruðum
hold	halda, haldast, haldit, heldi, hölða	hung	hengu
		hunger	gráðr, hungri
holding	halda	hungry	ómett
holy	heilug, helga	hunt	veiða
home	heim, heima	hurry	skunda
home-drawn	heimdregi	hurt	grand
home-following	heimanfylgja	hurts	standi
honour	sæmd, sæmdar, samira, þegnsköpum, virðing	husband	manns
		husto	hústó
		hvitabaer	hvítabæ, hvítabær
honourable	tignum	hvitserk	hvítserk, hvítserki, hvítserkr
hood	höttr		
hoods	höttu		
hope	ván	**I, i**	
hoped	vænta		
horda-knut	hörða-knút, hörða-knútr	i	ek, í, mér, mik
		i-am	ek
horn	horn, horni	ice	ís, ísinn
horns	hornum	i-die	deyja
horse	hesti	if	at, ef, er, hvárt
horses	hesta, hesti, hestum	ill	ill, illa, illr, illt
host	lið	ill-doing	illgjarn
hostility	ófriðr	ill-like	illilig
hot	heitr, heitt	ill-tempered	illgjarn
house	hús, húsum		

English	Old Norse	English	Old Norse
image	mynd	iron-side	járnsíða
impossible	ófarar	is	er, ér, eru, hvárt, sé
improved	síða	is-being	sé
in	á, at, at, en, er, í, inn, inni, inum, því, um, við	is-it	er
		island	eyri
		islands	eyland
in-bed	rekkju	it	á, at, enn, er, hana, hann, hitt, hún, í, þar, þat
incite	óttu		
increased	jóku		
infancy	ómegð	it-be	vera
in-front-of	framan, fyrir	it-concluded	enda
ingibjorg	ingibjörg	it-is	er
inheritance	ættleifð, erfi	it-is-said	kveða
in-him	honum	it-might	mætti
injure	granda, meiðir	it-seemed	sjá
injury	grandi	it-was	er, sem, þat, væri, var
inlet	vági		
inndyr's-island	inndyris-eyju	it-would-be	væri
inner-lands	innanlands	iva	ívu
innocent	saklausan	ivar	ívar, ívari, ivarr, ívarr, ívars
insane	ærir		
inside	innan, inni	ivar's	ívars
intend	ætla, ætlar		
intended	aætlaði, ætla, ætlaði, ætlar, ætlat, ætluðu, vísi		

J, j

English	Old Norse
intentions	ætlar, fyriraetlan
in-the-boy	sveini

English	Old Norse
jaws	gin
jewels	gersimum
joints	fellingum
in-the-day	dags
into	í
journey	færi, fara, ferð, ferðar, för, leið
in-vain	ván
invasion	herskátt
journeyed	fór
invitation	boð
journeying	leiðangr
invite	báðuð, biðr, boð, býði
journeys	ferr
jumped	stökk
invited	bað, bauð, biðr, bjóða, buðu, býðr
jutland	jótland, jótlandi, reiðgotaland
ireland	írlandi

K, k

English	Old Norse
irish	íra
iron	járn
iron-shoes	járnskó
keep	halda, haldim, lætr
ironside	járnsíða, járnsíðu
kept	heldi

English	Old Norse	English	Old Norse
kill	bana, drep, drepa	know-you	veistu
killed	dræpi, drap, drápu, drápuð, drepa, drepin, drepit	knut	knúti, knútr, knúts
		knutsson	knútsson
		kraka	kráka, kráku
killer	bana	kraku	kráku
kill-you	drepa		
kindled	kveykja		
kinds	konar	**L, l**	
king	buðlungi, konung, konungr, konungs, siklingr		
		lacking	vanr
		lad	sveinn
kingdom	konungdóm, ríki, ríkinu, ríkis	lads	sveinar
		lady	kona
kingdoms	ríki, ríkis	laid	lá, lægi, lætr, lagðak, lagði, lagðr, lagiðr, látit, leggja, leggr, lét, létta, létu, létum, leyfðu, liggr, lögð, lögðu, lögðum
kings	konunga, konungar, lofðunga, lofðungar		
king's	konungr, konungs		
king's-assembly	konungastefnu		
kingship	konungdóm		
king's-sons	konungssynir	lair	ból
kinsmen	frændr	lament	sýtira
kissing	kyssa	laments	sýtir
klakk-harald	klakkharaldr, klakkharalds	lance-meeting	fleinþings
		land	land, landi, landinu, landit, lands, lönd, löndum
knee	kné		
kneeled	hníga		
kneeling	hníga	land-ruling's	landráða
knees	hné, knjám	lands	landi, landinu, lönd, löndum
knew	kennast, kenndi, kennir, kunni, skildu, veit, vissa, vissi, vissu, vita, viti		
		lands-folk	landsfólk
		landsmen	landsmanna, landsmenn
knew-they	kenndust	land-snakes	barðhjarls
knife	knífi	land-warriors	landherrinn
knorrs	knarra, knerrir, knörru, knörrum	land-way	landveg
		land-ways	landveg
know	kunna, kunni, kynni, sé, skilja, veist, veit, víst, vit, vita, vitir, vitu	large	mikill, mikit, stórar
		large-ships	stórskipum
		last-night	gærkveld
		later	síðan, síðar, síðari
knowing	kunna, veit, vita, viti, vitum	laughing	læjandi
		launch	skjóta
known	kenna, kennt, kunnigt, þekk, veit, víst	launched	skaust

English	Old Norse	English	Old Norse
law	lög	likened	líkari
lay	lá, lagðist, lágu, láta, lét, liggja, liggr	likeness	líktist
		limbs	limum
laying	lá, lægis, leggja	lindesnes	líðandisness
lay-out	láta	lindiseyri	lindiseyri
leader-less	höfðingjalaust	lineage	ættar
leaders	formenn	linen	líndúk
learned	numit, spurði, spyrja, spyrr, spyrst	listen	hlýða
		lit	kveykt, kveyktr
learn-of	spyrja	little	fæðu, fátt, lítill, lítils, lítit, litla, litlu, lítt
least	minnst		
leave	láta	little-as-possible	síst
led	leiddi	little-be	lítill
leek	lauk, lauks	little-snake	yrmling
left	ferst	live	líf, lifa
lejre	hleiðru	lived	bjó
less	hlut, miðr, minna, minni, minnr, síðr	lives	ævi, lífi
		located	stefnt
lesser	minni, minnum	lock-bow	lásboga
less-fair	óvænni	locked	læst
less-famous	ófrægri	lombardy	lúmbardí
let	læt, lætr, láta, látið, látin, leggr, lét, léta, létk, létu, lögðis	london-city	lundúnaborg
		long	langa, langa, langr, langt, lengi, löng, löngu, löngum, síða, sitt
let-down	leyst		
let-us	látum		
let-us-lay	leggjum	longer	lengr
let-us-see	sjám	longships	langskip, langskipum
let-us-settle	ráðumst		
let-us-think	hyggjum	look	líta, lítist
level	stigum	looked	gáðu, horfðu, hyggr, sjá
lidar	líðum		
life	ævi, líf, lifa, lífi, lífs	looking	bragði, litit
life-laying	lífláti	looking-after	sýslu
life-less	líflátnir	looks	yfirlitum
life-loss	líflát	loose	laus
lifted	lypt	loose-fee	lausafé
light	léttr	loot	hlut
lighter	léttari	lord	herra
like	líkr, líkt, líst	lord-of-the-land	landherr
liked	leist, líkaði	lose	láta, týna
likely	líkendi, líkligt	lost	týndi, týndist

English	Old Norse	English	Old Norse
lothbrok	loðbrókar	many-men	fjölmennr
lothbrok's	loðbrókar	marital-status	hjúskaparfar
loudly	hátt, óhljóð	mark	mark, marka
love	ást, ástir	marked	marka, merkðan
loved	ann, unni	mark-of	merki
loved-friend	ástvinr	marks	marka
lucky	sælir	marriage-proposal	ráðahag
luna	lúna	married	átti, fekk, gift, kvángaðr
lungs	lungun	marry	fá, fáir
lust	girnd	marstan	marstan
lying	leggja, liggi, löginn	mass	messu
		matched	maki
		matted	þæfð
		matter	efni, mæla, mál, mála, máls

M, m

English	Old Norse	English	Old Norse
mad	óðari	matters	mæla, málum
made	ger, gera, gerða, gerði, gerir, gert, gervir, látit, létum, liggr, verit	matured	bráðgerr
		may	má, mætti, mátti, mátti, máttu, mega, megi, megim, megin, megir, megu, meguð, megum
made-he	gerðist		
maid	mey, meyja		
maiden	mær, mey	may-be	má
maidens	mær	may-have	mega
maiden's	meyjar	me	meir, mér, mik, mín, minn, mínu
majority	þorri		
make	gera, leggja	meal	verðar
man	karl, maðr, mann, manna, manni, menn, mönnum	measure	alnar
		meat	bráð
		meet	fund, fundar, hitt, mæta, mót, móti
manner	lund		
man's	hal, karls, manns	meeting	fundum, hitt, mót, móti
man's-damage	mannskæðu		
man-slayer	mannsbani	meet-up	finnast
man's-son	mannsbarn	melt	bræddak
many	fjölda, fleira, manna, marga, margan, margar, margir, margr, margs, margt, menn, mikill, mikinn, mikit, miklu, mjök, mörg, mörgu, mörgum, ófáir	men	fólk, gotna, lið, liði, liðs, maðr, mann, mann, manna, manni, menn, mönnum
		men's	gumna, manna
		men's-heads	mannahöfðum
		mentioned	geti

English	Old Norse	English	Old Norse
mercy	grið, þyrma	moss-overgrown	mosavaxinn
messages	orðsending	most	flest, flestir, flestum, megin, mest, mesta, mestar, mesti, mestu, mjök
messengers	sendimenn		
met	fundust, hitta, hittast, hittir, hittist, hittust, mætast		
		most-beautiful	fríðust
metal	malmr	most-handsome	fríðastr
metallic	malmi	mostly	mest
might	mælti, mætta, mætti, mættir, mátti, máttu, mörg	most-virtuous	dyggligast
		mother	móði, móðir, móður
		mother-of-warriors	drengjamóður
might-be	væi	mother's	móðernis
mightiest	ríkasti	mother's-kin	móðurætt
mighty	mikill, mögnuð	mound	haug
mild	mildum	moustache	grön
mind	hug, hugða, hugr	mouth	mynni
minds	hugr	move	hræra
mine	mér, mik, mín, mína, mínir, minn, minna, minni, mínu, mínum, mitt	moved	fluttu
		much	mikil, mikill, mikilli, mikils, mikinn, mikit, mikla, miklar, miklir, miklu, miklum, mjök
mislaid	mislagðar		
mjosa	mjörs	munar-bay	munarvági
mock	háðum	murder	morði
molten	bræddum	must	mun, munt
monsters	óvættum	mustered	fylkt
monstrous	ferlíki	must-have	munduð
month	mánuð	my	mér, mik, mín, mína, mínir, minn, mínu, mínum, mitt
mood	skap		
moon	máni		
more	fleira, fleiri, meir, meira, meiri	my-life	lífit
		myself	mér, sjálfr
more-advisable	ráðligra		
more-famous	frægri		
morning	morgin, morgininn, morginn, morgni, myrgininn		

N, n

English	Old Norse
nail	nagl, nagli
name	nafn, nafni
named	heita, heiti, heitinn, heitir, hét, héti, hétu, nefndr, nefnir
morning-gift	morgingjöf
morning-shear	morginskœru
morning-while	morginstund
mortal-wound	benstara
mortar	lím
moss	mosa
name-fastening	nafnfesti
namesake	nafni

English	Old Norse
naming	heitit
narrowest	mjóvasta
nature	aðal
naval-force	skipaher
near	hjá, nær
nearby	hjá
nearer	nær
nearest	næst
nearly	náliga
near-lying	náliga
neck	háls, hálsi, halsum, svíra
need	gagns, þurfa
needed	þarf, þörf, þurfa, þurfti, þurftu
neighbour	granni
neither	hvárki, hvergi
never	aldri, aldrigi, aldrlagi
new	nýir, nýjari, nýju
news	fregit, frétt, fréttir, fréttum, spurdaga, tíðenda, tíðendi, tíðendum
news-of-war	hersaga
new-take	nýtak
next	annan, næsta, næstum, síðasti
nickname	kenningarnafn
night	náttar, nótt
nights	nætr, nátta
nine	níu
njörun	njörun
no	eigi, einkis, ekki, enga, engan, engar, engi, engum
no-man	manngi
no-more	engrar
none	eigi, ekki, enga, engan, engi, engir, engis, engum, síst
none-of	engi
non-fighting-men	óvígr
no-one	eigi, engi

English	Old Norse
nor	né
north	norðan, norðr
northern-lands	norðrálfu, norðrlönd
north-lands	norðrlönd
northumberland	norðhumbrulandi
northumbria	norðhumrulandi, norðimbralandi
norway	noreg, noregi, noregs
norwegians	norðmönnum
not	eigi, ekki, enga, engi, engrar, engu, né, nú
not-any	nakkvat
not-born	óbornir
not-done	óbúit
not-far	ofarliga
nothing	einkis, ekki, engi, engu
not-lacking	óvant
not-strange	ókynligt
not-to	ekki
now	nú
nowhere	hvergi

O, o

English	Old Norse
oath	eiða, svardaga
obligations	kvöð
observed	hyggja
obstacles	kanntu
obvious	auðsætt, auðvitat
occasion	sinn
occupation	iðju
ocean	ægir, sollinn
odin	óðinn, óðins
odin's	óðinn, óðins
of	á, af, at, en, er, frá, í, of, ok, ór, þeira, til, um, við
of-all	allra
off	af

English	Old Norse	English	Old Norse
of-fair	*fögr*	only	*einir, einu, enga*
offer	*bjóði*	onto	*á*
offered	*bauð*	open	*upp*
offered-tree	*böðheggr*	open-handed	*örr*
of-his	*sinna*	opposition	*andvíga*
of-ill	*illr*	or	*eða, ella, elligar, né*
of-me	*mér*	ordeal	*raunar*
of-men	*manna*	ordered	*bað*
of-news	*tíðenda*	orders	*boði*
often	*opt, optar*	ore	*malms*
of-that	*þærs*	origin	*uppruna*
of-the-flame	*leygjar*	origin-of	*uppruna*
of-the-journey	*fararinnar*	orn	*örn*
of-the-kingdom	*ríkr*	other	*aðra, aðrir, ella, fleira, öðru, öðrum, önnur*
of-them	*þeim, þeira*		
of-the-ships	*skipanna*	others	*aðra, aðrir, annan, öðrum, öndrum*
of-the-world	*heimsins*		
of-this	*þess, þetta*	other-things	*annat, öðru*
of-use	*gagn, gagni*	otherwise	*annarr*
of-which	*er*	our	*okkarrá, okkart, okkra, vár, várar, vér*
of-winters	*vetra*		
ogmund	*ögmundr*	our-lives	*ævi*
olaf	*ólafs*	our-own	*eigu*
old	*fornan, fornir, gamall, gamli, gamlir, gömul*	ours	*okkarr, okkars, okkr, oss, ossar, várar, várn, várs, várt, váru, várum*
old-age-died	*ellidauðr*		
old-bull	*öldungshúð*	ourselves	*sjálfum*
old-bull's-hide	*öldungshuð*	out	*ór, út, utan, utar, úti*
old-man	*karl*	outer	*yst*
old-woman	*kerlingu*	outermost	*yst*
on	*á, í*	out-from	*ór, undan, út*
once	*eitthvert*	outlives	*lifir*
one	*annarr, ein, eina, einn, einnar, einnhvern, einni, einu, einum, eitt, eitthvert*	outnumbered	*ofrliði*
		out-of	*á, ór, utan, útan*
		outside	*utan, utar, úti*
		out-to	*ýta*
one-day	*sinn*	over	*af, efra, ór, yfir*
one-of	*einnhverr*	overgrown	*vaxinn*
one's	*eins, sér*	overkill	*ofrkapp*
on-land	*foldar*	overwhelming	*ofrefli*

English	Old Norse	English	Old Norse
overwhelming-force	ofrefli	played	leiki, léku
own	eiga, eignast	plays	leiki
owned	átt, eigu	pleased	blíðr
owning	eiga	pleasing	geðsligra
		pledge	heit
		pledged	hétu
		plenty	œrna
		plenty-of	ærit

P, p

English	Old Norse	English	Old Norse
pale	bleikr	point	odd, odda, oddar
palms	palmi	poison-full	eitrfullir
part	hlut, hlutr, þorra	poles	stöngum
parted	skildust, skiljast, skilnaði	pools	tjör
parts	deili, hluti	poor	fátæka
parts-of	hluta	poor-beggar	stafkarl
pass	leið	popular	alþýða, vinsæll
passed	leið, líða, liðin, liðnar, líðr	populous	fjölmenn
passes	líðr	possible	hægt
passing	liðnar	pour	byrla
peace	friði, friðr, fritt, rönum	poured	hellti
peaceful	kyrrðum, spektar	poverty	fátæki
peasant's	karls	powerful	ríkr, völd
people	fólk, fólkit, manna, menn, mönnum	precious	gersimar
		prepare	búa, búast, búumst
people's	fira	prepared	bjó, búa, búast, búin, búinn, búit, búna, búnar, búnir, býst, skipat, skipuð
perch	hríslu		
performed	framðar, vann		
person	maðr, mann, manni		
pierced	nistir, stungit	present	fyrir, staddir
piercing	smýgra	present-to	tjá
piglets	grísir	prevail	ráða
place	leggja, stað	prey	bráðir
placed	bar	prince	hilmi, þengill
places	stað, staðar	princes	hildingar
plan	ráð, ráða, ráði, ráðs	problems	vandamálum
planed	skefr	promised-for	festum
plank-fence	skíðgarðr	promising	heitim, vænligt
planned	ráða	promisingly	vænligt
plans	ráð, ráða	property	gós
play	leiki	propose	biðja
		proposed-to	beðit
		prospect	efni

English	Old Norse	English	Old Norse
protect	verja	ran	hlaupa, hleypr, hlupu, rendi, renna
protected	hlífa	randalin	randalín
protection	hlíf	ranks	fylkingar, fylkingum
prove	ræsis, sanni	rapid	sviðr
providing	kveða	rather	heldr
provisions	föngum, vistir	rats	rottar
provoke	etja	raven	hrafn, hrafni
puffins	lunda	ravens	hrafns, rafnar
punished	hegningar	raven's	hrafni
punishment	hegning	raw-wet	hráblauta
purpose	annk	reached	seilist
pursue	sýsla	reaching	ná
put	lét	react	bregðr, brygði
		readied	búin
		ready	búinn, búit
		realised	þykkjast

Q, q

English	Old Norse
quarrel	skœru, þœfðar
quickest	skjótast
quickly	bráðast, hratt, skjótt

R, r

English	Old Norse	English	Old Norse
rafn	rafn	reason	sök
rage	gný	received	tók
ragnar	ragnar, ragnari, ragnarr, ragnars	reconciliation	sættir
ragnar's	ragnari, ragnars	red	rauðan, rauðar, rauðr, rauðum, roðin
ragnhild	ragnhildar, ragnhildi, ragnhildr	redden	rjóða
rags	tötrum	reddened	rjóða, roðinn, roðna, ruðum
raided	herjat, herjuðu, ræna	redress	yfirbót
raiding	herfangi, herför, hernað, hernaði, herskildi	reduced	rýrt
		refuse	frýja
		refused	synjar
rain	regni	regarding	um
raise	safna	reidgotaland	reiðgotaland
raised	elr, fæddi, hafinn, hrundu, reisa, reisir, rista, safna	rejoice	fagna
		relatives	ættmanna
		released	leystr
		releasing	leysa
		remember	mank, mank, minnast, munk
rallied	fylkja	remembered	minntust, munat
		remembering	mundi
		renowned	ágætir
		repaid	launar
		repay	launa

English	Old Norse	English	Old Norse
reply	mót	room	herbergis, rúm, rúmi
resistance	viðtöku	rose	reistist, ríss
rest	hvíli, létta	rough	hart, rögguð
return	áðr, mót, móti	roughly	harða, hart
revealing	birtinga	route	leiðar
revenge	hefna, hefnd, hefnda, hefndina, hefnið, hefnt	rule	ráða, ríkjum
		ruled	ráðandi, ráðinn, ræðr, réð, réði, réðu, ríkt
review	rifja		
reward	launi	ruler	jöfra, jöfurr
rhine's	rínar	ruler-of	réð
ribs	rifin	ruling	ráðagerðar, ræðr, réð, veldi
rich	ríka		
ride	ríð, ríða	run	hlaupa
riders	riddara	running	hlaupi
riding	ríða	rushed	geyst
riding-men	riddaralið		
right	hægri, réttir		
ring	baugs, baugum, hring		

S, s

English	Old Norse
ringerike	hringaríki
ring-like	hringleginn
rings	bauga, baugi, hringa
rise	reisa
risen	risit
risked	hætt
river	á
roared	glumði, grenjuðu
rocks	björgum
rode	reið, reiddi
rognvald	rögnvaldr
rognvald's	rögnvalds
rogue's	skalk
rolled	vals, veltist
roller	vals
rollers-red	hlunnroð
roller-warships	hlunnalungum
roman-world	rómaveldi
rome	róms
rome-city	rómaborgar
rongvald	rögnvaldr

English	Old Norse
sacrifice	blótim, blótum
sacrificed	blótinn
sacrificed-to	blótat, blótin
sacrifices	blót, tafn, tafni
sacrificial-places	blótstaðr
safe-conduct	griðum
safely	heill
saga	saga
said	kjeðst, kvað, kvaðst, kváðu, kváðust, kvæði, kveðr, kveðst, mælt, mælti, sagði, sagt, seggir, segi, segir, segja, sögð, sögðu, sögn
said-they	kváðust
said-to	segja
sailboards	snekkjur
sailboats	snekkjur
sailed	siglðum
sail-yard	rá
sake	sák, sakir
salmon	lax

English	Old Norse	English	Old Norse
salt	salti	see	sá, sé, sjá, sjám
same	einu, sama, sömu	seeing	sjá
samso	sámsey, sámseyju	seek	leita, leitat, sækja
sand	sand, sandr	seeker	sækitík
sands	sanda	seekers	veiðivitjar
sat	sat, sátu, sest, setit, setr, setst, sitja, sitr	seeking	leitat
		seek-to	sækja
sated	mett	seem	þykkja
savage	ólmr	see-me	sé
savagery	grimmleik	seemed	þætti, þótti, þóttust, þykkir, þykkist
save	spari		
saw	sá, sæi, sák, sér, sét, sjá	seems	sýnisk, sýnist, þætti, þykki
say	kveðir, mæla, mál, seg, segið, segja, segjum, sjá, sögn	seems-to	þykki
		seem-to	þykkjast
		seen	sæi, sér, sét, sjá, sjást, sú, sýnum
say-of	segja		
say-to	segja	seen-you	sáttu
scarborough	skarðaborg	see-this	sjá
scarcely	trautt	self	sjálfan
scattered	dreif	send	gera, senda
scattering	dreif	sending-men	sendimenn
schlei-river	slés	sends	sendar
scored	skera, skorin, skorit	sense	vit
scotland's	skotlands	sent	fara, senda, sendi, sendir, sent
scraped	skóf		
scream	gjalla	separate	skilja
screaming	hlakkar	separated	herskildi
sea	ægi, haf, hafa, hafs, sæ	separately	herskildi
		separation	skilnaði
seagulls	máva	serpent	lyngölun, naðri, orma, ormi, orminum, ormr, ormrinn
seagull's	mávangs		
sea-kings	neskonungum		
search	leita		
sea-serpents	ófni	serpents	ormar, ormarnir, ormr
season	misseri		
seasoned	röskva	serpent's	orminum, ormsins
seat	sætis, sat	servant-maids	þjónustukonur
seated	leggr	servants-of	þjónustumenn
seaworthy	sæfært	serve	þjóna
secret	leynt	served	gegnir, þjónuðu
secretly	leyniliga		

English	Old Norse	English	Old Norse
set	setja, setr, sett, setti, settist, settr, settumk, sitja	ship	skip, skipa, skipum, skipunum
set-out	setja	ship-preparing	skipabúnað
settle	búast, byggja, sætta	ships	herskipum, skip, skipa, skipanna, skipin, skips, skipum
settlement	byggð, byggja, sætt		
settles	byggvir	ship's-stem	stafni
seven	sjau	shirt	serk
sewn-and-stitched	saumaðan	shiver	hrolla, spán
shabby	vesallátan	shocked	bregðr, lostinn
shaft	skapt, skaptit	shook	hristir, skelfr, þokar
shaggy-breeches	loðbrækr, loðbrók	shore	strönd
shaggy-cape	loðkápa	short	skamma, skammt, skemmr
shaking	hristir		
shall	mun, muni, munt, munu, munum, skal, skalk, skalt, skuli, skulu, skulum, skyli	shortage	skorti
		shortage-of	skorti
		short-distance	skammt
		shortly-distance	skammt
shall-be	skal	short-way	skammt
shallows	útgrynnis	shot	skaut, skotit, skutu, skýtr
shame	klækjum		
shaped	telk	should	knátti, man, mun, mundi, muntu, munu, munum, munut, skal, skulu, skuluð, skylda, skyldi, skyldu, skyli
share	hlut		
sharp	hvass, hvassir, hvell		
sharpened	snarbrýnir		
sharply	snarpir		
shaved	koll		
she	hana, henni, honum, hún	should-be	mun, skulu, skyldi, skyli, væri, yrði
		shoulders	herða
shear-lancet	skœrubíldr	should-it	skyldi
sheath	slíðra	shouldit-be	mundi
sheath-flame	slíðrloga	should-to	munuat
she-is	hana	shouted	æptu
she-was	hana, hún	shouting	óp
she-wolf's	ylgr	show	sýna
shield	brynjur, randar, rönd, skildi, skjöld	showed	sýndu, sýnt
		shown	sýnt
shields	randar, skildi, skildir, skjöld, skjöldu, skjöldum, skjölduna, skjómar	sibilja	síbilja, síbilju
		sibilja's	síbilju
		sickness	sótt
		sickness-death	sóttdauðr
shimmering	bliku	side	síðu
shining-sworded	svarðmerðlingar		

English	Old Norse	English	Old Norse
sides	*síður*	sleeves	*ermar*
sighvat	*sighvatr*	slender	*mjó*
sign	*merkja*	slept	*sefr, sofnar, sváfu*
signed	*signuð*	slew	*vá*
sigurd	*sigurðar, sigurði, sigurðr*	slipped	*smó*
		smaland	*smálönd*
sigurdarson	*sigurðarson*	small	*smátt*
sigurd's	*sigurðar*	smaller	*smæri*
silence	*hljóð, þegi*	smear	*ríða*
silenced	*þagnaði*	smiths	*smiða, smiði*
silent	*þagði, þegði*	snake	*orm, ormr, orms*
silk	*silki*	Snake-in-the-eye	*ormr-í-auga*
silk-shirt	*silkiskyrtu*	snake-pit	*ormgarð*
silver	*silfd, silfr, silfri*	snakes	*ormarnir, ormr, snákar*
since	*sem, síðan, síðir, því*	snoring	*hrytr*
singing	*sungu*	so	*í, sá, samir, sé, sér, sjá, slíka, sú, svá, svát, þat, þat*
sit	*sætis, set, sit, sitja*		
sits	*sitr*		
sitting-next-to	*sessunautum*	so-as	*svá*
six	*sex*	so-did	*svá*
skald	*skáld*	softened	*bleyta*
skane	*skáni*	so-great	*mikla*
skarpa-skerries	*skarpa-skerjum*	so-is	*sás*
skilfully	*hagliga, næfri*	sole-ruling-king	*einvaldskonungr*
skilled	*gervar, reyndir*	some	*eitthvert, nokkura, nokkurn, nokkurrar, sumir, sumra, sumt, sumu*
skin	*hörund*		
skjoldungs'	*skjöldunga*		
skogul's	*sköglar*		
skulls	*hausa*	somehow	*nokkurn*
slain	*svelta, valr*	some-of	*sumt*
slain-blood	*valblóði*	someone	*nokkurr, nokkurs*
slain-fall	*valfalli*	something	*nokkut*
slain-offering	*valtafn*	something-else	*annat*
slaughter	*morði, snerru*	sometime	*nokkuru*
slayer-of-fafnir	*fáfnisbana*	some-time	*eitthvert*
slaying	*fell, vígi*	sometimes	*lotum*
sleep	*sofa, svefn, svefni, svefns*	somewhat	*nakkvat, nokkut*
		so-much	*svá*
sleeping-house	*svefnhúss*	son	*son, sona, sonar, sonr*
sleeping-quarters	*svefnskemmu*		
sleepy	*syfjaðan, syfjaðr*	song	*syngja*

English	Old Norse	English	Old Norse
son-of	*syni*	spear-tip	*spjóti, spjótinu, spjótit*
son-of-hring	*hringssonar*	spear-tree	*geirtré*
son-of-ingi	*ingasonar*	speech	*mál, máli, ræðu, tölu*
son-of-ingjald	*ingjaldssonar*	spine	*hrygg*
sons	*burir, mögr, mögum, sona, sonu, sonum, syni, synir*	split	*klýfr, renna, stökk*
		spoke	*kvað, kveðr, mæla, mælir, mælti, mæltu, segir*
sons-of	*synir*		
sons-of-haekling	*hæklings*	spoken	*kveðit, mælt*
soon	*brátt, snart*	sported	*leik*
soonest	*skjótast, snemmst*	sports	*íþróttir*
sorcery	*blótskap, blótskapr, tröllskapnum*	spread	*breiða, spyrjast*
		spread-in	*víða*
so-that	*svát*	sprinkled	*ausinn*
sought	*beið, leita, leitat, sóttan, sóttu*	spurted	*stökk*
		spying	*njósn*
sound	*sundi*	stab	*slíta*
sounded	*gjalla*	stand	*staðar, standa*
south	*suðr, sunnan*	standing	*standa*
southern-lands	*suðrríki, sunnanverðri*	stands	*stendr*
		stand-up	*uppi*
south-islands	*suðreyjum*	stand-you	*standast*
sow	*gyltan*	stare	*kaga*
spangarheid	*spangarheiði*	started	*hafinn*
spangarheith	*spangareiði*	startled	*brá, brást*
spare	*spara, spari*	stay	*standa*
speak	*mæla, mælir, tala*	stayed	*stóð*
speaking	*mælti, mæltu, tilkvæði*	steadfast	*staðist*
		steed	*mars*
speaks	*mæli, mælir*	steel	*stáli*
spear	*geira, spjót, spjóti, spjótinu, spjótit*	steered	*styr, stýrði*
		steerer	*sveif*
speared	*frák*	steering	*styr*
spear-nail	*geirnagla*	stein	*steins*
spear-point	*odd, odda*	step-mother	*stjúpmóðir*
spear-points	*odda, spjótsoddum, spjótsoddunum*	stepsons	*stjúpsona, stjúpsonu*
		stern	*stafn*
spears	*geira, geirr, oddr, spjót, spjótin, spjótunum*	stiff	*stirðar*
		stifling	*mollu*
spear-shaft	*lag, spjótskapt, spjótskaptinu, spjótskepti*	still	*enn, kyrr, kyrrir*

English	Old Norse	English	Old Norse
stole	ræntan	suffered	þyldi
stomach	mögum	summer	sumar
stood	stæði, standa, stendr, stóð, stótt, studdist	summoned	safnar, stefnir
		summons	stefnu
		sun	sólar
stop	stöðva	supper	náttverð
storehouse	skemmu	supports	stoðar
storm	dyn, hríðar	suppose	ætla
story	sögu	supposed	ætla, ætlar, ætluðu
straight	gegnt	surf	brim
straightaway	þegar	surpassed	bar
straight-away	þegar	surprisingly	furðu
strange	endemlig, undarligum, undarn	svolnir's	svölnis
strategy	brögðum	swear	sverja
strength	kraptr, magni	sweat	sveita, sveiti
stretch	teygði	sweden	svíaríki, svíþjóð, svíþjóðar, svíþjóðu
stretched	þenja		
strike	slá	swedes	svíar
striking	högg	sweet	sýtandi
string	streng, strengr	swell	svella
string-laid	strenglágar	swept	ræstr
stripped	fletta, flettr, hroðinn	swiftly	skjótt
strong	sterka, sterki, stinn	swine-worth	svívirðing
stronger	sterkari	swollen	sollinn, þrútinn
strongest	sterkasta, sterkastr	sword	bröndum, mæki, sverð, sverða, sverði, sverðinu
stronghold	fastgarðr		
strongly-built	harðger	sword-hart	brandahjört
struck	hjó, hjoggum, hneit, höggvit, lustu, sló	sword-point	blóðrefilinn
		swords	bröndum, hjörvi, sverð, sverða, sverði, sverðs, sverðum
struck-off	höggvins		
subjected	lögðu		
submitted	undir		
substantial	drjúgr	swore	sverr
success	sigr	sworn	svarit
successful	sigr	symptoms	sóttar
such	slíka, slíkan, slíkar, slíkir, slíkrar, slíkri, slíkt, slíku, slíkum, svá		

T, t

English	Old Norse
such-as	sem
sucked-at	sogit
table	borð
table-game	tafl

English	Old Norse	English	Old Norse
tail	sporð, sporðr	that-kind-of	þessarar
take	nema, tæki, taka, takast, tek, tekr	that-she	hún
		that-was	er, váru
take-care-of	annast	that-way	þanninn
taken	drepit, nema, nemst, taka, tekin, tekinn, tekit	that-which-is	þat
		that-you	þáttu
taken-care-of	annast	the	á, at, at, en, er, hins, í, in, ina, inir, inn, inna, innar, ins, inum, it, né, sá, sitt, sú, þá, þann, þat, þat, þau, þeim, þeir, þetta, því
takes	tekr		
tales	órunum		
talk	ráði, talar, tals		
talked	hjalar, telr		
talking	málug		
tar	biki, tjöru	the-assembly	þing, þingit, þings, þingsins, þingstefnu
taste	bergja, bragði		
tax	skatta	the-battle	bardaga, bardagi, bardaginn, orrostunni
tear	slíta		
tears	gráti, tár		
tell	segir, segja	the-before	fyrr
telling	segið	the-beginning	upphafi
temperament	skapsmuni	the-black	svarti
ten	tigu, tíu	the-boneless	beinlausi
tender	mildri	the-box	eskinu, eskit
tens	tøgum	the-boy	sveininn, sveininum, sveinn, sveinninn
tents	tjöld, tjöldum		
terror	ófriðr	the-boy's	sveininum
test	reyna, reyndi	the-braver	fræknligast
tested	reyna	the-bread	brauðit
tha-may	má	the-brothers	bræðr, bræðra, bræðrum
than	en, er, heldum, sem, þá		
		the-bullocks	kvígendin
thane	þegn, þegni	the-bulls	naut
thanks	þökk	the-business	ráð
that	á, at, at, en, er, ér, hvat, í, sem, sér, sinn, sú, svá, þá, þangat, þann, þann, þat, þat, þats, þau, þeim, þess, þetta, því, til, við	the-cabin	skemmuna, skemmunnar, skemmunni
		the-chief	höfðingi
		the-chieftain	höfðinginn
		the-city	borg, borgarinnar, borgin, borgina, borginni
that-had	hafði	the-city-walls	borgarveggi, borgarveggina, borginni
that-is	þat		
that-it-is	þat	the-company-of	lið

English	Old Norse	English	Old Norse
the-cooks	matsveinar	the-guardsmen	hirðmenn
the-cow	kúna, kúnni, kýr, kýrin	the-hairy-side	háram, hárham
the-crew	lið	the-hall	höllina, höllu, höllunni
the-crowd	fjölmennis	the-hall-floor	hallargólfinu
the-danes	dana, danir, dönum	the-harp	hörpuna, hörpunnar, hörpunni
the-danger	hætta	the-hart	hjörtr
the-daughter	dóttir	the-heart	hjartat
the-daughter-of	dóttir	the-high-seat	hásætit
the-day	daginn	the-house	húsinu, húsit, húss
the-dead	dauða	the-hut	skálann
the-death-of	dauða	their	sinn, sinnar, sínu, sitt, þeim, þeir, þeira, þeirar, þeiri
the-deck	lypting		
the-din	gnýinn		
the-dog	hundinn, hundrinn	theirs	sín, sína, sínar, sinn, sinna, sinnar, sinni, síns, sínum, sitt, þeim, þeira
the-doors	dyrr		
the-eagle	örn		
the-earl	jarl, jarli, jarlinn		
the-earl's	jarls, jarlsins	the-keen	hvassi
the-earth's	jarðar	the-king	fylkingum, konung, konungi, konunginn, konunginum, konungr, konungrinn, konungs
the-estate	bæjarins, býjar		
the-evening	aptanninn		
the-eye	auga		
the-eyes	auga, auga		
the-farm	bær	the-kingdom	ríki, ríkin, ríkinu
the-feast	veislu	the-kingdom-of	ríki
the-fence	skíðgarðinn	the-king's	konunganna, konungr, konungs
the-field	völl		
the-fields	völlunum	the-knife	knífrinn
the-fire	bál, eldinn	the-lady-of-the-house	húsfreyja
the-fleshy-side	holdrosu	the-land	land, landi, landinu, landsins
the-forces	her, herinum, liðinu		
the-foremost	öndvegi	the-lands	lönd, löndum
the-forest	skóg, skóginn, skóginum	the-lap-of-cloak	skikkjuskaut
		the-lineage	ætt
the-fort	vígi	them	sér, sik, þá, þau, þeim, þeir, þeira
the-gathering-of	safnaðar		
the-girl	mærin, meyjunni, meyna	the-maiden	meyjunni
		the-man	karl, karls
the-gods	ásum, goðum	the-matter	mæla, mál
the-gold	gullit	the-men	liðinu, liðit, menn
the-greatest	ágæst, mestr	the-messengers	sendimenn

English	Old Norse	English	Old Norse
the-morning	morgin	the-river	á
the-most	mest, mesta, mesti	the-rollers	hlunni
the-most-beautiful	fríðust	the-saga	sögu
themselves	sér, sik, sín, sínu, sjálfir	the-saga-of	sögu
		the-salt	salta
then	á, at, en, enn, er, inn, sá, síðan, sinn, sinnum, þá, þann, þar, þás, þat, þau, þegar, þeir, þenna, þó, því	the-same	samt
		the-same-time	jafnlengd
		the-sand	sandinum
		the-saxons	saxa
		these	ina, it, sér, þau, þeir, þenna, þess, þessa, þessar, þessi, þessir, þessum
the-name	heitit		
the-nature	náttúra		
the-news	tíðenda, tíðendin		
the-night	njóta, nótt, nóttina	the-sea	hafinu
the-noise	gnýr	the-serpent	orminn, orminum, ormrinn
then-one	þann	the-serpent's	orminum
the-norns	norna	the-shaft	skaptit
the-northern-lands	norðrlönd, norðrlöndum	the-shield	skildinum
		the-ship	skipa, skipi, skipunum
the-north-lands	norðrlöndum		
the-ocean	ægir	the-ships	skipa, skipum
the-oldest	ellstr	the-ship's-cook	matsveinar
the-old-man	karl, karli, karls	the-shirt	serknum
the-old-woman	kerling, kerlingar, kerlingu	the-sides	hlið
		the-skin	húðina
the-other's	annars	the-slain	vals
the-people	mann, manna	the-sleeping-room	skemmuna, skemmunni
the-piglets	grísir		
the-pillars	súlur	the-snake	orminum
the-pupil	sjáldrit	the-sound	sundi
the-pyre	bálinu	the-southern-kingdom	suðrríki
the-queen	drottning		
the-ranks	fylking, fylkingar, fylkingu	the-spear-head	spjótit
		the-spear-point	spjótit
there	hingat, sitt, staðinn, þá, þaðan, þær, þangat, þar, þars, þat, þau, þegar, þeir, þeirar, þeiri	the-spears	spjótin
		the-spear-shaft	skaptinu
		the-spear-tip	spjótit
		the-spine	hrygg, hrygginum
thereafter	síðan	the-storm	andviðri
therefore	fyrir, því, við	the-story	saga
there-was	var, varð	the-strength	hagleik
the-ring	hringinn	the-sun	sólar

English	Old Norse	English	Old Norse
the-swedes	svía	thora	Þóra, Þóru
the-swift	hvati	thora's	Þóru
the-townspeople	borgarinnar, borgarmenn	thord	Þórðr
		thorn	Þorn
the-tree	trénu	thorns	Þyrni
the-trees	mörkina, viðinn	those	inir, it, Þann, Þat, Þeim, Þeira
the-walls	veggirnir		
the-way	leiðar	thoug	Þó
the-will-of	vilja	though	en, Þó, Þótt
the-wise	horskum	thought	álits, börðust, hug, hugat, hugðak, hugði, hugðist, hugðu, hugðum, hyggja, hyggr, íhugar, sýndist, sýnist, sýnum, Þættist, Þó, Þótti, Þóttist, Þóttu, Þóttust, Þykki, Þykkir, Þykkist, Þykkjast
the-wisest	vitrastr		
the-woman	kona, konan, konunni		
the-woods	skógar		
the-world	veröldin, veröldu		
the-worst	verr, verst		
the-wound	sárinu		
they	eru, fyrir, hafa, Þeir, sem, sín, sitt, Þá, Þar, Þat, Þau, Þegar, Þeim, Þeir, Þeira, Þeiri, Þetta		
		thought-cowardly	hugblauðum
		thought-fit	sýndist
they-had-parted	skilnaði	thoughts	hug
they-were	eru, Þau, Þeir	thousand	Þúshundraða
thin	mjóst	three	Þrenna, Þriggja, Þrimr, Þrír, Þrjá, Þrjár, Þrjú
things	hluti		
think	hug, hygg, hyggja, hyggr, Þykki, Þykkja, Þykkjumst		
		three-times	Þrisvar
		three-winters	Þrévetr
third	Þriðja, Þriðji, Þrimr	threw	köstuðu
third-of	Þriðjung	through	á, at, gegnum
this	at, hins, í, inn, sinnar, sinni, sitt, sú, Þá, Þann, Þann, Þat, Þat, Þenna, Þess, Þessa, Þessar, Þessarar, Þessi, Þessu, Þessum, Þetta, Því	thrust	stakk
		thyra	Þyri
		tidings	tíðenda
		tie	binda
		tightly	fast
		timber	mörk
		time	stund, stundr, stundum, tíma
this-is	Þess	times	tíma
this-time	tíðar	tired	mæddan, móðr
this-way	leið	to	á, at, fyrir, í, innan, of, sér, til, undir, við
this-who	sás		
thong	Þvengr		

English	Old Norse	English	Old Norse
to-all	allra	took	heldr, námu, nema, nemr, tækist, taka, tekr, tekst, tók, tókk, tókst, tóku
to-all-who	allir		
to-ask	boð		
toasts	fagnaðaröl		
to-away	brott	took-care-of	annast
to-battle	bardaga	to-open	upp
to-be	at, er, vera	tore	slíta
to-bed	rekkju	tore-up	sleit
to-be-sick	sóttar	tortured	píndr, pínuðu
to-cast	kasta	to-rule	ráða
to-come	ganga	to-sea	hafa
to-death	bana	to-see	sér, sjá
to-die	deyja	to-sit	sitja
to-do	færa, gerst	to-take	taka
to-each	hverr	to-talk	hjala
to-escape	flóttann	to-tell	spjöll
to-fight	berjast	to-them	þeim
to-find	finna	to-the-other	öðru
to-follow	fylgja	to-travel	ferðinni
together	sama, saman	touched	tók
togetherness	samför	tough	harðfengt
to-give	gefa	toughness	harðfengi
to-go	fara, gengr	to-wait-for	bíða
to-guard	gæti	towards	at, fram, móti, til
to-have	hafa	townspeople	borgarmanna, borgarmenn, borgarmönnum
to-her	henni, hún		
to-him	hann, honum, sér	to-you	þér, yðr, ykkr
to-injure	granda	to-your	þér
tokens	jarteinir	trade	iðnar
to-know	vita	trail	slóð
told	sagði, sagt, segir, segja, sögð, sögðu, talað	travel	fara, fari, fer
		travelled	fara, farinn, farit, farnir, fer, ferr, ferst, fór, fóru, fórum
told-to	sögð	travelling	fara, fari, farinn, ferð, fóru
to-look-at	yfirlits		
to-me	mér, mik	travel-weary	farmóðr
to-meet	finna, hitta, móti	treacherous	ótrúligt
tongue	tungu	treasure	lausafé
too-early	ofsnemma	tree	tré
		trees	viðinn
		trial	mannraun

English	Old Norse	English	Old Norse
tribute-paying-land	skattlönd	un-decayed	ófúinn
trick	brögð	under	und, unda, undan, undir
trickery	brögnum	understand	skiljum
tricks	brögð, brögðum	understood	skildi, skildu, skilja
tried	freistat	undone	ógert
trod	stíga	unexpected	óvænt
troll-like	tröllskap	unfairly-behaved	óþokkuliga
troubled	tregar	un-friends	óvinum
true		unheard-of	endemi
true-like	trúleiki	un-invaded	óherskátt
truly	sannliga	unless	nema
trumpets	lúðr	unlike	ólíkar
trust	trúa	unlikely	óvænlig
trusted	treystist, treystust	un-right	óráðligt
trustworthy	trúnaði	unseeing	ósýnna
truth	satt	un-talkative	óðamálug
tunic	namk	until	áðr, er, til, tll, uns
turn	hverfa	un-warned	óvart
turn-back	hverfa	unworthy	óvirðuligar
turned	horfit, hverfa, sneri, sneru, snerust, snúa, snýr, stýrir, undum	up	upp, uppi, yfir
		up-going	uppgöngu, uppgöngur
turned-his	snýr	upon	á
turned-out	orðit	uppermost	efstr
twelve	tólf	upper-sweden	uppsvíaveldi
twenty	tvítøgir	uppland	upplöndum
twin	tvíbura	uppsala	uppsala, uppsölum
two	tvá, tvær, tvau, tveggja, tveimr, tveir	up-to	at, undir
		urge	hváta
		us	oss
		use	gögnum, kostar
		useful	njóta
		users	nýtinjótar
		usually	vani

U, u

English	Old Norse
ullr-acres	ullarakri
unafraid	ógndjarfr
unbelievable	bregða
unborn	óbornir
un-careful	óvarlig
unclothed	óklædd
unconquerable	óvígan
un-cowardly	óblauðan

V, v

English	Old Norse
valkyrie	valmeyjar
valley	dal
valour	hreysti

English	Old Norse	English	Old Norse
valthjof	valþjófr	war-clothes	herklæði
valued	virðir	war-cry	herópi
various	ýmsa, ýmsi, ýmsum	war-declaration	hersögu
venom	eitri	warfare	herför
verse	vísu	war-going	herför
very	einkar, harðla, mjök	warm	varmar
vestfold	vestfold	warmed	bakaðist, bakast
victory	sígr, sigrast, sigrs	war-men	hermenn
vidrir's	viðris	warrior	hermaðr
vifil	vífill	warrior-man	hermaðr
vifilsborg	vífilsborg, vífilsborgar	warriors	drengir, drengs, fyrðar, gram, rekkar
vikaskeid	víkaskeiði	war-shields	herskildi
viken	víkin, víkina	war-slings	valslöngur
vikings	víkingar	war-taken	harðfengnir
village	þorps	wartooth	hilditönn
villages	þorp	war-voyage	herferð
visit	tíðar, vitja	wary	varr
voice	rödd	was	á, at, er, eru, gerist, sá, sé, væri, var, varð, vark, váru, vas, vasat, vask, vera, verða, verðr, verit
volnir	völnir		
voyage	för		
voyages	ferðum		

W, w

English	Old Norse	English	Old Norse
		was-bitten-by	bitu
		was-concluded	lýkr
		was-displeased	líkar
waded	óð	was-given	gaf
wage-war	herja	was-heard	spyrjast, spyrst
wagon	vagn	washed	þvær
wait	bíða, biðim	washing	laugar
wales	valland	was-married	kvángast
walk	ganga	was-named	hét
walking	ganga, geng	was-not	eigi
wand	gand, völdr	was-said	mæltu
wanted	vildi	was-seen	sá
wanted-to	vill	was-this	þetta
war	her, hers	was-thought	þótti
warband	her, herr	watch-holders	varðhöld
war-band	her, herr	water	vatni
war-booths	herbúðir	waterfalls	vatnföllum
war-camp	herbúðir	waterford	veðrafirði

English	Old Norse	English	Old Norse
water-ice	vatnsísinum	wept	grét
water's-edge	vatnsbakkanum	were	er, ér, eru, es, væri, var, varu, váru, verða, verðr, vígr
waves	bára, hrannir		
way	hætti, leið, leiðar, veg		
		were-afraid	óttaðist
ways	hætti, megin, vega	were-given	gaf, gefr
way-to	til	were-they	eru, þeim
we	oss, várum, vér, vit	we-sliced	skífðum
weak	veikan	west	vestr
weakness	lasi	west-gautland	vestra-gautland, vestra-gautlandi
wealkings	argan		
wealth	auðr, fé, fjár, lausafé, ófafé	we-told	tölðumk
		what	at, er, hvat, hver, hverja, hverr, hversu, því
wealthiness	fátæki		
wealthy	auðig	whatever	hvat, hvetvetna
weapon	vápn	when	at, en, er, es, ok, sem, þá, þegar, var, vark, váru
weapon-capable	vápnhæft		
weapon-clothes	vápnföt		
weapon-handy	vápnhæft	where	en, er, hvaðarr, hvar, sem, þar, var
weapons	vápn, vápnum		
weapons-prepared	vápnabúnað	wherever	hvar, hvert
we-are	erum	whether	hvart, hvárt
wearing	hirðik	which	en, er, es, hverjum, hverr, sem, vilkat
weather	veðr		
weather's	viðris	whichever	hváriga
wedding	brullaup	while	hríð, meðan, stund, stundu
wedding-feast	brúðlaup, brullaup		
we-drink	drekkum	whined	umði
weeks	vikna	whistling	þjóta
weep	grætr	white	hvítar, hvítum
we-know	vitum	who	er, hver, hverir, hvern, hverr, sem, var
welcomed	fagna, fagnat		
well	hress, vel		
		whole	heill
well-enough	bjargvel	whom	hvern
well-mannered	kurteisust	whose	hverrar
		who-was	er
wendland	vindland, vindlandi	why	hví
went	færi, fara, fari, farit, ferr, fór, fóru, ganga, gangi, gekk, gengr, gengu, gerði, gerðu, varð	wicked	illa
		wickedly	illa
		wide	vítt
		widely	breiða, víða
went-they	fáðir	wide-travelled	viðfarar

English	Old Norse	English	Old Norse
widow	ekkju	without	án
wield	valda	without-vengeance	óhefnt
wielded	veldr	withstand	standa, standast
wife	kona, konu, kvánar	withstood	staðist
wild	ólmir	withstood-us	frýðu
wild-animals	dýr, dýrum	woken	vakna
wildest	ólmasti	wolf	ulfi, vargi, vargr
will	mun, mundi, mundu, veiti, vil, vili, vilið, vilir, vilja, viljum, vill, vilt	wolves	ulfa, vargi, vörgum
		woman	kona, kvenna
		woman-ruled	kvánríki
		women	konum, konur, kvenna
will-be	verði	won	fingum, gagn, unnar, unnit, unnu, vann, vinnr, vinst, ynni
willed	vilda, vildi, vildu, vili, vilja, vill		
willed-it	vildi	wondered	hyggr
willed-to	vill	wonder-like	undarligt
william	vilhjálmr	wondrous	kyns
willing	gerr, gjarn	won-we	unnum
wills	vildi, vill	wood	storðar
will-you	viltu	wooden-man	trémaðrinn, trémann
win	unnit, vinna	woods	skógar
wind	byri, veðr	word	orð
wine	vín	words	orð, orða, orðit
wine-beaker	vínkers	word-sending	orðsending
wine-leek	vínlauk	wore	bar
winning	unnit	work	sýslu, unnit, verk, verki, verkit, vinni, vinnir
winter	vetrinn, vetrum		
winters	vetra, vetrum		
wisdom	speki	worked	vinnst
wise	spekingr, vitr, vitrust	work-on	vinna
wise-like	vitrliga	world	heimsala
wisest	vitrustu	worn	slitnaðan
wish	væntum, vil, vilja, viljum, vilt	worse	verr, verra, verri, verstr
wished	skyldi, vildi, vilja, vill	worst	verst
wished-to	vill	worth	verð, vert
wish-to	viljum	worthily	virðuliga
wit	vit	worth-of	verði
with	á, af, í, með, sinni, því, við, vit	worth-price	verðkaupit
		worthy	vert
with-him	honum		
with-his	sínum		

English	Old Norse	English	Old Norse
would	áverkann, mun, mundi, mundu, munu, skal, skyldi, skyldu, væri, vildi, vildu, vill, yrði	yours	þín, þína, þínir, þinn, þinna, þínu, þínum, þitt, yðar, yðarn, yðarra, yðarrar, yðarri, yðr, yðru
would-be	mundi, mundu, munu, væri	yule	jól
would-have-been	hefði		
wound	ben, sár, sára, sárinu		
wounded	sár, sárr, sárum		
wound-flame	undleygs	zealand	selund, selundi
wounds	sár, sára, sárum		
woven	ofnu		
wrangle	þræta		
wrap	vefja		
wrecked	brýtr		
wretched	ælig		
written	rítr		
wrong-doing	rangendum		

X, x

Y, y

yawn	gein
yet	enn
yngvarr	yngvarr
york	jórvík, jórvíkr
you	þér, þik, þit, þú, yðar, yðarn, yðr, ykkr
young	ung, unga, ungi, ungr, ungu, yngstr
younger	yngri, yngrum
your	ert, þik, þín, þína, þinna, þínum, yðarra, yðvarn

Z, z

www.ingramcontent.com/pod-product-compliance
Lightning Source LLC
Chambersburg PA
CBHW051403070526
44584CB00023B/3273